T0316961

National Competitiveness of Vietnam: Determinants, Emerging Key Issues
and Recommendations

SCHRIFTEN ZUR WIRTSCHAFTSTHEORIE UND WIRTSCHAFTSPOLITIK

Herausgegeben von
Klaus Beckmann, Michael Berlemann, Rolf Hasse,
Jörn Kruse, Franco Reither, Wolf Schäfer,
Thomas Straubhaar und Klaus W. Zimmermann

Band 39

PETER LANG

Frankfurt am Main · Berlin · Bern · Bruxelles · NewYork · Oxford · Wien

Hien Phuc Nguyen

National Competitiveness of Vietnam: Determinants, Emerging Key Issues and Recommendations

PETER LANG
Internationaler Verlag der Wissenschaften

Bibliographic Information published by the Deutsche Nationalbibliothek
The Deutsche Nationalbibliothek lists this publication in the
Deutsche Nationalbibliografie; detailed bibliographic data is
available in the internet at <http://www.d-nb.de>.

Zugl.: Leipzig, Univ., Diss., 2008

Printed with financial support of
DAAD (German Academic Exchange Service).

15
ISSN 1433-1519
ISBN 978-3-631-59135-2

© Peter Lang GmbH
Internationaler Verlag der Wissenschaften
Frankfurt am Main 2009
All rights reserved.

www.peterlang.de

Acknowledgements

In order to complete this thesis, I owe a great debt of gratitude to many people. First and foremost, I would like to express my deep gratitude to Prof. Dr. Rolf Hasse for his kindly care, generous help and encouragement. Without the great comments and valuable guidance of Professor Hasse I would have not been able to complete this research.

I am greatly indebted to Dr. George Quaas for his kind help and significant comments, especially involving the empirical study section of the research. I would also like to express a special thank to Dr. Minh Khuong Vu (Harvard) for his great help and guidance. Although he has not been in Germany, we have had significant discussions via email which have helped me to complete the research.

I would also like to thank Prof. Dr. G. Schnabl, Prof. Dr. U. Vollmer, and my colleagues at both the Institute for Economic Policy and Institute for Theoretical Economics, whose constructive opinions and arguments in the PhD seminars helped me to develop my thesis.

I am grateful to the Vietnamese Government and German Academic Exchange Service (DAAD) whose financial support made my research possible.

I would like to thank all the business leaders, local and government officials, and academics, who spent their scarce time in answering my survey questionnaire. I am also grateful to my colleagues and friends in Vietnam for collecting data and conducting the survey. For correcting the draft, I am very thankful to Mrs Julie Sliva (America) and Ryan Young (Australia) who kindly and enthusiastically helped me to correct the dissertation. The result would have been limited if I hadn't had their help.

On this occasion, I also would like to express my special thanks to Prof. Dr. F. Quaas, Mrs Martina Kussatz, Mr. M. Rauch, S. Preissler, and Mrs R. Kohlmann who have assisted and encouraged me in many ways to complete this research.

Finally, I would like to thank my parents and parents in-law for their help in collecting data and continuous encouragement. I am also indebted to my older sister, who has been very caring and encouraging to me. Last but not least, I want to thank my young wife, Ha, for her patience and wholehearted support for me to overcome challenges during the time of the study course.

Table of Contents

List of Abbreviations

ADB	Asia Development Bank
APEC	Asia-Pacific Economic Co-operation
ASEAN	Association of South-East Asian Nations
ATC	Agency for Technical Coorperation
BOT	Build - Operate and Transfer
CAV	Custom Valuation Agreement
CCIA	Central Committee on Internal Affairs
CIEM	Central Institute of Economic Management
DAF	Development Assistant Fund
EVN	Electricity of Vietnam
FDI	Foreign Direct Investment
GSO	General Statistics Office of Vietnam
GTZ	Gesellschaft fuer Technische Zusammenarbeit
IAS	International Accounting Standard
IBEA	International Business and Economic Activities
IMD	Institute for Management Development
IMF	International Monetary Fund
IPO	Initial Public Offering
IPPs	Independent Power Producers
IT	Information Technology
LUR	Land Using Right
MNCs	Multinational Corporations
MOF	Ministry of Finance
MOLISA	Ministry of Labor, Invalid and Social Affair
MONRE	Ministry of Natural Resource and the Environment
MPI	Ministry of Planning and Investment
NAFTA	North America Free Trade Agreement
NGO	Non – Governmental Organization
NICs	New Industrialized Countries
NPLs	Non-Performing Loans
NTBs	Non-Tariff Barriers
OECD	Organization for Economic Co-operation and Development
PAR	Public Administration Reform
QRs	Quantitative Restrictions
R§D	Research and Development
S&T	Science and Technology
SAV	State Audit of Vietnam
SCIC	State Capital Investment Company

11

SEDP	Social Economic Development Plan
SMEs	Small and Medium-Sized Enterprises
SOCBs	State Owned Commercial Banks
SOEs	State Owned Enterprises
SVB	State Bank of Vietnam
UEL	Unified Enterprise Law
UNCTAD	United Nation Conference on Trade and Development
UNIDO	United Nations Industrial Development Organization
VCCI	Vietnam Chamber of Commerce Industry
VNC	Vietnam National Competitiveness
VND	Vietnamese Dong
VNPT	Vietnam Post and Telecommunication
WB	World Bank
WEF	World Economic Forum
WIR	World Investment Report
WTO	World Trade Organization

List of Figures

List of Tables and Boxes

Chapter 1:   Introduction

1.1 Research Context and Problem

The "Doi moi" policy has brought expressive economic fruits and radical changes within the Vietnamese economy. The GDP growth remained relatively high, having an average annual rate of 7.5% between 1990 and 2007. Physical infrastructure and human resource have been improved compared to the previous phase, and the financial market has been initially set up. International trade and foreign investment activities have become more liberal and open, and as a result they have performed remarkable achievements. The business environment has become more attractive due to simplification of administrative procedures. All of the above factors have led to an improvement in Vietnam's national competitiveness and productivity. However, Vietnam's competitiveness, productivity, and economic growth in the new context reveal some concerned problems that need to be examined and clarified.

Firstly, national competitiveness has become a central preoccupation of policy makers and business leaders in both developed and developing countries. Although its importance has been acknowledged, national competitiveness remains a widely unaccepted concept (Porter 2004, p 19) and it has been a controversial issue among professional economists who are often skeptical of the concept (Lall 2001a, p32) while governments and policy makers are particularly interested in the issue of competitiveness (Lall 2001a, p 2), specifically the policies that can improve it. Governments have established councils and competitiveness committees have written white papers and organized conferences on the subject (ADB 2003, p204). In fact, national competitiveness is a real concept (Lall 2001b) and the most meaningful concept of competitiveness at national level is national productivity (Porter 1990, p 6). Productivity is a fundamental for national competitiveness and a nation's living standard in the long term. Productivity will secure sustained economic growth and citizens' improvement in living conditions (Porter 2004, p 21). The central challenge in economic development then is how to create the conditions for rapid and sustained productivity growth (Porter 2003, p 25).

Secondly, although Vietnam has had a relatively high growth recently, it should not be complacent and needs to pay continued attention to being competitive (Dapice 2003). The clearest evidence that Vietnam could develop even faster comes from a comparison with China (Vu 2003, p1); both countries have followed a similar way and institution from a planned to a market oriented economy, but economic growth in China has typically exceeded Vietnam's by about two percentage annually (Figure 1.1) and inflows of foreign direct investment (per capita) in China are higher two fold than that in Vietnam. This view was widely held in the words of United Nation Development Program resident representative in Hanoi, Jordan Ryan, "Vietnam should not be lulled by its success...[It] can and must do much better as it faces intense global competition"[1].

Thirdly, the principle economic goal of a nation is to produce a high and rising standard of living for its citizens. The ability to do so depends on its competitiveness and productivity with which a nation's resources (labor and capital) are employed (Porter 2003, p 25). Productivity is a value of the output produced by a unit labor and capital. It depends on both the quality and features of products (which determine the prices they can command) and the efficiency with which they are produced (Porter 2004, p 22). In line with economic growth, labor productivity performance (defined and measured as output per employee) in Vietnam has improved over time (Figure 1.2). However, labor productivity performance in Vietnam still lags behind neighboring countries, especially with China. If in 1990 labor productivity level between two countries was not quite different, now there is a significant difference in productivity level (Figure 1.2). Obviously, China has made a greater progress in productivity and competitiveness than Vietnam, and China's labor productivity growth is much higher than the rate of its counterpart. What causes lead to this issue need to be understood.

Fourthly, there are some emerging key issues of Vietnam's national competitiveness such as production resources shortage, out-dated technology, dominance of SOEs and slow their reform, red-tape and corrupt administration. These issues impact negatively the productivity and competitiveness as well as sustainable economic growth in the long-term. At the same time, Vietnam cannot do everything to improve its competitiveness due to a limitation of resources and competence. Furthermore, national competitiveness is a large scope concept relating to many areas of an economy. Therefore, the problem is that we have to point out the most urgent key issues and the top priorities measures to enhance Vietnam's national competitiveness and productivity as well as sustain its economic growth.

The key to success in the coming years is that the Vietnamese government should design strategies to take full advantage of the potential benefits that globalization and competition offer. The government and its enterprises need to understand what competitiveness means and how it fits in the development process.

---

1   As reported by Agence France Press, August 13, 2003

Figure 1.1 Annual GDP Growth, % (1990-2007)

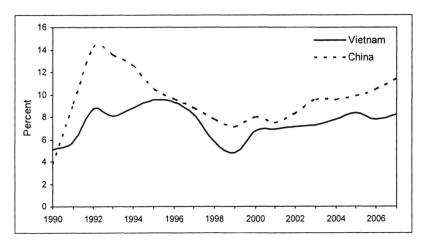

Source: ADB

Figure 1.2 Labor Productivity Performance

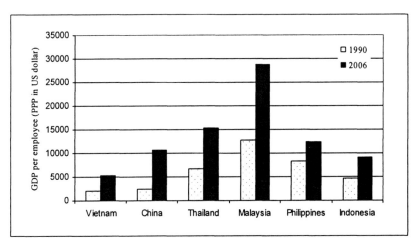

Source: ADB and IMF

Fifthly, the rapid globalization during the last few decades has opened up many opportunities. Vietnam's joining the WTO organization has affected every level of its economic activities. The lowering of tariffs and the dismantling of other restrictions to trade has generated intense competition and strong incentives for perceptive entrepreneurs. The result is that most domestic markets are being subject to increased competition from foreign firms. At the same time, a collaborative world in which countries seldom make complete products from start to finish offers plenty of opportunities. World trade barriers are breaking down and economic instabilities are better understood than in the past (ADB 2003, p208). In addition, competitiveness is considered by all countries to be a prerequisite for maintaining high levels of income and employment. Greater competitiveness allows Vietnam to diversify away from dependence on a few primary-commodity exports and move up the skills and technology ladder, this being essential in order to sustain rising wages and permit greater economies of scale and scope in production (UNCTAD 2002, p117). In this context, the Vietnamese government needs to rethink how to catch the opportunities and avoid challenges brought by globalization and to maintain the national competitiveness of Vietnam as well as its long run growth prospects. It possibly provides sound macroeconomic policies and necessary reforms in the financial and state owned enterprise sectors as well as public institution.

Due to the importance of the competitiveness in development processes in Vietnam, there have been a number of studies and conferences focusing on this problem. Le, Dang Doanh (2001) examined Vietnam's national and product competitiveness. Nguyen, Phuc Hien (2002) proposed some recommendations for enhancing the competitiveness of Vietnamese enterprises in the context of international economic integration. CIEM[2] (2003) took on the project of enhancing the national competitiveness of Vietnam. Vu, Minh Khuong and Johnathan Haughton (2003) conducted a study of the competitiveness of Vietnam's three largest cities (Hanoi, Hai Phong and Ho Chi Minh city). Wen-Jen Hsieh and other Vietnamese scholars (2004) carried on an analysis of national competitiveness: the perspective from Vietnam. Chiang Kao and other scholars (2007) measured the national competitiveness of Southeast Asian countries (included Vietnam). However, most of these studies remain descriptive and concentrate on specific impacts or aspects of Vietnam's competitiveness. A comprehensive analysis of the role of the competitiveness and its determinants as well as its emerging key issues in the development process in Vietnam are still lacking and policy recommendations are thus not very effective and feasible. This study is therefore to fulfil this gap: it investigates and analyzes drivers driving Vietnam's national competitiveness so as to propose measures to enhance its competitiveness.

---

2   Central Institution for Economic Management

1.2 Research Objectives

The overall purpose of this study is to examine Vietnam's national competitiveness as well as its determinants. The concrete intents of the study are:

1. To examine determinants driving Vietnam's national competitiveness.
2. To analyze and evaluate Vietnam's national competitiveness through using the combination of hard and survey data.
3. To point out emerging key issues of Vietnam's national competitiveness.
4. To propose some solutions and policy implications to enhance Vietnam's national competitiveness and sustain its economic growth.

1.3 Research Questions and Hypotheses

In order to reach the above objectives of this thesis, the main hypotheses of this study that are: (1)competitiveness approach is in the long run, (2)the fluctuation of exchange rate is excluded, (3) the Vietnamese economy is in the process of regional and global integration.

Research questions need to be answered that are:

1. What factors drive the national competitiveness of Vietnam? How does each factor influence Vietnam's national competitiveness?
2. How is the state of Vietnam's national competitiveness?
3. What are emerging key issues of Vietnam's national competitiveness?
4. What need to be done to enhance Vietnam's national competitiveness and sustain its growth?

1.4 Methodology

In order to answer the questions, multimethodology[3] or mixed methods research are used in this study. Mixed methods research is a combination of qualitative and quantitative methods (Creswell 2003, p 208). This combination is very common in sociology. It in the most general sense may involve multiple methods, multiple investigators, and multiple methodological and theoretical frameworks (Denzin, 1970 quoted in Fielding and Schreier 2001, p12). The value of the combination of qualitative and quantitative methods in a research is that qualitative and quantitative methods can validate or supplement each other and may result in illuminating

---

3   http://en.wikipedia.org/wiki/Multimethodology

insights about the investigated social phenomena (Kelle 2001, p1). This method is used to investigate determinants of Vietnam's national competitiveness. In addition, methods of analytical analysis, synthesis, statistics, and evaluation are used in analyzing and assessing the state of Vietnam's national competitiveness.

Data resources In order to conduct this study, we use both hard and survey data. Due to systemic and interdisciplinary nature of the theoretical framework and poor statistics of Vietnam, we could not rely on statistic data sources alone. We were forced to use survey data sources in order to match the wide variety of the theoretical frameworks and understand the research further. Hard data is collected from international and domestic organizations (ADB, WB, IMF, GSO, etc). Survey data is collected from WEF and conducted in Vietnam (see further in section 4.2.2).

1.5 Structure of the Thesis

This thesis is structured in seven chapters. *Chapter 1* presents an introduction, including research problem, objective, hypothesis and question, methodology and structure of the thesis.

In *Chapter 2*, we first discuss the conceptual frameworks of national competitiveness. Scholars and institutions have been very prolific in proposing their own definitions of competitiveness. Relying on multifaceted opinions, a condensed concept of national competitiveness is proposed. The evolution of competitiveness and the causes of competition among nations are included in this section.

In the second and third sections of this chapter, Porter's Diamond model and the stages of competitive development are presented. The model is a dynamic of competitiveness and it is also comprehensive because it aggregates all the ideas of competitiveness from classical to modern. The last section examines the "golden" rules of competitiveness that are fundamental to the analysis in the following chapters.

Chapter 3 examines determinants of national competitiveness and its roles. Relying on the above mentioned theoretical frameworks, six determinants of national competitiveness will be explored: Production Resources, Technology Development, Market Conditions, International Business and Economic Activities, Government Role and Company's Strategy and Operation. The interdependence among these determinants as a dynamic of national competitiveness also will be examined in this chapter. These determinants will provide most of the independent variables for our empirical study in the second section of chapter 4.

In *Chapter 4*, in the first section of this chapter, we discuss the economic development in Vietnam since its reform. This section shows us an outlook of expressive economic performance of Vietnam as well as its background and integration into the regional and global economy in two decades. In the second section, we empirically test all of the determinants presented in the previous chapter and above-mentioned summary. We do this by using a model of multiple linear regression. Models 1-3 will be conducted using hard data of time series from 1990-2005 with GDP per capita as the dependent variable. Models 4-6 will be done using survey data from 154 respondents with VNC[4] as the dependent variable. These results of the regression will provide empirical evidence which determines the drive of national competitiveness in Vietnam. The result is also a basic for analyzing the competitiveness of the Vietnamese economy in the following chapter.

In *Chapter 5*, we will analyze the state of Vietnam's national competitiveness relying on six identified determinants. We also evaluate Vietnam's competitiveness progress in the last two decades and the remaining weaknesses compared to some selected regional countries. Some main indicators are used to illustrate this analysis and assessment. This chapter is fundamental to point out some emerging key issues and to propose some solutions enhancing Vietnam's national competitiveness in coming years in the next chapter.

In *Chapter 6*, we first point out some emerging issues of Vietnam's competitiveness based on the analyzing of the previous chapter. These include production resource shortage and low quality, outdated technology, bureaucratic and corrupt administration, and slow SOEs reform. In the second section of the chapter we propose some solutions to enhance the competitiveness of Vietnam such as: addressing production resources shortage and quality; developing an independent and vibrant domestic private sector; strengthening public institution and government effectiveness. Each above mentioned solution includes some detailed recommendations.

Conclusions and findings of the thesis are presented in *chapter 7*.

---

4   VNC, standing for Vietnam national competitiveness, is identified by each respondent (see Appendix 5)

Chapter 2: Theoretical Frameworks of National Competitiveness

In this chapter, we first discuss the concept of national competitiveness. Scholars and institutions have been very prolific in proposing their own definitions of competitiveness. Relying on multifaceted opinions, a condensed concept of national competitiveness is proposed. The evolution of competitiveness and the causes of competition among nations are included in this section.

In the second and third sections of this chapter, Porter's Diamond model and the stages of competitive development are presented. The model is a dynamic of competitiveness and it is also comprehensive because it aggregates all the ideas of competitiveness from classical to modern. The last section examines the "golden" rules of competitiveness that is fundamental to the analysis in the following chapters.

2.1 The Concept of Competitiveness

In recent years, the concept of competitiveness has emerged as a new paradigm in economic development. Competitiveness captures the awareness of both the limitations and the challenges posed by global competition. Although its importance is acknowledged (Porter 2004, p 19), competitiveness has been a controversial topic among economists and scholars, especially competitiveness at national level.

2.1.1 National Competitiveness

National competitiveness has become a widely used term in economic literature in recent years. However, the wide and frequent usage of the term is not always based on a clearly defined meaning, and a lot of misunderstandings and contradiction are based on this terminological non-exactitude (Reiljan 2000, p7). In almost all papers concerning the competitiveness of a nation, it is not clearly determined what the target of a nation's competitiveness is. There is no accepted definition of competitiveness, and the term seems to mean different things to different researchers – some may stress a country's technological leadership, whereas others stress export shares, productivity or its growth rate (Boltho 1996, p 2; Fröhlich 1989, p 22; OECD 1992; Porter 1990, p 25). This refers to the typical treatment of the issue, meaning that instead of defining the competitiveness of a nation, various factors that influence competitiveness are explored. Most of the studies mentioning the competitiveness of a nation present the factors used to measure the competitiveness, however the concept itself is not defined. It is impossible to implement a correct measurement and interpret the results adequately when the target is not defined (Reiljan 2000, p9). On the basis of such studies it is hard to derive theoretically proven and practically applicable proposals.

The necessity of improving national competitiveness, its maintenance and emerging issues are being intensively discussed in both economic theories and practical life. The market economy is the competitive economy and therefore different theories consider competition to be an important part of economic activity. The increasing importance of national competitiveness can be explained by strongly economic integration and globalization, that also requires a constant growth of competitive strength (Reiljan 2000, p10).

Some economists have expressed very serious reservations about its meaning as they believe the idea to be very elusive. One of them is Krugman. He argued that definition of national competitiveness is a futile exercise and a dangerous obsession. National economies are not in direct competition with one another. One nation cannot go bankrupt in the way firms do. He argued that the notion of national competitiveness makes no sense (Krugman 1994, p 44). In addition, Reich (1990) stated that national competitiveness is one of the rare terms of public discourse that have gone directly from obscurity to meaninglessness without any intervening period of coherence.

Confusion in terminology and problems with defining competitiveness are not reasons for eliminating the term or ignoring practical analyses of the competitiveness of a nation. Fortunately, their arguments have not stopped thinking and research on national competitiveness (Hämäläinen 2003, p3). Lall (2000b) argued that national competitiveness, in fact, is a real issue that can be defined and measured. Porter stated that the concept of national competitiveness is meaningful and it is explained by national productivity (Porter 1990, p6). According to Porter, in order to understand competitiveness, the beginning point must be the sources of a nation's prosperity. A nation's standard of living is determined by the productivity of its economy, which is measured by the value of goods and services produced per unit of the nation's human, capital, and natural resources. The World Economic Forum defined competitiveness as ability of a country to achieve sustained high rates of growth in GDP per capita (WEF 1996, p19). In the World Competitiveness Yearbook (2003), IMD clarified that national competitiveness is the ability of a nation to create and maintain an environment that sustains more value creation for its enterprises and more prosperity for its people. This concept emphasizes a climate in which firms compete.

In contrast, OECD expresses a country's export share in international markets. National competitiveness is defined as ability of a nation to, under free trade and fair market conditions, produce goods and services which meet the test of international markets, while simultaneously maintaining and expanding the real income of its citizens over the long term. This makes competitiveness as a zero-sum game, because one country's gain comes at the expense of others. This view of competitiveness is used to justify intervention to skew market outcomes in a nation's favor (Porter 2003, p25).

Some others argued that economies may become more competitive by keeping their currencies undervalued through nominal depreciations. In the short-term there can be important gains in price competitiveness due to exchange rate fluctuations largely resulting from short term speculative capital flows. These exchange rate changes are much more volatile than productivity. The result is there can be sudden dramatic changes in price competitiveness without any change in the fundamentals. A strategy of keeping currency undervalued, however, will most likely be unsuccessful in the long-term since it may only mask and perpetuate a lack of productivity in the country's firms (UNIDO 2002). Countries that systematically rely on devaluation to maintain their competitiveness often fail to improve productivity and sustain economic growth in the long term.

Boxes: 2-1 Definitions of competitiveness

"Competitiveness, a field of economic knowledge, which analyses the facts and policies that shape the ability of a nation to create and maintain an environment that sustains more value creation for its enterprises and more prosperity for its people" (IMD's World Competitiveness Yearbook, 2003).

"Ability of a country to achieve sustained high rates of growth in GDP per capita" WEF, Global Competitiveness Report, 1996, p19.

"National competitiveness refers to a country's ability to create, produce, distribute and or service products in international trade while earning rising returns on its resources" (Scott, B.R: and Lodge, G.C.,"US competitiveness in the world economy", 1985, p3).

"Competitiveness includes both efficiency (reaching goals at the lowest possible cost) and effectiveness (having the right goals). It is this choice of industrial goals which is crucial. Competitiveness includes both the end and the means toward those ends" (Buckley, P.J. et al "Measures of International Competitiveness: A critical survey" Journal of Marketing Management, 1998).

"Competitiveness should be seen as a basic means to raise the standard of living, provide jobs to the unemployed and eradicate poverty" (competitiveness advisory group "Enhancing European Competitiveness" second report to the

President of the Commission, the Prime Ministers and the Heads of State, December 1995).

"Competitiveness is the degree to which a nation can, under free trade and fair market conditions, produce goods and services which meet the test of international markets, while simultaneously maintaining and expanding the real income of its people over the long-term" (OECD)

"The ability to produce goods and services that meet the test of international markets while citizens earn a standard of living that is both rising and sustainable over the long-run" (the First Report to the President and Congress, 1992. US Competitiveness Policy Council)

"Competitiveness implies elements of productivity, efficiency and profitability. But it is not an end in itself or target. It is a powerful means to achieve rising living standard and increasing social welfare – a tool for achieving targets. Globally, by increasing productivity and efficiency in the context of international specialization, competitiveness provides the basis for raising people's earnings in a non-inflationary way" (Competitiveness Advisory Group – Ciampi Group, Enhancing European Competitiveness, first report to the President of the Commission, the PM and the Heads of State, June 1995)

"Competitiveness should be seen as a basic means to raise the standard of living, provide jobs to the unemployed and eradicate poverty" (Competitiveness Advisory Group – Ciampi Group, Enhancing European Competitiveness. Second report to the President of the Commission, the PM and the Heads of State, June 1995
Source: IMD

In general, the studies from different scholars and organizations mention different aspects of the concept of national competitiveness. However, the concepts of competitiveness involving productivity and living standard are more widely accepted. In this study, the concept of national competitiveness is based on the following academic views of competitiveness from well-known different economists and organizations, which has inspired our research on national competitiveness.
National competitiveness refers to a nation's ability to create and sustain economic growth, and raises the standard of living of its citizens by improving national productivity in condition of a market economy[5].

---

5   The definition is based on the concept of the WEF, IDM, the report to the President and Congress, 1992 US Competitiveness Council, and the notion of competitiveness by M.Porter.

Obviously, productivity is fundamental to national competitiveness and a nation's living standard in the long term. Productivity will secure sustained economic growth and improvement in citizens' living conditions. Productivity depends both on the value of a nation's products and services, measured by the prices they can command in open markets, and the efficiency with which they can be produced (Porter 2003, p25). Productivity growth leads to rise in real incomes and living standards (Haque 1995, p23). Productivity is the target, not exports *per se*. Only if a country expands exports of products or services it can produce productively will raise national productivity (Porter 2003, p26). The productivity of nations is ultimately set by the productivity of their companies (Porter 2000, p 41). An economy cannot be competitive unless companies operating there are competitive, whether they are domestic firms or subsidiaries of foreign companies. The productivity of the entire economy matters for the standard of living, then, not just the trade sector (Porter 2004, p35).

The world economy is not a zero-sum game. Many countries can improve their prosperity if they can improve productivity (Porter 2004, p 21). Productivity allows a nation to support high wages, a strong currency, attractive returns to capital, and with them a high standard of living (Porter 2003, p26). It would be a delusion to consider that it is possible to gain competitiveness in conditions of low productivity. Developing countries, like Vietnam or China, have internationally competitive industries because the low cost of production is stem from the lower real wages. However, low wage based competitiveness is fleeting (Porter 1990). It would be wrong to consider a nation to be competitive if it is gained on the ground of low labor cost, decreasing wages and irrelevant working conditions. It rather refers to low level of competitiveness of a country because it is not able to guarantee higher income to its citizens (Mosley 1993, p 225). The central challenge in economic development, then, is how to create the conditions for rapid and sustained productivity growth (Porter 2003, p 25).

Ultimately, the target of national competitiveness is "general welfare". All other interpretations, including trade issues, are seen as major factors of competitiveness (Kitnmantel 1995, p106). The competitiveness of a nation is described by welfare of its citizen and economic growth. According to Fagerberg, competitiveness reflects the ability of a country to secure a high standard of living for its citizens relative to the citizens of other countries (Fagenberg 1996, p48). Landau's approach emphasizes the growth of citizens' living standard in line with relatively equal distribution of wealth, providing jobs to everyone who is able and willing to work; and doing it without harming the living standard of the next generation (Landau 1992, p299). Improving the standard of living and general welfare are considered to be final objectives of competitiveness (Tellisuuden Kestkusliitto 1989, p3). Success in foreign trade and foreign investment inflow can be seen as determinants that influence national competitiveness (see further in the next chapter).

Industry Competitiveness

Competitiveness of an industry, formed by the set of enterprises with similar activities could be to a certain extent similar to that of enterprise's competitiveness (Reiljan 2000, p14). Meanwhile, the industry is competing with other industries in the internal economy. In terms of the international economy, industry competes with similar foreign industries in other countries. The competitiveness of an industry is to a great extent determined by the economic and political framework. There are several factors that contribute to the growth of a certain industry's competitiveness such as the tax system, subsidies or import export terms etc. The overall research of economic and political benefits or restrictions and their impact allows one to evaluate where the industry operates efficiently, or just relies on benefits.

Enterprise Competitiveness

At the level of firm, competitiveness can be defined rather simply. Firms are competitive, if their products and their prices fit the requirements of the relevant markets, and they remain profitable in their business.

Enterprise competitiveness is the ability to sustain a market position by inter alia supplying quality products on time and at competitive prices through acquiring the flexibility to respond quickly to changes in demand and through successfully managing product differentiation by building up innovative capacity and an effective marketing system (Altenburg 1998). The competitiveness of a firm is the ability to do better than comparable firms in terms of sales, market shares and profitability, and is achieved through strategies. Buckley argued that a firm is competitive if it can produce products and services of superior quality and lower costs than its domestic and international competitors. Competitiveness is synonymous with a firm's long-term profit performance and its ability to compensate its employees and provide superior returns to its owners (Buckley 1998, p176).

The main difference between the competitiveness of an enterprise and that of a nation is that the enterprise will go bankrupt if it remains uncompetitive for long whereas a nation never goes out of business no matter how badly it is managed or how uncompetitive it is. When an economy loses its competitiveness, this is reflected in its declining employment, economic recession, rising inflation and deteriorating welfare rather than elimination from the market (Reiljian 2000, p 27). A nation remains competitive when it maintains some competitive industries and firms, and a competitive climate in which its firms compete. In turn, a competitive industry encompasses a firm or some firms which remain competitive in both domestic and international markets.

2.1.2 Motivations of Competition among Nations

Nations compete because world markets are open (IMD 2005, p 610) and they become more open over time. Why did nations finally agree to lower their barrier, at least for economic reasons? The answer probably lies in the aftermath of the Great Depression. Many scholars, J.M. Keynes in particular, have shown that an economic slowdown in 1929 developed into a worldwide depression in the 1930s because nations adopted protectionist policies. In order to prevent such a situation happening again, the Bretton Woods agreement, in 1944, sought to liberalize international trade. Today, tariffs on goods are less than 4% among members of the World Trade Organization (WTO). Moreover, the OECD, since its creation, has fostered the development of the free movement of capital, goods and services, at first among developed countries and then worldwide. Finally, free trade areas such as NAFTA and regional integration organizations such as NAFTA and regional integration organizations such as the European Union have reinforced this development.

Technology and globalization have accelerated the trend toward a World, which is not only open, but also transparent and immediate. Enterprises now benefit from an enormous choice in selecting their business locations. Consequently, nations need to promote their comparative advantages in various areas. For instance, competitiveness used to only focus on the ability to show aggressiveness on world markets through exports and foreign direct investment (FDI). Today, competitiveness also emphasizes the ability to develop attractiveness, both to foreign and local firms, for activities that generate economic wealth. (IMD 2005, p 611). There is no common recipe for competitiveness in every nation. Each individual country needs to adapt them to their own environment. Competitiveness strategies succeed when they balance the economic imperatives imposed by world markets with the social requirements of a nation formed by its history, value systems, and traditions. Some scholars claim that nations themselves do not compete, rather, their firms do. There is no doubt that competitive firms are main engines of a nation's competitiveness. They are at root of wealth creation. Nevertheless, over the last decades governments' role has increased to such an extent that it is simply impossible to ignore their influences on modern economics. Several recent studies continue to underline the key role of nations in shaping the environment in which firms operate. A significant part of the competitive advantage of nations stems from far-reaching incentive policies which are designed to attract foreign investment.

2.1.3 Evolution of Competitiveness Concept

Different goals and social values have been stressed at different stages of the development of economic thought and by different economic schools. Therefore the methods and means proposed for achieving high level of competitiveness have been also different. It explains also the difference between schools on the definition of competitiveness and its formation. In other words, the concepts of competitiveness is result of a long history of thoughts, which will help to define the various aspects of this more modern and complex concept (IMD 2005 p 617).
Representatives of the Mercantilist attitude do not consider the concept of competitiveness to be ambiguous. It seems obvious to them that countries compete with each other in the same way as corporations do. To a Mercantilist competitiveness means country's ability to export as much as possible and the "winner" is the one whose export volume exceeds import.

The classical model considers imports to be the purpose of trade. Exports are a cost to the country - produced but not consumed. Or to put it differently, exports are an indirect way to produce imports, because it is more efficient than the producing imported goods itself (Krugman 1996, p17-25). Representatives of classical school have expressed in several theories, especially the importance of achieving cost advantages. Adam Smith stated in his theory of absolute advantage that the one who is able to produce with the lowest cost in the world has the absolute advantage and thereby it determines basis of competitiveness (Smith 1776). David Ricardo explored comparative advantages in international trade. According to his view, international trade and specialized productions are implemented if comparative ratios of production costs by countries are different. This means that basis of exports can be only a relative advantage. Ricardo's view is that international trade is created by difference of labor productivity among countries (Ricardo 1817, p 89-105).

The Neo-classical school understands the limitations of both the Classical and the Mercantilist position. They find the arguments for intervention in economical processes unimpressive. Representatives of the Neo-classical school are cynical about the likelihood that subtle arguments for intervention can be translated into productive policies in the real world (Krugman 1996, p20). David Ricardo explained that comparative advantage arises from differences in labor productivity, but did not satisfactorily explain why labor productivity is different between countries. Hecksher-Ohlin's neo-classical theory of relative advantage argued that comparative advantage arises from differences in resource endowments and a country should specialize according to resource-endowments. It means that a country should specialize in products which production costs are relatively low because the factors of production are abundant (Best 1993, pp. 188).

Economists of Keynesian school want government to support domestic firms wherever there seems to be a winner-takes-all competition for future monopoly profits. The competitiveness of nations, as well as corporations, is determined by the efficiency of governmental economic policy. Both Europe and Japan consider government policy to be an effective factor of economic growth (Thurow, L 1992, p35). It is believed that the role of the government is to provide necessary conditions so that everyone can enter the market by which competitiveness is enhanced (see further in the next chapter).

Finally, Michael Porter who has tried to aggregate all these ideas into a systemic model, called the "Diamond" model. He stated that the only meaningful concept of competitiveness at the national level is national productivity (Porter 1990, p6). According to Porter, national prosperity is created, not inherited. Therefore his model is a dynamic of competitiveness. Porter model is also comprehensive because it includes not only factor conditions, as most traditional theories, but also other important variables simultaneously (see further in the next section). His model has played an important role in analyzing and assessing as well explaining the competitiveness of a nation by researchers and international organizations in recent years.

2.2   Porter's Diamond Model

Michael Porter offers a well-known model, the diamond model, which can help understand the competitiveness of a nation in global and regional competition. It is the fundamental model for much recent research involving national competitiveness such as the global competitiveness report (WEF-World Economic Forum) and the world competitiveness yearbook (IDM-Institute for Development Management). To find out what drives the national competitiveness of Vietnam, we use this as our basic model.

2.2.1   Determinants in the Model

Why does a nation achieve international success in a particular industry? Why is one company more competitive than any other company in a particular industry and in a nation? Why do some nations remain more competitive than other nations? (Porter 1990, p 1-5).

The answer lies in the "Diamond" model which analyses the environment in which local firms compete.   The model takes four environmental factors into consideration.

1. The factor condition is the nation's position in factors of production, including skilled labor, natural resources or infrastructure, necessary to compete in a given industry.

2. The demand condition is the nature of the domestic demand for the industry's products and services.

3. The related and supporting industries denote the presence or absence in the nation of supplier industries and related industries that are internationally competitive.

4. The firm strategy, structure and rivalry are the conditions in the nation governing how companies are created, organized, managed and nature of domestic rivalry.

The determinants, individual and as a system, create the context in which a nation's firms are born and compete: the availability of resources and skills necessary for competitive advantage in an industry; the information that shapes what opportunities are perceived and the directions in which the resources and skills are deployed; the goals of owners, managers and employees that are involved in or carry out competition; and most importantly, the pressure on firms to invest and innovate.

When a national environment permits and supports more rapid accumulation of specialized assets and skills– sometimes simply because of greater effort and commitment – companies gain competitive advantages. When a national environment affords better ongoing information and insight into product and process needs, companies reap competitive advantages. Ultimately, nations succeed in particular industries because their home environment is the most dynamic and the most challenging and it stimulates and prods firms to upgrade and widen their advantage over time.

Nations are most likely to succeed in industries or industry segments where the national "Diamond", a term Porter uses to refer to the determinants of a system, is the most favourable. The "Diamond" is a mutually reinforcing system. The effect of one determinant is contingent on the state of others. Favourable demand conditions, for example, will not create competitiveness unless the state of rivalry is sufficient to cause firms to respond to them. Advantages in one determinant can also create and upgrade advantages in others (Ibid., pp 132).

Chance and government, two additional determinants, can affect other determinants in differently important ways. Chance events are developments outside the control of firms, such as pure inventions or breakthroughs in foreign market demand. Government, at all levels, can improve or reduce from the national advantage. This role is seen most clearly by examining how policies influence each of the determinants.

2.2.2 The Diamond Model as a System

Each of these four determinants defines a point on the diamond of national advantages. The effect of one point often depends on the state of others. Sophisticated buyers will not translate into advanced products, for instance, unless the quality of human resources permits companies to meet buyer needs. Selective disadvantages in production will not motivate innovation unless rivalry is vigorous and company goals support sustained investment. At the broadest level, weakness in any determinant will constrain an industry's potential for advancement and upgrading (Ibid., pp 144).

The determinants of the diamond are self-reinforcing. They constitute a system. The determinants, especially domestic rivalry, have the power to transform the diamond into a system–domestic rivalry because it promotes improvement in all the other determinants and geographic concentration because it elevates and magnifies the interaction of the four separate influences.

The role of domestic rivalry illustrates how the diamond operates as a self-reinforcing system. Vigorous domestic rivalry stimulates the development of unique pools of specialized factors, particularly if the rivals are all located in one city or region. For example, the University of California at Davis has become the world's leading centre of wine-making research, in line with the California wine industry. In furniture and shoes industries, Italian consumers have learned to expect more and better products because of the rapid pace of new product development that is driven by strongly domestic competition among hundreds of Italian companies (Ibid., pp 146). Domestic rivalry also promotes the formation of related and supporting industries.

Figure 2. 1: Porter's Diamond Model

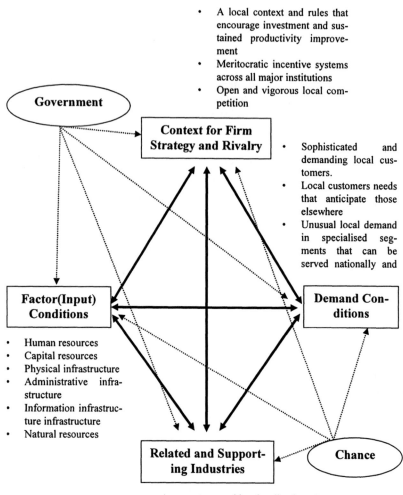

- A local context and rules that encourage investment and sustained productivity improvement
- Meritocratic incentive systems across all major institutions
- Open and vigorous local competition

Government

Context for Firm Strategy and Rivalry

- Sophisticated and demanding local customers.
- Local customers needs that anticipate those elsewhere
- Unusual local demand in specialised segments that can be served nationally and

Factor(Input) Conditions

Demand Conditions

- Human resources
- Capital resources
- Physical infrastructure
- Administrative infrastructure
- Information infrastructure infrastructure
- Natural resources

Related and Supporting Industries

Chance

- Access to capable, locally based suppliers and firms in related fields
- Presence of clusters instead of isolated industries

Sources: Porter (1990) and The Global Competitiveness Report 2004-05

The effects can work in all directions: sometimes suppliers become new entrants in the industry that they have been supplying, in turn, highly sophisticated buyers may themselves enter a supplier industry. Another effect of the diamond's systemic nature is that nations are rarely home to just one competitive industry; rather, the diamond creates an environment that promotes clusters of competitive industries. Competitive industries are not scattered helter-skelter throughout an economy but usually linked together through vertical (buyers and sellers) and horizontal (customers, technology and channels) relationships. One competitive industry can help to create others in a mutually reinforcing process. Japan's strength in consumer electronics, for example, drove its success in semiconductors toward the memory chips and integrated circuits these products use.

In general, the interplay among determinants encourages competitiveness among firms, industries and ultimately nations as described by Porter's diamond model (see Figure 2.1).

2.3 Stages of Competitive Development

National economic development or competitive development is a process of development stages. Each stage reflects the characteristic sources of advantages of a nation: productivity, a nation's competitiveness position, and national economic development level. Nations at different levels of development face distinctly different challenges (Porter 2004, p24).

The stages do not purport to explain everything about a nation or its development process. Some important concerns in development are inevitably left out, and no nation will fit a stage exactly. Instead, the stages are an effort to highlight attributes of a nation's competitiveness. Despite the diversity of most economies, we can identify a predominant or emergent pattern in the nature of a nation's competitiveness at a particular time. The pattern is reflected in the industries and segments in which the nation's firms can successfully compete as well as the types of strategies they employ.

A nation's competitiveness strategy is an art of balancing and enhancing a country's absolute advantage and comparative advantages. In each stage of development, the country has to decide *which factors to utilize; in which industries to invest; and where to innovate (Porter 1990, p 544-546).*

Therefore, defining stages of competitive development is important to derive strategic implications for a nation's competitiveness. Porter suggests four different stages of national competitive development: factor-driven; investment-driven;

innovation-driven and wealth-driven. In this section, we only introduce the first three stages, and analyze in detail the factor-driven and investment-driven development stages, which are the most meaningful for the research of developing countries (Figure 2.2).

Figure 2. 2: Stages of Competitive Development

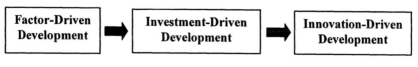

Sources: Porter (1990)

2.3.1 Factor-Driven Development

The resources-driven development is the initial stage, in which most companies from all internationally successful industries in a nation draw their advantages solely from basic resources of production such as: natural resources, or an abundant and inexpensive semi-skilled labor force. In the "Diamond" model only factor conditions are an advantage (Porter 1990, pp 546). This source of competitive advantage limits the range of industries and industry segments in which the nation's firms can successfully compete in international terms.

A nation's indigenous companies in such an economy compete solely on the basis *price* in industries that require either little product or process technology or technology that is inexpensive and widely available. Technology is sourced largely from other nations and not created. This occurs in some industries via imitation, import and foreign direct investment (Porter 2003, pp 28). More advanced product designs and technologies are obtained through passive investment in turn-key plants or are provided directly by foreign firms that operate production bases in the nation. In this stage, companies compete on price and few of a nation's companies have direct contact with end users. They have limited roles in valuce chain, focusing on assembly, labor-insentive manufacturing, and resource extraction. Foreign firms provide most of the access to foreign markets. Domestic demand for exported goods may be modest (Porter 1990, pp 546-548).

In this stage, an economy is sensitive to world economic cycles and exchange rates, which drive demand and relative prices. It is also vulnerable to the loss of factor advantage to other nations and rapidly shifting industrial leadership (Porter 2003, pp 28). While the possession of abundant natural resources may support a higher per capita income for a sustained period of time, a resources-driven economy is one with a poor foundation for sustained productivity growth.

The resources-driven stage is one that has characterized virtually all nations at some point time. Nearly all developing nations are at this stage, including transition nations such as China and Vietnam.

2.3.2 Investment-Driven Development

The next stage is investment-driven development. In this stage, national competitiveness is based on the willingness and ability of a nation and its companies to invest aggressively. Companies invest to construct modern, efficient, and often large-scale facilities equipped with the best technologies available on global markets. They also invest to acquire more complex foreign products and process technology through licenses, joint ventures and other means, which allow competition in more sophisticated industries and industry segments. Such technology is typically a generation behind international leaders, who are unwilling to sell the latest generation. In this stage, however, foreign technology and methods are not just applied but improved upon (Porter 1990, pp 549). The ability of a nation's industry to absorb and improve foreign technology is essential to reaching the investment-driven stage, and is the crucial difference between the resources- and investment-driven stages.

In this stage, basic resources become gradually advanced and a modern infrastructure is created through heavy investment from government, companies and individuals. Increasingly skilled workers and a growing pool of technical personnel, still paid relatively low wages, operate the sophisticated facilities and provide the internal capability to assimilate and improve technology (Porter 2003, p 29). Intense domestic competition in the industries in which the nation competes propels companies to invest continuously to push down costs, improve product quality, introduce new designs, and modernize production processes.

In the investment-driven stage, competitiveness is drawn from improving factor conditions as well as firm strategy, structure, and competition. While a nation's firms still retain competitive advantages in basic resources costs, competitive advantages widen to include low-cost but more advanced factors and the presence of well-functioning mechanisms for resource creation, such as educational institutions and research institutes.

The investment-driven stage, as its name indicates, is one where the ability and willingness to invest is the principal advantage rather than the ability to offer unique products or produce with unique processes. At this stage, companies still compete in *price-sensitive* segments of the markets, and product designs often reflect foreign market needs. Domestic demand in this stage is largely unsophisticated, because it exists in only a narrow and still emerging base of sophisticated industrial firms. A nation creates competitive advantage more from supply push than demand pull. Related and supporting industries are largely undeveloped in the nation at this stage. Production is almost solely based on foreign technology, foreign equipment, and even foreign components. As a result, process technology is modern but behind that of global leaders, and dependence on foreign suppliers constrains the pace of innovation. Typically, industries are relatively mature and produce either end products, basic components or undifferentiated materials. In mature industries, foreign rivals' plants may be obsolete, providing opportunities for a nation's firms to gain an advantage because of greater willingness to invest in modern assets.

The investment-driven stage is characterized by rapid gains in employment and the bidding up of wages and factor costs. Loss of competitive position in the most price-sensitive industries and segments begins. An investment-driven economy is concentrated on manufacturing and on outsourced service exports (Porter 2003, p 28). The economy becomes less vulnerable to global shocks and to movements in exchange rates than in the resources-driven stage, but it remains fragile.

The proper role of government in this stage reflects the sources of national competitiveness. Given that competition still rests heavily on factors and the willingness to invest, government's role can be important. It can be important in such areas as channelling scarce capital into particular industries, promoting risk taking, providing temporary protection to encourage the entry of domestic rivals and the construction of efficient scale facilities, stimulating and influencing the acquisition of foreign technology and encouraging exports. Government, at this stage, must also usually take the lead in making investments to create and upgrade resources, though companies and individuals must begin to play a growing role as well (Porter 1990, p 549-552).

2.3.3 Innovation-Driven Development

In the third stage, innovation-driven competitive development, all the determinants are at work and their interaction are at the strongest. This stage is called innovation-driven because firms not only appropriate and improve technology from other nations but create them (Ibid., pp. 554). National competitiveness due to factor costs becomes less important. Instead of factor cost advantages, the ability of produce innovative products and services at the global technology frontier using the most advanced methods becomes the dominant source of competitive advantages (Porter 2003, p 28). New mechanisms emerge to create advanced and specialized factors and continually upgrade them. Favorable advanced factors, demand conditions, and the presence of related and supporting industries in the nation allow firms to innovate and sustain innovation (Porter 1990, p 555). Consumer demand becomes increasingly sophisticated because of rising incomes, higher level education, increasing desire for convenience, and the invigorating role of domestic competition.

In this stage, firms compete internationally in more differentiated industry segments. They continue to compete on cost but now it depends not on factor costs but on productivity due to high skill level and advanced technology. The markets of price-sensitive segments are gradually transfered to firms from other nations. Companies also compete with self-contained global strategies and possess their own international marketing and service networks along with growing brand reputation abroad (Porter 1990). Foreign manufacturing develops in those industries whose structure favors a dispersed value chain either to reduce cost or to enhance marketing effectiveness in other nations. This stage also marks the onset of significant foreign direct investment.

In the innovation-driven stage, world-class related and supporting industries develop in important clusters. The clusters started in the factor and investment-driven stages become deepened and widened. In this stage, particularly, sophisticated services succeed in international competition and it becomes an important part of the economy.

This stage is also the most resistant to macroeconomic fluctuation and exogenous events. Industries are less vulnerable to external shocks and exchange rates movements because they compete on technology and differentiation. Firms' global strategies provide a buffer against such fluctuations. The proliferation of successful industries reduces dependence on any one sector.

Government's role in this stage is markedly different from the previous one. The appropriate philosophy and types of intervention change. Allocation of capital, protection, licensing control, export subsidy, and other forms of direct intervention lose relevance or effectiveness in innovation-driven competition (Porter 1990). In this stage, a government must rely more on the private sector. As an economy broadens and deepens, government cannot hope to keep track of all existing and new industries and all the linkages among them. Instead, government's efforts are best spent in indirect ways such as stimulating the creation of more and more advanced resources, improving the quality of domestic demand, encouraging new business formation, preserving domestic rivalry, and other areas.

2.4 The "Golden" Rule of National Competitiveness

In order to achieve a sustainable economic growth in the long run, it is essential for a nation to further build and sustain its productivity and competitiveness. Competitiveness is a multi-faceted phenomenon, which involves economic, social, political and international dimensions and relates to all players in the economy. Competitiveness cannot in the long-term be sustained unless all the dimensions contributing to it are properly addressed. It is however often the case that these dimensions result in conflicting priorities, especially in the short-term where, for instance, the attainment of social objectives may conflict with economic efficiency considerations. The achievement of competitiveness across all these dimensions in a sustainable manner will depend upon golden rules that could result in win-win situations for economic players in the long-term. The golden rules for competitiveness therefore cover virtually all aspects of economic policy and require inputs from all social partners (IMD 2005, p 615).

2.4.1 Creating a Stable and Predictable Legislative Environment

There are two fundamental legislative factors that strongly influence competitiveness. One is the orientation of legislation toward business in areas such as property rights and the burden and predictability of taxation. Such legislation and taxation must be as non-burdensome and as business-friendly as possible. It must be stable and predictable to minimize the possible risks to business. In addition, legislation has to be directly geared to stimulate business activity and promote competitiveness, by voiding distortions in product and factor markets, enforcing product safety and environmental standards and encouraging business competition.

The second aspect is the efficiency with which the rule of law is enforced. This entails adequate security and judicial services and the absence of corruption. An essential requirement for the conduct of business and investment is the respect of property rights in a country, the minimization of corruption and the upholding of the rule of law in general. Although these issues may appear obvious, they constitute the principal reason why a number of countries with relatively low costs, significant economic potential and substantial resources fail to attract the investment required to realize their competitiveness.

2.4.2 Working on Flexible and Resilient Economic Restructure

This involves, first and foremost, sound and disciplined pubic finances. A lower share of government expenditure in the national output allows more resources to be profitably used in the private sector, directly as government absorbs fewer labor and financial resources and indirectly, by leading to a lower tax burden. The second aspect of a macroeconomic structure conducive toward competitiveness is to have consistent and credible monetary and exchange rate policies. The third aspect is a market-oriented structural policy where resources are allowed to find their most profitable employment via the price mechanism and where markets are encouraged to function efficiently and competitively.

2.4.3 Investing in Physical and Technological Infrastructure

Infrastructure services should be provided at good quality and competitive costs in order to sustain competitiveness. Such services span beyond the provision of essential utilities and include information and communication technology needs. Of crucial importance within this context is a sound national financial system that enjoys a good reputation among market players and which effectively channels saving funds into investment while providing an efficient payments system.

2.4.4 Promoting Private Savings and Investment (Domestic and Foreign)

Attracting investment and foreign direct investment in particular, involves a proper mix between offering fiscal and other financial incentives and providing an appropriate economic climate for business in line with the golden rules for competitiveness discussed here. National competitiveness is nowadays increasingly dependent on the latter, as countries vying for international investment are all offering more or less equally attractive financial investment packages.

2.4.5 Developing Ability to Sell on the International Market (Exports)

This involves market aggressiveness and a pro-active approach to take advantage of potential opportunities, so as to anticipate the dynamics of demand and continuously balance the marketing mix in the most effective manner possible. This may involve substantial and on-going restructuring activities, particularly if these were previously oriented toward captive domestic markets.

2.4.6 Focusing on Transparency in Government

The quality and efficiency of public administration can make a substantial impact on business costs and competitiveness. Public administration provides a number of essential services to business as well as performing a regulatory role. It is important for a nation's competitiveness strategy that such services will be provided as efficiently as possible, while regulation is kept to the minimum required to achieve its aims, thereby resulting in the lowest possible burdens on the business sector. Administrative procedures faced by businesses should be reviewed toward this end. Transparency and procedure simplification facilitate the efficient operation of businesses and enhance their competitiveness.

2.4.7 Harmonizing a Relationship between Wages Levels, Productivity and Taxation

Competitiveness requires that labor costs remain within the bounds of the growth of its productivity. The role of the social partners is to ensure that efficient work practices are sought at all times, to enable firms to succeed in the competitive challenge, making it possible to share the benefits of higher profits and higher wages, reaped via increased productivity and competitiveness. It is important that wages do not move out of line with productivity, especially in the public sector where a hard budget constraint does not exist, as is normally the case in private sector operations. At the same time, the effect of taxation as a wedge between the productivity of labor and the reward received for work effort is to be minimized as much as possible by, amongst other things, moderating direct tax progressiveness to the extent possible.

2.4.8 Preserving the Social Structure by Strengthening the Middle Class

Social cohesion is important in its own right, but it is also indispensable for a country to sustain its competitiveness and its international image as a suitable and stable place where to invest and conduct business. In this respect, the welfare system has a role to play by moving away from all-encompassing schemes toward more focused programs aimed at fulfilling genuine needs. Efforts toward improving tax compliance by the higher-income earning stratum of society would also allow an easing of tax burdens on other segments of society and improve social consensus on measures aimed at improving national competitiveness.

2.4.9 Investing Heavily in Education

In an increasingly globalized world where physical and financial resources are highly mobile across countries, the quality of human capital accounts for a significant part of the competitive success of a country. Human capital availability is not only an important determinant of business investment, but is also the main engine of knowledge dissemination and innovation.

Chapter 3:   Determinants of National Competitiveness

In the previous chapter, we discussed the conceptual frameworks of national competitiveness such as the nature of national competitiveness; the development of ideas about competitiveness and international trade; the levels of competitiveness including firm, industry and nation; the "golden" rules of national competitiveness. Porter's diamond model and stages of competitive development were introduced in the chapter.

In this chapter, relying on the above mentioned theoretical frameworks, six determinants of national competitiveness and their role will be presented: Production Resources, Technology Development, Market Conditions, International Business and Economic Activities, Government Role and Company's Strategy and Operation. The interdependence among these determinants as a dynamic of national competitiveness also will be examined in the last section.

In the previous chapter we noted the diamond model which offered the basic understandings of the competitive advantages of nations and the mechanisms for creating these advantages. However, it must be said that the model is limited more or less in its application to developing nations (Cho 1994 and Moon 1998), such as China or Vietnam. Thus, the model's determinants need to be modified to be applied to developing or less developing countries, because these countries create national competitiveness based mainly on resource advantage, international business and economic activities, and government support (Cho and Moon 2000, and Hämäläinen 2003). As a result, six determinants are determined based on the diamond model and stages of competitive development. They are: production resources, technology development, market conditions, international business and economic activities, company's strategy and structure, and government role.

3.1 Production Resources

Each firm, industry and country possesses what economists have termed production resources (factor of production). Production resources are nothing more than the necessary inputs to compete in any firm, industry and nation such as labor, natural resources, capital, and infrastructure. Although the fundamental structures in industrialized economies have been changing, production resources will remain an important determinant of national competitiveness (Hämäläinen 2003, p 100). A nation's endowment of production resources clearly plays a role in economic growth and national competitiveness such as the rapid growth of manufacturing, productivity and competitiveness in low-wage countries such as Hong Kong, Taiwan, and Singapore, and more recently, Thailand, China, and Malaysia. But the role of production resources is different and far more complex than is often understood (Porter 1990).

3.1.1 Endowment of Production Resources

The endowment of production resources has been the cornerstone of the analysis of national competitiveness and economic growth since establishment of the classical school (Hämäläinen 2003, p. 101). As our review of economic growth and international trade theories revealed, classical economists divided production resources into relatively broad classes. The economists devoted the major parts of their works to analyzing the nature, origin and returns of three 'cores of production': land, labor and capital. In this research framework, production resources can be grouped into a number of categories: human resources, infrastructure, capital resources and natural resources.

Human resources is *a core* of a nation's competitiveness. It includes the quantity, skills, and cost of personnel, and takes into account standard working hours and work ethic (Porter 1990). Human resources are a fundamental that develops all other factors such as technology, advanced infrastructure, knowledge resources, and so on. Human resources can be divided into unskilled, semiskilled and skilled labor, of which skilled labor is the most important, and it has been given the most attention by economists in recent decades. Skilled labor can be classified into a myriad of categories such as skilled workers, graduate engineers, scientists, management, and so on. Two aspects of the quality of human resources require attention and investment. *The first* is investment in people's health. Current studies conducted in a variety of developing countries have confirmed the adverse effects on productivity of poor health and nutrition (Strauss, J., 1986, Deolalika 1988). *The second* is investment in education and training such as primary and secondary school, and tertiary education. Investment in education has become the prerequisite for any nation wanting to develop technology, productivity, competitiveness and economic growth, while technology has become inevitable for bringing education to society.

In the Global Competitiveness Report (2000), Horst Siebert, President of the Kiel Institute of World Economics in Germany, emphasized that improvement of national systems for human capital formation was a major determinant of competitiveness and economic growth. In the same vein, David Bryer, Executive Director of Oxfam, confirmed that the World Bank regards education as the single most valuable development intervention (Oxfam 2000, session 55 and session 25).
A study uses India's experience with the green revolution to shed light on this issue (Foster and Rosenzweig 1996, Foster.A.D and M.R. Rosenzweig) Using data on rural households, farming inputs, and crop yields, Foster and Rosenzweig

find that farmers with a primary education were in general more productive than their uneducated counterparts. Their findings strongly suggest that the benefits of education are greatest in the context of changing circumstances.

Infrastructure refers to the type, quality, and user cost of available infrastructure that affects competition, including the transportation system (road, ship, air, and railway), the communication system, mail and parcel delivery, payments and funds transfer, health care, and so on (Porter 1990). Infrastructure also includes the quality of life and the attractiveness of a nation as a place to live and work.

Capital resource refers to the amount and cost of capital available to finance firms and industries. Capital is not homogeneous, but comes in various forms such as unsecured debt, secured debt, bonds, equity, and venture capital. There are varying terms and conditions attached to each form. The total stock of capital resources in a country, and the forms in which it is deployed, are affected by the national rate of savings and by the structure of national capital markets, both of which vary widely among nations (Porter 1990, p. 75). The globalization of capital markets, and the large capital flows among nations, are slowly making national conditions more similar. However, substantial differences currently remain and are likely to remain indefinitely.

Natural resources refers to the abundance, quality, accessibility, and cost of a nation's land, water, mineral, and timber deposits, hydroelectric power sources, fishing grounds, and other physical traits. Climatic conditions can be viewed as part of a nation's physical resources, as can a nation's location and geographic size. Location, relative to other nations that are suppliers or markets, affects transportation costs and the ease of cultural and business interchange. For example, proximity to Germany has had an important historical influence on Swedish industry. The time zone of a nation relative to other nations may also be significant in a world of instantaneous global communication. London's position between the United States and Japan is often identified as an advantage in financial service industries, because London-based firms can do business with both Japan and the United States during a normal working day (Ibid., pp 76).

The combination of resources employed differs widely among firms and industries. A nation's firms gain competitiveness if they possess low-cost or uniquely high-quality resources of the particular types that are significant to competition in a particular firm and industry. For example, Singapore's location on a major trading route between Japan and Middle East has made it a centre for ship repair (Ibid., pp 154).

The role of resource endowment is more complicated than we often understood. Competitiveness from resources depends on *how efficiently* and *effectively* they are deployed. This reflects the choices made by a nation's firms about how to mobilize resources as well as the technology used to do so. Therefore, the value of particular resources can be dramatically altered by choice of technology (see the next section). Not only *how* but also *where* factors are deployed in an economy is important, because technological expertise and the most capable human resources can often be utilized in a variety of industries.

In the context of current globalization and regionalization has made local availability of some factors less essential. Natural resources, human resources, knowledge and capital factors can be mobile among nations through the modern global corporation. Once again, it is not mere access to resources but the ability to deploy them productively that takes on central importance to competitiveness. However, resource advantages, such as natural or low-cost labor, have facilitated nations to maintain economic growth and improve national competitiveness in the initial phase of economic development (Ibid., pp 545-548).

3.1.2 Classification of Production Resources and their Role

To explore the role of production resources in national competitiveness, production resources need to be classified clearly. Since the days of Adam Smith, production resources were classified into three broad factors: labor, land and capital. Porter (1990) has criticized the broad classification of resources for not being very helpful in explaining competitiveness in particular industries. He argues that a nation's firms gain competitiveness if they possess the specific resources that are significant to competitiveness in particular industry. This leads him to propose a new hierarchy of resources which defines the characteristics that determine their significance to particular industries. Dunning (1992) independently suggested a similar hierarchy of resources.

Basic and advanced resources. Basic resources include natural resources, climate, location, unskilled and semiskilled labor, and debt capital. They are important in extractive or agriculturally-based industries and in those where technological and skill requirements are modest and technology is widely available. Porter's research showed that competitiveness based on basic factors (low-wage cost) succeeded in the initial period of development, for example, construction industry in Korea[6], but the success is fleeting (Porter 1990).

---

6   Korean firms have enjoyed international success in the construction of civil projects, based in part on the availability of low-cost and disciplined Korean labor. However, firms from nations with even lower wages are supplanting Korean firms, and competitors from more

Advanced resources include modern digital data communication infrastructure, highly educated personnel such as graduate engineers and computer scientists, and university research institutes in sophisticated disciplines. They are now the most significant resources for competitiveness. They are necessary to achieve higher-order competitiveness such as differentiated products and proprietary production technology. They are scarcer because their development demands large and often sustained investment in both human and physical capital. The institutions required to create truly advanced resources (such as educational programs) themselves require sophisticated human resources and/or technology. Advanced resources are also more difficult to procure in global markets or to tap from afar via foreign subsidiaries. They are integral to the design and development of a company's products and processes as well as its capacity to innovate, which best takes place at the home base and must be closely connected to the firm's overall strategy (Porter 1990, pp 74-80).

A nation's advanced resources are often built upon basic factors. A supply of doctoral-level biologists, for instance, requires a number of talented university graduates in the field. This means that basic factor pools, while rarely a sustainable competitiveness in and of themselves, must be of sufficient quantity and quality to allow for the creation of related advanced resources.

Generalized and specialized resources. Generalized resources consist of the highway system, a supply of debt capital, and a number of well-motivated employees with college educations. They can be deployed in a wide range of firms. Specialized factors include narrowly skilled personnel, infrastructure with specific properties, knowledge bases in particular fields, and other resources with relevance to a limited range of or even to just a single firm (Porter 1990, p 78).

Specialized factors based competitiveness is more sustainable than generalized factors based competitiveness. Generalized factors provide a support only more rudimentary competitive advantages in the initial stage of development process. They are often available in many nations and tend to be more easily nullified, circumvented, or sourced through global corporate networks. Activities based on generalized factors (such as labor-intensive assembly operations requiring semi-skilled employees) can often be readily carried on at a distance from home base (Ibid., p 78).

---

advanced nations such as Italy are sourcing cheap labor pools locally in nations where they bid on international contracts or from developing countries, nullifying the Korean advantage. The result is that the Korean construction industry is in sharp decline (Porter 1990)

Specialized factors need more concentrated, and often riskier, private and social investment. In many cases they depend on already having a root of generalized factors. Both of these things make them scarcer. Specialized or advanced factors are necessary in more complex or propriety company activities, and they are necessary to remain the competitiveness sustainable (Ibid., p 79).

When a nation possesses both advanced and specialized resources for competing in a particular industry, that nation's competitiveness becomes more significant and sustainable. In contrast, competitiveness based on basic or generalized factors is unsophisticated and often fleeting. The specialization's standard is also biased to rise, hence today's specialized resources are prone to become tomorrow's generalized resources (Porter 1990).

In the sophisticated industries that form the backbone of any advanced economy, a nation does not inherit but instead creates the most important factors of production, such as skilled human resources or a scientific base. Moreover, the stock of resources that a nation can enjoy at a particular time is less important than the rate and efficiency with which it creates, upgrades and deploys them in particular firms and industries (Ibid., pp 81).

Created and specialized resources tend to be human capital and skill-intensive. Charles Sabel has argued that organizations need more skilled employees in uncertain environments where the information processing requirements are more demanding (Sabel 1990). He expects to find such environments where the product market fluctuations are wide, each product is more or less unique or produced in small batches, there is rapid technological change, or raw materials and parts are not available in a standardized form. Many of these uncertainties have increased since the early 1970s as a result of macroeconomic instability and a shift in the techno-economic paradigm (Piore and Sabel 1984; Freeman and Perez 1988).

The demand for created and specialized resources is also increased by the changing nature of production processes. The increasing specialization and complexity of production processes decreases the importance of direct production activities relative to transaction and coordination activities (costs) (Wallis and North 1986). Since many transaction and coordination activities require advanced technology (airplanes, telecommunications equipment, computers etc.) and highly skilled human capital (manager, engineers, lawyers, traders etc.), the demand for knowledge-intensive, created and specialized resources are prone to increase at higher levels of economic development. At the same time the increasing specialization, mechanization and efficiency of production processes reduces the demand for basic raw materials and unskilled labor, and increases the demand for well-trained technicians, machine operators and service personnel.

In general, the increasing specialization and division of labor in modern value-adding systems has increased organizational uncertainties by making the production systems more complex and interdependent. The increasing complexity and interdependence of production systems increases the information processing needs of organizations and puts growing demands on the skill level of workers and managers. As a result, the demand for well-trained and knowledgeable workers and managers is likely to increase in economies characterized by an extensive division of labor.

3.2 Technology Development

Historically, many developing countries have attracted trade and foreign investment primarily due to their advantages in low-cost raw materials and cheap, unskilled labor. Since approximately the mid-1980s, there has been a trend toward export-oriented development, and many governments have attempted to bias foreign investment and domestic business enterprise toward exports rather than import substitutions (Abdullah, 1995, UNIDO). These policies often require offering incentives to firms to invest in technologies which are internationally competitive. As firms in developing countries acquire new technology but also become more exposed to international competition, there will be further need to combine technological and human resources in ways which enable them to compete at home and abroad (Abdullah, 1995; Tung 1994).

3.2.1 Technology and Competitiveness

At a given period of the time, the competitiveness, productivity and growth of an economic system is determined by technology in two ways. First, the efficiency and costs with which the system transform its productive resources into growth-creating outputs is shaped by the available *process technologies*. Second, the *existing product technologies* are important determinants of consumer value, productivity, competitiveness and growth. As a result, technology influences both the *price and non-price* competitiveness of firms and economic systems (Hämäläinen 2003).

The importance of technological innovation for productivity, competitiveness and economic performance has been recognized at least since Joseph Schumpeter's seminal works[7] (Schumpeter 1934). Schumpeter was particularly critical of the

---

7   Although Schumpeter's name is usually mentioned in the context of technological innovation, his own definition of innovation was much broader. It includes five categories of inno-

prevailing neoclassical theory of the early twentieth century which explained economic growth in terms of resource accumulation.[8]

Both Schumpeter and Keynes' critiques of the neoclassical paradigm were published in the turbulent 1930s. During the postwar years, the stabilization of the macroeconomic environment and the relatively smooth evolution of technologies provided a more fertile ground for elaboration and policy application of the Keynesian macroeconomic theory than the Schumpeterian innovation theory. However, during the past three decades, the situation has changed quite dramatically as the macroeconomic theories and policies proved insufficient in the face of the growing macroeconomic problems of the 1970s and a sign of a new technological revolution has become stronger in the 1980s. As a result, the research on national productivity and competitiveness has recently begun to emphasize the importance of technological innovations for economic performance.

It is widely accepted in the economics literature that technology plays a significant role in productivity, competitiveness and economic growth. Partly due to its own fast-changing nature and partly because of the increasingly integrated world economies, technology per se has moved to the centre stage in economic analysis. Rapid technological advancement is quickly shifting the frontiers of technology, leading to tremendous improvement in the competitive strength of firms and industries. Increased globalization of economies is necessitating further improvements in the competitiveness of firms and industries by intensifying international competitive pressures. The competitiveness of a firm can be taken to be its ability to do better than comparable firms in sales, markets shares, or profitability (Lall 2001). In highly competitive environments and in the context of international integration, the competitiveness of firms and industries depend primarily on technology. Technology makes higher sales possible in many ways, either through the introduction of a new and superior product; by improving the quality of existing products, or through efficient utilization of resources-productivity improvement resulting in cost reductions; by improving access to customers, or through a combination of all of the above. In other words, technology enables firms and industries to expand their sales in both domestic and foreign markets by making it possible for them to supply increasing quantities of quality products at cheaper prices.

---

vations: product innovation, process innovation, market innovation, supply innovation, and organizational innovation.

8   The slow and continuous increase in time of the national supply of productive means and of savings is obviously an important factor in explaining the fact that development consists primarily in employing existing resources in a different way, in doing new things with them, irrespective of whether those resources increase or not (Schumpeter 1934, p. 68)

3.2.2 The Processing of Technology Development

The productivity and competitiveness impact of new technology is determined by a *two-phased process of transfer and innovation*. The relative importance of transfer and innovation of technology for a particular economy depends on its indigenous technological resources and capabilities vis-à-vis those of the rest of the world. Thus small and developing nations are relatively more dependent on the transfer and diffusion of foreign technologies than on innovation and diffusion of indigenous ones.[9] However, all economic systems are likely to need some indigenous innovation activities since their 'absorptive capacity', the ability to utilize technologies developed elsewhere, depends critically on such the activities (Cohen and Levinthal 1989; OECD 1996a).

Absorption and diffusion are two aspects of the transfer of technology. Absorption refers to technology users who import technology from other countries, often developed countries. In contrast, diffusion refers to technology exporters who create new technologies. The two next sections analyze the phases of transfer, absorption and innovation, and their roles in productivity and competitiveness.

3.2.2.1 Technology Transfer

Technology absorption is vital to developing countries. They import new technology, equipment, patents and so on from developed countries, but they have to learn to use these imports effectively. Using new technology is not an automatic and simple process. It entails the conscious building of technological capabilities: a mixture of information, skills, interactions and routines that firms need in order to handle the tacit elements of technology. If an economy does not build its capacity for technology absorption, technology transfer becomes less effective and wastes resources. As a result it reduces national productivity and competitiveness.

Transferring technology effectively is not easy, not costless or automatic (UNCTAD 2003). Micro-level research on developing countries, based on the evolutionary theories of Nelson and Winter (1982), shows how complex and demanding the task can be. Technology is not sold in embodied forms. Its tacit elements need effort and time to master. Its efficient use cannot therefore be assumed for poor countries that expose themselves to more world markets and technologies. Technological mastery entails building costly new capabilities; it takes time and investment and is uncertain. Technology transfer requires supporting changes in factor markets, i.e., in the creation of skills to access, master and improve upon

---

9   According to OECD small nations depend on imports for more than 50 percent of their acquired technology, OECD 1996.

new technologies. Enterprises cannot therefore develop capabilities in isolation (UNCTAD 2003). They need to coordinate with government, and local and foreign institutions. There are two broad approaches: fostering learning by domestic firms (autonomous) and depending on FDI to drive technological upgrading. Both entail the extensive use of foreign technologies, but the different agents for fostering learning involve different strategies to import, absorb and build upon new technologies.

Transferring and using new technology requires investment and conscious effort. Much of the effort lies has to be undertaken by the firms themselves, however, a significant part of the effort must be undertaken by other firms, factor markets and support institutions. While the transfer and capability-building process is essential in both developed and developing countries, it tends to be more difficult in the latter, due to weak enterprises, networks, markets and institutions. Furthermore, mastering new technology is not a one-off task. Most developing economies start with comparatively simple, labor-intensive technologies where skill needs are low, learning is short and relatively less risky, and there is little inter-firm or inter-industry coordination. Once mastery is achieved, continued development involves the upgrading and deepening of technologies. Otherwise, countries that establish a competitive niche in a low-technology activity may stagnate at the bottom of technology ladder. To sustain competitiveness, they must move into more advanced technologies and technological functions. The below salient features of technology and learning help us to understand further technology transfer and its roles as well.

Box 1 The salient features of technology and learning

1. Technological learning is a real and significant process. It is conscious and purposive than automatic and passive. Firms using a given technology for similar periods need not to be equally proficient: each would travel on a different learning curve according to the intensity and efficacy of its capability building efforts.

2. Firms do not have full information on technical alternatives. They function with imperfect, variable and rather hazy knowledge of technologies they are using.

3. Firms may not know how to build up the necessary capabilities — learning itself often has to be learned. The learning process faces risk, uncertainty and cost. For a technological latecomer, the fact that others have already undergone the learning process is both a benefit and a cost. It is a benefit in that they can borrow from the others' experience. It is a cost in that they are relatively inefficient during the process.

4. Firms cope with uncertainty not by maximizing a well-defined function but by developing organizational and managerial "satisfying" routines (Nelson and Winter, 1982). These are adapted as firms collect new information, learn from experience and imitate other firms. Learning is path–dependent and cumulative.

5. The learning process is highly technology-specific, since technologies differ in their learning requirements. Some technologies are more embodied in equipment while others have greater tacit elements. Process technologies (like chemical) are more embodied than engineering technologies (machinery and automobile) and demand different effort. Capabilities built up in one activity are not easily transferable to another.

6. Different technologies have different spillover effects and potential for further technological advances. Specialization in technologies with more technological potential and spillovers has greater dynamic benefits than specialization in technologies with limited potential.

7. Capability building occurs at all levels: shop-floor, process or products engineering, quality management, maintenance, procurement, inventory control, outbound logistics and relations with other firms and institutions. Innovation in the sense of formal R&D is at one end of the spectrum of technological activity; it does not exhaust it. However, R&D becomes important as more complex technologies are used: some R&D is needed just for efficient absorption.

8. Technological development can take place to different depths. The attainment of a minimum level of operational capability (know-how) is essential to all activity. This may not lead to deeper capabilities, an understanding of the principles of technology (know-why): this requires a discrete strategy to invest in deepening. The deeper the levels of technological capabilities aimed at, the higher the costs, risk and duration involved. The development of know-why allows firms to select better the technologies they need, lower the costs of buying those technologies, realize more value by adding their own knowledge, and develop autonomous innovative capabilities.

9. Technological learning is rife with externalities and inter-linkages. It is driven by links with suppliers of inputs or capital goods, competitors, customers, consultants, and technology suppliers. There are also interaction with firms in unrelated industries, technology institutes, extension service, universities, associations and training institutions. Where information flows are particularly dense, clusters emerge with collective learning for the group as a whole.

10. Technological interactions occur within a country and with other countries. Imported technology is generally the most important initial input into learning in developing countries. Since technology changes constantly, moreover, access to foreign sources of innovation is vital to continued technological progress. Technology import is not, however, a substitute for indigenous capability development — the efficacy with which imported technology is used depends on local efforts to deepen the absorptive base. Similarly, not all modes of technology import are equally conductive to indigenous learning. Some come highly packaged with complementary factors, and so stimulate less learning.

Source: Lall, S. 2000.b

The literature on technology transfer and diffusion distinguishes between two distinctions: *internalized and externalized, and disembodied and equipment embodied* technology transfer (UNCTAD, 2003; OECD, 1992, 1996a). Internalized technology transfer proceeds from a multinational company to affiliates under its control. In the case of externalized technology transfer the process occurs between independent firms. While internalized modes necessarily involve MNCs, externalized ones may also involve MNCs selling technologies on contract (MNCs are the largest sellers of licensed technology). The sale can take a variety of forms: minority joint ventures, franchising, turnkey projects, sale of equipment, licences, technical assistance, subcontracting or original equipment manufacturing arrangements. Internalized transfers bring with them a package of supporting inputs to ensure their efficient deployment. Externalized transfers may involve additional inputs by the technology seller, but generally tend to call for greater learning effort by the recipient.

In general, internalized technology flows are a very efficient means of transferring a package of capital, skills, information and brand names to developing countries. For many new technologies, internalized transfers are the only possible mode of transfer, since innovators are unwilling to part with them to unrelated parties. Even where technologies are available at arm's length, internalization may be the most efficient way of transferring the tacit knowledge involved because of the commitment of transferor and its capability to support learning. If the technology is changing rapidly, internalization provides the most direct access to improvements. If the activity is export-oriented, internalized transfers offer the additional advantages of international marketing skills and networks, established brand names or, of increasing relevance, access to integrated production structures spanning several countries.

However, internalized technology transfers also carry costs. Profits are realized by the MNCs on the package as a whole rather than just the innovation component. If the host country already possesses other elements of the package, it may be cheaper to buy the technology separately.[10] In general, the more standardized and diffused the technology and the more capable the buyer, the more economical externalized modes will be. However, there is a more subtle reason: the existence of learning benefits, deepening and externalities may tilt the choice in favor of externalization, even for relatively complex and difficult technology. For these activities, reliance on foreign investment can shorten the learning period but reduce the other benefits of technology transfer and capability building (UNCTAD 2003).

One advantage of internalized forms of technology transfer lies in the long-term commitment of foreign partners to the project and its ability to provide the elements needed to operate new technologies. At the lowest level, therefore, foreign investment is a very efficient way of transferring technology. Since all technolo-

---

10   Economies such as the Republic of Korea and the Taiwan Province of China did this because their enterprises had the necessary capabilities to master the technology.

gies need adaptation and improvement, foreign affiliates, with their base of high-level management and technical skills, tend to be in the forefront of such activity in developing countries. In addition, MNCs have the experience of other affiliates in the developing world to draw on, and can shift knowledge and personnel across countries to help with the upgrading of local capabilities.

Disembodied technology transfer is the process whereby new technology is spread through channels other than embodiment in machinery and equipment. It results from knowledge spillovers that characterize innovation processes. Equipment-embodied or hard technology transfer, in turn, is the process whereby innovations spread in the economy through the purchase of technologically intensive machinery, components and other equipment.

Disembodied diffusion may be organized, e.g., when firms license innovation or when MNEs transfer new process or product knowledge to their foreign subsidiaries. More often, however, it is a by-product of the firm's innovative activities as new knowledge "spills over" to other firms. In either case knowledge transfer takes place mainly through research channels (OECD 1996b).

Knowledge spillovers occur when innovating organisations cannot appropriate fully the benefits of their innovations. As we will see, the weak appropriability[11] of technological innovation stems from its public-goods characteristics. Innovation tends to leak into the public domain through channels such reversing engineering, trade publication and patent application, conferences, seminars, turnover of R&D personnel, and inter-firm cooperation. As a result, the private and public benefits of innovatory activities differ and policy makers must weigh the benefits of a strong appropriability regime[12] against those of more rapid transfer and diffusion of innovations[13].

The *equipment-embodied* transfer of technology is typically related to a few key industries that act as suppliers of new technologically intensive machinery, equipment and components to several "downstream" industries, consumers and government. These industries, which receive little inflow of embodied R&D from other industries, are mainly in the R&D intensive manufacturing sector[14]. On the other hand, service sectors are the main acquirers of technologically sophisticated machinery and equipment (OECD 1992, 1996a).

---

11   Appropriability regimes will be discussed in next section.
12   A strong appropriability regime provides incentive for innovation.
13   A weaker appropriability regime provides greater macroeconomic benefits.
14   Some examples are: electrical machinery, drugs, medicines, chemicals, instruments, communications, and information processing equipment.

The equipment-embodied transfer of technology is particularly important for developing countries which usually lack indigenous R&D capabilities and must acquire foreign technology (OECD 1996a). An OECD study on technology diffusion shows that the bulk of acquired technology comes from the cluster of industries related to information technology, and the importance of this industry has increased over time. This is the fastest growing technology cluster. Moreover, certain types of technology tend to gravitate to certain sectors: information technology to high technology manufacturing, communication, services and finances, insurance and real estate; transport technology to transport service; consumers good technology to wholesale and retail trade; materials technology to agriculture and to medium and low technology manufacturing; and fabrication technology to mining, utilities and construction (OECD 1996b).

The above discussion suggests that the processing of technology transfer and capability building are fundamental for following phase-technology innovation.

3.2.2.2 Technology Innovation

Most technological innovation is carried out by profit-oriented firms that weigh their innovatory investments in terms of expected profits (Pavitt 1987). Since outputs of an innovation are positively related to its inputs (Dosi 1984), the conditions for successful innovation are related to factors that influence the expected return and costs of innovatory investments. In this section, we discuss five such factors: market potential; technological opportunities; appropriability regime; organizational capabilities; and incentive mechanism (Hämäläinen 2003).

Market potential Other things being equal, innovatory investments and output will be positively related to the size of the potential market. One of the earliest references to the effect of the market potential on technological innovation can be found in Adam Smith's *Wealth of Nations*, where it was argued that one of three main advantages of economic specialization was the "invention of a great number of machines which facilitate and abridge labor, and enable the one man to do the work of many" (Smith [1776]1998). More importantly he emphasized that advantages of specialization were limited by the 'extent of the market'. Thus Smith was probably the first to suggest that technological innovation is driven by market potential.

More recently, Jacob Schmookler (1966) has made a persuasive argument that links the increasing output of innovatory activities to the growth of markets in the United States. His time series and cross-sectional data show that technological innovations are driven by the market potential of the products and services involved. Schmookler's argument is consistent with Nelson and Winter's (1977) observation that major technological trajectories tend to be characterized by a wide scope for specialization, division of labor and mechanization. Market potential affects the innovation process in three different ways: first, it provides the selection criteria among the alternative technological paradigms; second, it defines the precise trajectory of advance within an established paradigm; and third, it determines the rate of technical progress along the trajectory (Dosi 1988).

Technological opportunities Schmooklers's 'demand-pull' argument has been criticized by scholars who believe that the set of potential technological trajectories is quite limited by the rules, technical imperatives and specific scope of advance of each technology (Rosenberg 1976; Mowery and Rosenberg 1979; Freeman 1982) These scholars argue that technological opportunities are limited in the short term, and market conditions only stimulate, hinder and focus the research for new technological paradigms. Instead of demand-pull they emphasize the "technology-push' argument where scientific discoveries open up new possibilities for technological innovation. Salter explains:

An industry may be born around some scientific principles. Subsequently there is a great potential for improvement around the same basic principle. A specialized technology arises and, for a period at least, brings forth a continuous flow of significant improvement and modifications... At any one time, some industries are in this stage of rapid improvement, while others, more mature, find significant advances less frequent and less rewarding (Salter 1960).

As suggested by Salter, the technology-push argument recognizes that technological opportunities, and thus the expected returns of innovatory activity, are sector-specific and depend on the maturity of the technological paradigm (Dosi 1988).

Appropriability regime refers to the environmental factors that govern an innovator's ability to capture the profits generated by his innovation (Teece 1987). Since most technologies have public-good characteristics, the nature of the appropriability regime, whether it is tight or weak, is an important determinant of the expected return of innovatory activities. Factors that affect the appropriability of innovations are related to: the properties of the technological knowledge (e.g., tacit versus codified); market structure; (oligopolistic versus competitive); legal environment (enforcement of patents, copyrights, trademarks, etc.); and access to necessary complementary assets. These factors are also likely to vary among industrial sectors and technologies (Magee 1977; Teece 1987; Dosi 1988).

The degree to which knowledge is tacit or codified affects the ease of imitation by competitors. Tacit knowledge is more difficult to transmit and receive than codified knowledge and thus offers better protection against potential imitators (Teece 1987). Market structure determines the intensity of imitation pressures faced by innovators and thus the expected quasi-rents from a given innovatory investment. In general, the more competitive the industrial environment, the lower are the quasi-rents of the innovator (OECD 1992). The property rights regime is another, but often over-emphasized, determinant of appropriability. Secrecy, lead times, imitation costs, learning, scale economies, superior sales, and servicing efforts are often more important for appropriability (Levin et al 1987; Mansfied 1986; Dosi 1988). Finally, the appropriability of innovation may also depend on the innovator's access to important complementary assets (Teece 1987). This factor becomes more important at higher levels of economic specialization where the complementary assets are increasingly firm-specific and dispersed in the production system.

Organizational resources and capabilities Firms possess a unique bundle of resources and organizational capabilities. Since a high proportion of technological innovation takes place within firms, their unique resources and capabilities become an important determinant of technological innovation. In particular, firms that are successful innovators tend to focus their innovatory efforts in areas that are close to their existing organizational strengths (Cooper 1983; Maidique 1983). Thus, technological change becomes a cumulative process where a firm's new technologies are constrained by its past innovatory activities. If these cumulative and firm-specific patterns of technology can be identified, measured and explained, it is possible to predict the future evolution of technological innovations in firms, industries and nations (Pavitt 1987; Dosi 1988).

Incentive mechanism As with any other economic activity, the efficiency of innovatory activities depends on positive or negative incentives. Besides the key role of competition, the technological innovation literature identifies the following 'incentive mechanisms': technological bottlenecks; scarcities of critical inputs; abundance of particular resources (e.g., energy and natural resources); major shocks in prices or supplies; composition, change and growth of demand; industrial conflicts; close user-producer interaction; and tight regulatory standards. These factors stimulate technological innovation, however, incentive mechanism depends on the specific nature of technology and institutional context of each nation.

In sum, technology plays crucial role in improving productivity and competitiveness. It influences strongly other determinants of competitiveness, by creating dynamics for the competitiveness of firms, industries and nations. These influences will be analysed further in section 3.7.

3.3 Market Conditions

Market conditions are frameworks that create a competitive environment in which firms can compete and operate in order to achieve their goals. Market conditions have played a critical, if not decisive, role in improving a firm's competitiveness as well as a nation's one. A nation does not remain competitive unless it creates good market conditions (Porter 1990, pp 86-96). In this section, we analyze market conditions as the density of domestic competition.

Domestic competition is competition among firms in a local market. Porter's study showed that nations with a leading world position often have a number of strong internal competitors, even in small countries such as Switzerland or Sweden. This is true not only in fragmented industries but also in industries with substantial economies of scale. It is also true in the United States in the computer and software industries. Nowhere is role of fierce competition more apparent than in Japan.[15] Domestic competition is arguably the most important for the competitiveness of a firm, industry and nation because of powerfully stimulating effect it has on the others.

Static efficiency is much less important than dynamic improvement, which domestic competition uniquely spurs. Domestic competition, like international market competition, creates pressure to innovate and improve. The competition of local rivals leads to lower costs, improve quality and service, and create new products and processes. But unlike competition with foreign competitors, which tends to be analytic and distant, local competition goes beyond pure economic and business competition and becomes intensely personal. Domestic competitors engage in active feuds. They compete not only for market share but also for people, for technical excellence, and perhaps most importantly for "bragging rights" (Porter 1990). One local competitor's success proves to others that advancement is possible and attracts new competitors to the industry.

Domestic competition not only creates pressures to innovate but also to innovate in ways that improve the competitiveness of a nation's firms (Porter 1990). The presence of domestic rivals nullifies the types of advantages that come simply from being in the nation, such as factor costs, access to home market, a local supplier base, and cost of importing that must be borne by foreign firms. If there are a number of Korean rivals in an industry, for instance, none gets an advantage simply because of low labor costs or low-cost debt financing. This forces a nation's

---

15   where there are more 112 companies competing in machine tools, 34 in semiconductors, 25 in audio equipment, 15 in cameras-in fact, there are usually double figures in the industries in which Japan boasts global dominance (Porter 1990).

firms to seek higher-order advantages and ultimately it becomes a sustainable source of competitiveness. Firms must seek propriety technologies, reap economies of scale, exploit national advantages more effectively than the competitors, and create their own international market networks. Intense domestic rivalry helps to break the attitude of dependence on factor-based competitiveness (Porter 1990).

Home competition also enhances the competitiveness of firms and industries which in turn improves the national competitiveness. A group of domestic competitors tries alternative approaches to strategy and creates a range of products and services that cover many segments. This enhances innovation and productivity, and a breadth of products and approaches builds defences against foreign penetration. The competitiveness of an industry is made more sustainable by removing some avenues for entry by foreign competitors. Good ideas are imitated and improved upon by local competitors, raising the overall rate of industry innovation. The stock of knowledge and skills in the industry accumulates as firms imitate each other and as personnel move among firms. Ideas diffuse faster within a nation than across nations because it is difficult for firms from other countries to tap into such a process. Though individual firms cannot keep innovation proprietary for long, the entire national industry progresses faster than foreign competitors, and this supports profitability for many of the nation's firms (Porter 1990).

A geographic concentration of competitors in a city or region within a nation both shows and strengthen the improvement of national competitiveness (Porter 1990). In such an environment, popular luncheon spots are patronized by executives from several companies, who eye each other and trade the latest gossip. Information flows with enormous speed. Firms must move fast to sustain their competitiveness, whereby the overall national competitiveness improves.

The competition in a nation not only creates advantage but helps to avoid disadvantages in sustaining the competitiveness of a nation. With a group of domestic competitors following various competitive strategies, there is a check against forms of government intervention that stifle innovations and blunt competition (Porter 1990).

Another benefit of domestic competition is the pressure it creates for constant upgrading of the sources of competitiveness. The presence of home competitors automatically cancels the types of advantage that come from simply being in a particular nation-factors costs, access to or preference on home market, or costs to foreign competitors who import into the market. Companies are forced beyond them, and as a result, remain more sustainably competitive. Moreover, competing domestic rivals will keep each other honest in obtaining government support. Companies are less likely to get hooked on the narcotic of government contracts or creeping industry protectionism. Instead, the industry will seek, and benefit from, more constructive forms of government support, such as assistance in opening markets, as well as investment in focused educational institutions or other specialized factors (Porter 1990).

Furthermore, vigorous domestic competition that ultimately pressures domestic companies to look at global markets and toughens them to succeed. Particularly when there are economies of scale, local competitors force each other to look outward to foreign markets to capture greater efficiency and higher profitability. Also, having been tested by intense domestic competition, the stronger companies are well equipped to win abroad.

3.4 International Business and Economic Activities-IBEA

National competitiveness is driven by internal (domestic) and external (international) activities. International business and economic activities are considered to be an external driver of competitiveness. They have played a significant role in improving productivity and competitiveness, by influencing all other identified determinants of competitiveness. For analytical purposes IBEA can be divided into two groups: Foreign Direct Investment (FDI) and International Trade (imports and exports). In this section, we focus generally on introducing the static IBEA activities. The IBEA as a dynamic will be examined in more detail in section 3.7.

3.4.1 Foreign Direct Investment (FDI), Multinational Corporations (MNCs), and Competitiveness

Foreign Direct Investment (FDI) is defined as an investment involving a long-term relationship and reflecting a lasting interest and control by a resident entity in one economy. FDI implies that the foreign investor exerts a significant degree of influence on the management of the enterprise resident in the other economy. Such investment involves both the initial transaction between the two entities and all subsequent transactions between them and among foreign affiliates, both incorporated and unincorporated. FDI may be undertaken by individuals as well as business entities.

Flows of FDI are classified into inward and outward. They comprise capital provided (either directly or through other related enterprises) by a foreign direct investor to a FDI enterprise, or capital received from an FDI enterprise by a foreign direct investor. FDI has three components: equity capital[16], reinvested earnings[17] and intra-company loans[18] (UNCTAD 2005).

FDI stock is the value of the share of their capital and reserves (including retained profits) attributable to the parent enterprise, plus the net indebtedness of affiliates to the parent enterprise. FDI flow and stock data used in the WIR (world investment report) are not always defined as above, because these definitions are often not applicable to disaggregated FDI data. For example, in analysing geographical and industrial trends and patterns of FDI, data based on approvals of FDI may also be used because they allow a disaggregation at the country or industry level. Such cases are denoted accordingly.

Foreign Direct Investment (FDI) is the largest source of external finance for developing countries. It has the potential to generate employment, transfer skills and technology, raise productivity, enhance competitiveness and exports, and contribute to the long–term economic development of the world's developing countries. More than ever, countries at all levels of development seek to leverage FDI for development[19].

Multinational Corporations (MNCs) are incorporated or unincorporated enterprises comprising parent enterprises and their foreign affiliates. A parent enterprise is defined as an enterprise that controls assets of other entities in countries other than its home country, usually by owning a certain equity capital stake. An equity capital stake of 10 per cent or more of the ordinary share or voting power for an incorporated enterprise, or its equivalent for an unincorporated enterprise, is normally considered as the threshold for the control of an asset[20]. In the WIR

---

16   Equity capital is a foreign direct investor's purchase of shares of enterprise in a country other than its own.

17   Reinvested earnings comprise the direct investor's share (in proportion to direct equity participation) of earnings not distributed as dividends by affiliates, or earnings not remitted to the direct investor. Such retailed profits by affiliates are reinvested.

18   Intra-company loans or intra-company debt transactions refer to short or long-term borrowing and lending of funds between direct investors (parent enterprises) and affiliate enterprises.

19   UNCTAD, available at
     http://www.unctad.org/Templates/Startpage.asp?intItemID=2068&lang=1

20   In some countries, an equity stake of other than 10% is still used. In the United Kingdom, for example, more of the ordinary shares or voting power for an incorporated or unincorporated enterprise in which an investor, who is a resident in another economy, owns a take that permits a lasting interest in the management of that enterprise (an equity stake if 10 per cent for an incorporated enterprise, or its equivalent for an unincorporated enterprise.

(2005), subsidiary enterprises, associate enterprises and branches-defined below-are all referred to as foreign affiliates or affiliates (UNCTAD 2005).

Box 2 Noticeable features of recent FDI

1. FDI flows are growing faster than other economic aggregates such as national gross fixed capital formation, world trade and GDP. International production (by MNCs and affiliates) is steadily increasing its share in global production.

2. MNCs increasingly dominate world trade: around two thirds of visible trade is handled by MNCs, and the share is growing particularly in activities with significant scale of economies in production, marketing or innovation.

3. Of the visible trade handled by MNCs, between 30 and 40 percent is within MNCs' systems, between affiliates and parents or among affiliates. Such internalized trade contains the most dynamic exports today, moving within integrated international production systems, where TNCs locate different functions or stages of production to different countries. Affiliates participating in such systems produce on massive scales and use the latest technologies, skills and managerial techniques. The globalization of the value chains is likely to spread across many other industries, and linking local production chains to become a major source of growth, technology transfer and skill development.

4. Some MNCs are relocating non-production functions such as accounting, engineering, R&D or marketing to affiliates.These are high-value activities that feed into manufacturing competitiveness and local capabilities. This is what UNCTAD terms "deep integration" in international production, in contrast to earlier "shallow integration" where stand alone affiliates replicated many functions and related to other affiliate or parents via trade. However, the transfer functions such as R&D lags behind that of production, particularly in developing countries. For deep integration to occur, host countries have to be able to provide not just only cheap labor but also the whole array of modern skills, infrastructure, institutions, efficient business practices and suppliers networks that MNCs need in order to be fully competitive in world markets. Very few developing countries are able to meet these needs.

5. Large companies with transnational operations increasingly dominate the process of innovation: the creation of new technologies and organizational methods that lies at the core of competitiveness in all but the simplest activities. Most such companies originate in mature industrial countries. About 90 per cent of world R&D expenditure is in the OECD. Of this group, seven countries (led by the USA) account for 90 per cent. Access to new technologies thus involves getting knowledge from technological leaders in these countries. Thus, FDI becomes the most important, and often the only, way of obtaining leading edge technologies.

6. MNCs are central to exports by local firms of technology-intensive products. Many such products are difficult to export independently because of the need for expensive branding,

distribution and after-sales services. MNCs are also active in exports of low-technology products where factors such as scale of economies, branding, distribution and design are less important.

7. MNCs can help restructure and upgrade competitive capabilities in import-substituting activities. Where the facilities are already foreign owned, MNCs are often better able than local firms by investing in new technologies and skills. They can also help local suppliers to upgrade, or attract investment by their suppliers overseas.

8. FDI in services is rising rapidly as formerly homebound providers (such as utilities) globalize activities and take advantage of liberalization and privatization in their industries. The entry of service MNCs can provide rapid improvements in productivity and efficiency to host countries.

Source: WIR, UNTAD, 2003

The above features of FDI show that MNCs have been playing dominant roles in FDI activities. FDI acts mainly through MNCs such as mobile capital, technology transfer, training human resources, and so on.

A subsidiary is an incorporated enterprise in the host country in which another entity directly owns more than a half of the shareholder's voting power, and has the right to appoint or remove a majority of the members of the administrative, management or supervisory body.

An associate is an incorporated enterprise in the host country in which an investor owns a total of at least 10 per cent, but not more than half of the shareholders' voting power.

A branch is a wholly or jointly owned unincorporated enterprise in the host country which is one of the following: (i) a permanent establishment or office of the foreign investor; (ii) an unincorporated partnership or joint venture between the foreign direct investor and one or more third parties; (iii) land, structure (except structures owned by government entities) and/or immovable equipment and objects directly owned by a foreign resident; or (iv) mobile equipment (such as ships, aircraft, gas-or oil-drilling rigs) operating within a country other than that of the foreign investor for at least one year.

The main impact of MNCs on national competitiveness is related to their advanced technologies and skills, access to capital and final product markets, and participation in globalized systems of production and exchange. These influences become increasingly significant for industrialization in host developing countries.

As a result, many local firms in developing countries are becoming MNCs themselves, and are striking alliances with major players directly (UNCTAD 2000).

In generally, MNCs have been playing a major role in global R&D, technology transfer, human resource development, mobile capital, whereby they enhance the productivity and competitiveness of firms and nations. In other words, MNCs influence all other determinants of national competitiveness and create dynamics of competitive development. These affects will be analysed more concretely in section 3.7.

3.4.2 International Trade Activities and Competitiveness

Both economic theory and countries' experiences show that international trade (import and export) has been a major driver of economic growth in every open economy. As trade has been expanded, income has grown. Income growth depends heavily on a country's capacity to raise its productivity. Open economies have been able to harness the power to boost productivity and competitiveness, helping improve living standards and sustain economic growth. Openness to trade (imports and exports) strengthens the drivers of productivity and competitiveness via six crucial ways:

More efficient allocation of resources Trade enables each country to specialise in the production of those goods and services which it can produce most efficiently. Countries can raise overall consumption by exchanging their surplus for the surplus production of other countries which have a different comparative advantage.

Economies of scale In the absence of trade, economies of scale are constrained by the size of the domestic market. Trade removes this constraint, allowing industries and firms to produce on a more efficient scale than would otherwise be possible.

Similarly, *trade increases incentives for firms to innovate*, because of the rewards from successful innovation will be proportionately greater if firms are selling in larger (i.e. export as well as domestic) markets. Where highly productive firms expand as a result of exports, this boosts general productivity and competitiveness.

Greater competition Trade openness exposes domestic firms to greater competition. This helps to encourage the exit from the marketplace of the least productive firms; reduces monopoly rents; drives down margin; and reduces prices for consumers. Competition further reinforces incentives to innovate, helping to create more competitive firms which can then compete more effectively in the world. Trade can provide direct access to goods and services that incorporate new technologies particularly where more open trade regimes have led to different stages of the production process being undertaken in different countries.

Incentives for investment Better access to import and to export markets increases the scope for productive investment by creating new business opportunities. Foreign direct investment enables technology and innovation developed abroad to be applied to domestic production, enhancing competition and leading to a faster diffusion of more efficient and innovative processes

3.5 Company Strategy and Operation (Competitiveness)

Ultimately, only companies, not nations[21], directly create productivity and sustain competitiveness and the wealth of a nation (Porter 1990). To do so, they need appropriate strategies, goals and managerial approaches. The goals, strategies, and ways of organizing firms in industries vary widely among nations. It depends on the context and circumstance in which firms are created and organized. National competitiveness emanates from a good match between these choices and the sources of competitive advantages in a particular industry (Porter 1990, pp. 107-123).

3.5.1 Company Strategy

Companies are on the front line of international and domestic competition. They must increasingly compete regionally and globally. Internationally successful companies, for example, are not passive bystanders in the process of creating competitiveness. Their competitiveness results ultimately from an effective combination of national circumstances and company strategy. Company strategy has played an important if not decisive role in sustaining the competitiveness of company, industry and nation. The company strategy reflects the following aspects (Ibid., pp 107).

Competitiveness grows fundamentally out of improvement, innovation and change. Companies gain competitiveness over international competitors because they perceive a new basis for competing, or find new and better means to compete in old ways. It means that they must recognize the central role of innovation.

Innovation, in strategic terms, is defined in its broadest sense. It includes not only new technologies but also new methods or ways of doing things that sometimes

---

21   Government influences indirectly all six determinants to create an environment in which companies can compete and improve their competitiveness

appear quite mundane. Innovation can be manifested in a new product's design, a new production process, a new approach to marketing, or a new way of training or organizing. It can involve virtually any activity in the value chain.

In international markets, innovations that yield competitiveness anticipate not only domestic but foreign needs. Some innovations create competitiveness when a company perceives an entirely new buyer need or serves a market segment that competitors have ignored. Innovations that lead to competitiveness are also frequently based on new methods or technology that render existing assets and facilities obsolete. Competitors fail to respond because of a fear of speeding up the obsolescence of their past investments.

Competitiveness involves the entire value system. The value system is the entire array of activities involved in a product's creation and use, encompassing the value chains of companies, suppliers, channels and buyers. Close and ongoing interchange with suppliers and channels is integral to the process of creating and sustaining competitiveness. Competitiveness frequently comes from perceiving new ways to configure and manage the entire value system. Companies restructure or integrate their activities with suppliers, modify the strategies of channels, and recombine or integrate activities with buyers.

The importance of the entire value system to competitiveness is manifested by the prevalence of clustering. The presence of suppliers and users in a nation is an important asset, and is associated with international advantage in countless industries. The strongest competitive advantages often emerge from clusters that are geographically localized. Companies compete in ways that take advantage of presence of the national cluster. To maintain competitiveness, companies must often create and extend these clusters by stimulating the formation of suppliers, improving the needs of customers, or encouraging entry into related industries.

Competitiveness is sustained only via relentless improvement. Companies that remain a static target are eventually overtaken by competitors. Sometimes entrenched competitive positions can be held for years or decades once improvement stops, on the strength of early advantages such as established customers relationships, scale economies in existing technologies, and the loyalty of distribution channels. However more dynamic competitors ultimately find a way around these advantages by discovering better or cheaper ways of doing things.

Competitiveness is only sustained by a continual search for different and better ways of doing things. Ongoing modifications in firm differentiation strategy, for example, must find a stream of new ways to add to its differentiation, or, minimally, improve its effectiveness in differentiating in old ways. Yet the need for continuous innovation runs counters to organizational norms in most companies. Companies would rather not change. Particularly in a successful company, powerful forces work against modifying strategy. It takes strong pressures to counteract these forces. Rarely do these come exclusively from within an organization. Companies seldom change spontaneously; the environment jars or forces them to change. A company must expose itself to external pressures and stimuli that motivate and guide the need to act. It must create the impetus for change.

Competitiveness ultimately requires a global approach to strategy. A company cannot sustain competitiveness in international competition in the long run without exploiting and extending its advantages with a global approach to strategy. German chemical companies, for example, employ extensive foreign production and worldwide marketing networks to solidify their leadership.

A global approach to strategy involves a number of important elements. Firstly, it clearly means selling worldwide, not just in domestic market. However, international sales are viewed not as incremental business but as integral to strategy. The company builds an international brand name and establishes international marketing channels that it controls. Secondly, a global strategy involves locating activities in other nations in order to capture local advantages, or to facilitate local market penetration. Thirdly, and most importantly, a global strategy involves coordinating and integrating activities on a worldwide basis, in order to gain economies of scale or learning to enjoy the benefits of a consistent brand reputation, and serve international buyers. Simply operating internationally does not equate to a global strategy unless this sort of integration and cooperation takes place. A company must move toward a global strategy as soon as its resources and competitive position allow if it is competing in a global industry.

Creating pressures for innovation. A company should seek out pressure and challenge, not avoid them. Part of strategy is take advantage of the home nation to create the impetus for innovation. To do that, companies can sell to the most sophisticated and demanding buyers and channels; seek out those buyers with the most difficult needs; establish norms that exceed the toughest regulatory hurdles or product standards; source from advanced suppliers; treat employees as permanent in order to stimulate upgrading of skills and productivity (Ibid., pp. 109-115).

3.5.2 Company Goals and Management

Clear differences exist within and among nations in the goals that companies seek to achieve as well as the motivations of their employees and managers. Companies will succeed when goals and motivations are aligned with the sources of competitive advantage.

Company goals are most vigorously determined by ownership structure, the motivation of owners and holders of debt, the nature of the corporate governance, and the incentive processes that shape the motivation of business leaders. The goals of publicly held corporations reflect the characteristics of the nation's public capital markets. Capital markets vary a great deal across nations, such as identity of shareholders, the local tax regime. In addition, the role of shareholders and debt holders in corporate governance also varies. In Germany, for example, most shares are held by institutions for extended periods and are rarely traded. Banks are important holders of equity shares and play a prominent role on boards of directors, guiding corporate investments. Long-term capital gains have been exempt from taxation, reinforcing the tendency to hold shares for sustained periods. Management pays attention to the board, but day-to-day stock price movement are not viewed as particularly important. Because of local accounting rules, companies can establish substantial reserves to shelter income and provide a cushion in hard time.

In contrast, in the United States, most shares are held by institutional investors, but institutions are measured on quarterly and annual share price appreciation. Lacking full information about companies' long-term prospects and seeking stocks which will soon appreciate, investment choices stress quarterly earnings growth. Institutions trade frequently in order to realize capital appreciation, and account for most trading in larger company stocks. Long-term capital gains of investors are taxed at the same rate as ordinary income, shortening the time horizon of investment. Shareholders have little direct influence in the management of American companies because boards play little role in corporate governance. In practice, the only effective way to remove underperforming management or affect corporate direction is via takeover. In Korea, the public capital markets have been inefficient and poorly developed; government policy is the decisive factor in capital allocation, based on consideration other than short-term rate of return.

While we have concentrated on the goals of investors in public companies and their influence on management, private companies play an important role in many national economies. The goals of privately owed firms are more complex. Often pride and the desire to provide continuity to employees are important. Private owners frequently have a very long time horizon, are intensely committed to the industry, and operate with different profitability threshold. The attitudes toward debt holders also influence company goals. An important difference among nations is the extent to which debt holders also hold equity. In Germany, for example, regulations allow banks to hold corporate equity. Major lenders hold significant equity stakes and play an important role in corporate governance. By holding both, banks are motivated to be concerned with long-term company health rather than short-term cash flow and interest coverage.

Ownership structures, capital market conditions, and the nature of corporate governance in a nation have two broad influences on national competitiveness. The first grows out of the fact that industries have different appetites for funds, different risk profiles, different investment time horizons, and different average sustained rates of return. National capital markets will also set different goals for different types of industries. Nations will succeed in industries where the goals of owners and managers match the needs of the industry. The second, the influence of the capital markets varies with the need for funds. In industries where private ownership is feasible, for example, a nation can succeed despite public capital markets that set counterproductive goals (Ibid., pp 121-122).

3.5.3 Company Size

In the past decades, a great variety of models have shaped the discussions on management, in particular as regards the question of what size of company and what basic orientation are apt to offer the best promise of success in competition. It is inevitable that company size depends on the context and circumstances of a nation[22]. Company size influences robustly the competitiveness of the company. An optimal company size can take advantage of resources, seize new business opportunities and create competitiveness strongly in both domestic and international market, and vice versa. The discussions are stimulated by the emergence of a new techno-economic paradigm which seems to favour smaller companies.

The discussions on optimal company size have in recent years been marked by some experiences: developing efficient small and medium enterprises; competitiveness of Japanese corporate conglomerates; or corporate conglomerates with management problems and the exploding overhead costs in Western Industrial Countries. What is more important is the manner in which a company organizes its transactions.

Small and medium-sized enterprises (SMEs) In most countries, especially in less and developing countries, SMEs make up the majority of business and account for the highest proportion of employment (Fisher and Reuber 2001). SMEs are usually defined by the number of employees of the firm[23] and definitions vary between countries. The definitions used in developed countries often have higher size thresholds than those in less developed countries. Within the general SME category a number of sub-groups can be identified: self-employed persons with no

---

22 In Italy, for example, family owned companies are popular, so that most companies are small and medium enterprises

23 Some countries define SMEs on the basis of the value of sales or the value of assets. The differing definitions can make cross-country comparisons difficult.

employee, microenterprises with fewer than ten employees; small enterprises with eleven to forty-nine employees, and medium-sized firms with between 50 and 100 employees (Ibid., pp132)

The contributions of SMEs to development There is a general consensus that the performance of SMEs is important for both the economic and the social development of developing countries (Levy et al, 1999). From an economic perspective, SMEs provide a number of benefits (Ibid., pp 133):

SMEs, due to their size, can often easily adapt to changing demand patterns, trade patterns and macroeconomic conditions. This increases industrial flexibility.

SMEs have a reasonable ability to acquire technological capabilities and develop new products and processes and can thus contribute to national technological development and competitiveness.

SMEs can be an important vehicle for generating income and employment and so contribute to gross domestic product, economic growth and reduction in unemployment.

SMEs provide a setting in which assets and skills can be accumulated. This can lead to better economic opportunities for the individuals who acquire the skills, and for the household they help to support.

SMEs can decrease wage inequality. They do so largely by increasing economic participation among those in the lower half of income distribution.

A major corporation that maintains primarily conflict-oriented relations with its suppliers and customers will be less competitive than a smaller company that is integrated within a properly functioning network.

Japanese conglomerates are exceptionally efficient because they constitute the basis for long-term supplier relations, because joint R&D is easier to organize, because procurement of credit with conglomerate's bankers is relatively simple, and because there is here a large measure of tolerance for more or less protracted initial losses. Japanese conglomerates link a dense, long-term network of relationships with a low level of organizational rigidity. This distinguishes them from conglomerates in North America and Europe in which growth of scale has been associated with a multiplication of level of hierarchies, bureaucratization of decision-making processes, and explosion of overhead costs (Esser, Hillebrand, Messner, Meyer-Stamer 1996).

3.6 Government Role

Government plays an inevitable role in economic development because it affects many aspects of the business environment. Yet there has been a broad consensus among economists that the two major roles of government are to increase the overall efficiency and growth of national economies and reduce social inequities among their citizens (Hämäläinen 2003, pp 161). The first role stems from the presumption that, left on its own, a market economy cannot achieve rapid economic growth and efficient use of its production resources. Indeed it could be argued that without any government intervention a modern, highly specialized market economy could not even exist (North 1990). As a result, government activity is needed to overcome specific inefficiencies of the market mechanism, such as market failures. However, even efficient markets could not guarantee a fair distribution of income and opportunities in a society. Thus government activity is needed to ensure that the outcomes of market forces are socially more acceptable. The two principle duties of government have been given different weights in different countries and in different historical periods (Ibid., pp 162).

Historically, the classical (Adam Smith) and neoclassical schools neglect the role of government and have held the strongest belief in the efficiency of the market (price) mechanism. This view stems from Adam Smith's ideas:

According to the system of natural liberty, the sovereign has only three duties to attend to; three duties of great importance, indeed, but plain and intelligible to common understanding: firstly, the duty of protecting the society from the violence and invasion of other independent societies; secondly, the duty of protecting, as far as possible, every member of the society from the injustice or oppression of every other man of it, or the duty of establishing an exact administration of justice; and, thirdly, the duty of erecting and maintaining certain public works and certain public institutions which it can never be for the interest of any individual, or small number of individuals, to erect or maintain; because the profit could never repay the expense to any individual or small number of individuals, though it may frequently do much more than repay it to a great society (Smith [1776] 1998, pp180-181)

The first two duties of government establish the institutional foundations of markets which are prerequisite for an advanced division of labor and complex economic transactions (North 1990). The third duty of government involves public goods such as roads, bridges, canals, postal services and so on. This mechanism emphasized a view collapsed after the Great Depression and was replaced by Keynes' theory-macroeconomic theory. His theory got an enthusiastic reception from economists and policy makers. In essence, his theory involves government intervention through two major economic policies: fiscal and monetary policy.

It is important to note that Keynesian macroeconomics left the basic premises of neo-classical economics intact. Thus neoclassical scholars could continue their research relatively untouched with the managed flow of aggregate demand. Both neoclassical and macroeconomic approaches generally assume efficient competition (except for few monopolies) and a limited role for government at the micro-economic level. This is where the scholars of macro-organizational school disagree with their neoclassical and macroeconomic colleagues.

Government role in enhancing national competitiveness is inevitable. However, it depends on the stage of development and a country's particular circumstances. Porter argued that government role reduces gradually through each stage of development (Porter 1990). In the early phase, resources-driven development, government intervention is significant to improve infant firms' and industries' competitiveness. Korea government role provides a good example. In this framework, we note government role following two areas: Public Institutions and Government Policy.

3.6.1 Public Institutions

3.6.1.1 Institutional Concept

The term 'Institution' has different meanings for different persons. In the work *"Economic Institutions of Capitalism"*, Oliver Williamson defined institutions as alternative organizational mechanisms: markets, hybrids, and hierarchies (Williamson 1985). John R. Common viewed institutions as established societal organizations, which included inter alia universities, labor unions, churches, political parties and the government (Commons 1970). Douglass North argued that institution includes three major elements: informal behavioural constraints and incentives[24]; formal rules[25] and their enforcement (North 1990). In this study we focus on formal rules as a determinant which influences on national competitiveness.

Formal institutions consist of political, judicial and economic rules that complement and increase the effectiveness of informal institutions. The hierarchy of formal institutions extends from constitutions to statutes and common laws and further to government regulation, collective labor market agreements and individual contracts. Thus changes in formal institutions may originate from many different sources: the supreme court, federal and local legislatures and governments, regu-

---

24   Such as values, contracts and tradition
25   Such as constitutions, laws, regulations and contracts

latory agencies, collective bargaining and contracting organizations (Common 1970, North 1990).

Economic agents often attempt to manipulate the judicial, legislative, regulatory and bargaining processes in their self-interest. These 'rent-seeking' activities often have a detrimental effect on economic efficiency and competitiveness (Olso 1982). Since the profitability of rent-seeking activities depends on the prevailing economic environment and institutional arrangements, some economic systems are burdened with more rent-seeking than others.

Formal institutions are shaped by the judicial and legislative processes of the society, rent-seeking activities of special interest groups, collective bargaining between labor unions and employers, private bargaining between buyers and sellers and other private sector regulatory processes (Commons 1970, Oslo 1982). Although formal institutions are more easily changed by purposive action, the complexity of the above processes typically makes the evolution gradual. Hence drastic changes in the institutional framework are extremely rare.

North argues that modern economies where complex and impersonal exchanges are prevalent require efficient enforcement of contracts in order to achieve the maximum gains from economic specialization and trade (North 1990). He notes that institutions will break down if they are not enforced. Thus violations of institutional rules need to be detected and punished and institutionally sanctioned behaviour rewarded. Although North emphasizes the importance of coercive third-party enforcement, the enforcement of institutional rules may also depend on the possibility of losing one's reputation in case of defection or shirking.

The separate forces that shape informal and formal institutions may sometimes lead to an 'institutional disequilibrium' where they contradict each other (North 1990). The situation in Russia immediately after the collapse of the communist regime provides a good example. The institutional disequilibrium erodes competitiveness and may lead to chaos when it lasts for too long.

3.6.1.2 Institutions and Competitiveness

The institutional framework influences economic environment and competitiveness by shaping the individual and organizational incentives (North 1990, Porter 1990). These incentives shape the processes of resource accumulation and allocation, technology transfer and innovation, the interaction of buyers and sellers in the product markets, and the international business and economic activities. This section discusses the ways in which institutions can affect each of these processes and, through them, the national competitiveness.

Institutional incentives shape the quality and amount of productive resources created and acquired in the economic system. The incentives to accumulate physical resources (through investment and savings) and intangible assets (through education, training and learning) are determined inter alia by the national career preferences, social status of education, educational standards, tightness of property rights regime and tax laws[26]. Porter argued that the attractiveness of humanities among British students has been detrimental to the international competitiveness of British firms, while Japan has done very well with an institutional framework that encourages natural science education and applied research (Porter 1990).

Technology transfer and innovation is affected heavily by the institutional frameworks. The property rights regime is an important determinant of innovatory incentives. The better the innovator can appropriate the returns from his or her innovations, the better incentives he or she has to undertake innovatory activity (OECD 1996b). The approvability of innovations is also affected by the level of competition among producers which, in turn, is shaped by the prevailing regulatory regime and competition (anti-trust) laws. However it is not primarily through approvability that competition affects innovative behaviour but through its incentive effect.

Moreover the institutional incentives for physical investment will determine the pace of equipment-embodied technology transfer. In a similar way labor laws may affect firms' decisions to adopt new production technologies or organizational arrangements. The transfer of systemic technologies is facilitated by established industry standards. Industry standards may either encourage or discourage competition and technology transfer among firms (Hämäläinen and Laitamaki 1993). Finally, tight competition law can make it more difficult for firms to form close users and producers relationships, which detrimentally effects both transfer and innovation processes (OECD 1996b).

An efficient institutional framework directs productive resources to their socially most productive uses. Efficient institutions also facilitate rapid structural adjustment by speeding up the withdrawal of resources from uncompetitive and unproductive sectors and stimulating the investments into new and more promising sectors. On the other hand an institutional framework may also encourage rent-seeking behaviour where economic agents focus on redistributive rather than value-adding activities. The resulting misallocation of resources hurts national competitiveness (Olson 1982). The most serious misallocation problem is mass unemployment. Although there are many different factors behind this problem,

---

26   depreciation allowances, capital gains taxation, interest rate deduction

the institutional rigidities in labor markets clearly play a central role (OECD 1994).

The work effort of individuals depends on pressures and incentives strongly influenced by the institutional framework. As previously mentioned the competitive pressures on firms are shaped by the competition (anti-trust) laws, tariffs and regulation. Demanding regulatory standards can also pressure firms to become more efficient and gain 'first mover' advantages in new markets consequences of low effort levels and the working ethos in general are shaped by the cultural environment of society (Hämäläinen 2003).

In sum, institution is a juridical framework which strongly influences the competitiveness of firms, industry and the national economy.

3.6.2 Government Policy

In the continuing debate over the competitiveness of nations, no topic engenders more argument or creates less understanding than the role of the government policy. Many see the government as an essential helper or supporter of firms and industry, employing a host of policies to contribute directly to the competitive performance of strategic or target industries. Others accept the "free market" view that the operation of the economy should be left to the workings of the invisible hand. Both views are incorrect. Either, followed to its logical outcome, would lead to the permanent erosion of a country's competitive capabilities. On the one hand, advocates of government assistance for industry frequently propose policies that would actually hurt firms in the long run and create the demand for more assistance. On the other hand, advocates of a diminishing government presence ignore the legitimate role that government plays in shaping the context and institutional structure surrounding companies and in creating an environment that stimulates companies to gain competitiveness.

The central goal of government policy toward the competitiveness of the economy is to deploy a nation's resources with high and rising levels of productivity (Porter 1990, p126-128). Productivity is a fundamental factor in a nation's standard of living. To achieve productivity growth, an economy must be continually upgrading. This requires relentless improvement and innovation in existing industries and the capacity to compete successfully in new industries. New business formation is necessary to create jobs for new persons entering the workforce, to replace any jobs free up by productivity gains in other successful industries, and to replace jobs lost in less productive industries that have become uncompetitive.

Government's proper role is as a catalyst and challenger, it is to encourage- or even push-companies to raise their aspirations and move to higher levels of competitive performance, even though this process may be inherently unpleasant and difficult. Government cannot directly create competitive industries, only firms can do that. But government plays a critical role that is inherently partial, and that succeeds only when working in tandem with favourable underlying conditions. Yet, the government's role amplifies the drivers of the national competitiveness. Government policies that succeed are those that create an environment in which companies can gain competitiveness rather than those that involve government directly in the process, except in nations early in the development process. It is an indirect, rather than a direct role (Ibid., pp 140).

It is hard to understand why so many governments make the same mistakes so often in pursuit of national competitiveness: competitive time for firms and political time for governments are fundamentally at odds. It often takes more than a decade for an industry to create competitiveness; the process entails the long upgrading of human skills, investing in products and processes, building clusters, and penetrating foreign markets. But in politics, a decade is an eternity. Consequently, most governments favour policies that offer easily perceived short-term benefits, such as subsidies, protection, and arranged mergers-the policies that retard innovation. Most of the policies would make a real difference either are too slow and require too much patience for politicians or, even worse, carry with them the sting of short-term pain.

Policies that convey static, short-term cost advantage but that unconsciously undermine innovation and dynamism represent the most common and profound error in government industrial policy. In a desire to help, it is all too easy for governments to adopt policies such as joint projects to avoid "wasteful" R&D that undermine dynamism and competitiveness.

Government policy should be a signal. It can influence how firms compete by identifying and highlighting the important priorities and challenges they face. Government leaders have a stage from which they can define issues of national importance and shape attitudes toward particular problems in industry. Campaigns of the Japanese government, for example, elevated national attention to quality and overcame the stigma of "cheap" Japanese goods. One of the most visible elements of program was the establishment of Deming Prize. This prize carries enormous prestige and sends a strong signal to all Japanese firms about the requirements for competitive success.

Government in nearly all nations today are taking steps designed to improve competitiveness. Some of the most prominent and common policy thrust are the following (Ibid, pp 141): devaluation, deregulation, privatization, relaxation of product and environmental standards, promotion of interfirm collaboration and cooperation of various types, encouragement of mergers, tax reform, regional development, negotiation of voluntary restraint or orderly marketing arrangements, efforts to improve the general education system, expansion of government investment in research, government programs to fund new enterprises.

3.7 Interdependence among Determinants as a Dynamic of National Competitiveness

The determinants of national competitiveness reinforce each other and proliferate over time in fostering competitiveness. This interdependence determines the level of productivity. The level of productivity, in turn, sets a basis of competitiveness and citizens' standard of living (Ibid., pp 132). As this mutual reinforcement proceeds, the cause and effect of individual determinants become blurred. In reality, every determinant can affect every other determinant, though some interactions are stronger and more important than others. However, in this research framework, we solely analyse some of the strongest and most important influences among the determinants.

3.7.1 Effects on Production Resources

The types of production resources in a nation are influenced by other determinants, particularly those of resources most decisive for national competitiveness. Investment in generalized resources, such as transportation infrastructure and the secondary school system, are made virtually in every nation, normally as a natural outcome of public policy at various level of government. In turn, the size and quality of public investments in generalized resources can be and are influenced by the attitudes of business community and private citizens. What varies is a nation's rate of investment, its desired standard of performance, and how well the institutions involved in creating resources are administered. Though generalized resources are not a sufficient basis for competitiveness in advanced industries, they serve as the foundation from which advanced and specialized factors are created. Sustained national investment is therefore essential to national economic progress.

Production resources are perhaps most strongly influenced by *market conditions* (Porter 1990). A number of local competitors in robust competition stimulate the rapid development of skilled human resources, related technologies, market-specific knowledge, and specialized infrastructure. Companies invest in such resources themselves, singly or via trade association, under pressure not to fall behind. As important, however, is that a group of domestic competitors also triggers special programs in local school and universities, government-supported technical institutions and training centres, specialized apprenticeship programs, industry-specific trade journals and other information providers, and other types of investment in resources by government and other institutions. Domestic competition also stimulates job seekers to invest in gaining specialized skills. Human resource will be unusually rapid in industries viewed as prestigious or priorities, the attention of individuals, institutions, and government entities is most attracted. These effects will be most pronounced if the rivals are located in one region.

Production resources are also affected by *demand condition* (Porter 1990). A disproportionate level of demand for a product, or unusually stringent or sophisticated demand, tends to channel social and private investments into related production resources. Advanced and specialized resources of production grow up to help meet pressing local needs[27]. High or stringent local demand raises the likelihood of a consensus in government for making factor creating investment. It also focuses attention of individuals and firms on the need for making private investments.

A single *company* can have some effect on production resources, particularly if it is a major economic influence on town or region. However, a group of rivals usually provides far more stimulation.

Competition among local competitors spills over into efforts to court and develop relationships with educational institutions, research institutions and information providers. This competition will increase the rate of creating and allocating resources. The presence of a number of rivals not only signals the importance and potential of the industry, causing individuals and institutions to take notice, but also reduces the risk of investing in specialized facilities, programs, and knowledge. Rivals mitigate each other's bargaining power in sourcing specialized resources, promoting expended supply. The presence of some domestic competitors can elevate the support and consensus for investment in creating specialized resources by government.

The influences of a group of domestic competitors on advanced resources are more important and common, but far from automatic. Local companies must perceive the need for constantly upgrading the pool of resources, and work actively

---

27 For example, nations depend heavily on sea transport such as Sweden and Norway have well-developed specialized educational and scientific institutions geared toward oceanography and shipping

to stimulate investments in them. Robust domestic competition plays a special role on encouraging such an outlook as pressure from buyers.

The pool of resources and the rate at which they are created are also shaped the presence of clusters. The clusters draw on common inputs, skills, and infrastructure also further stimulates government bodies, educational institutions, companies, and individuals to invest in relevant factor creation or resource-creating mechanisms. Specialized infrastructure is enlarged, and spillovers are generated that upgrade factor quality and increase supply. Sometimes, whole new industries bring up to supply specialized infrastructure to such clusters. Such a mutually reinforcing process is occurring in the United States, where the existence of world-class industries in mainframe computer, minicomputer, software, logic circuits has sent public and private institutions scrambling to create software training centres and courses. The resulting pool of skilled human resources, knowledge, scientific centres and specialized infrastructure not only benefits this whole group of industries, but spills over to benefit other industries that depend on information technology.

Resource-creating investment in a nation cumulates over time. The role of the other determinants influencing educational, research and other institutions provides an ongoing and additive stimulus for specialized resources. Over time, differences in the rate and direction of such investments among nations can lead to wide national differences in the stock of specialized resources relevant to company, industry and nation.

International business and economic activities affect heavily on production resources via foreign direct investment and international trade.

Foreign Direct Investment. The availability of advanced, created, and specialized resources in the national economy is most clearly affected by inward foreign direct investment. Multinational corporations (MNCs) must have some ownership-specific advantages over and above those of local firms in order to compete successfully in a foreign location (Hymer 1960). These advantages may stem either from ownership-specific tangible and intangible assets or the firm's international network of operations (Dunning 1988). Both types of advantages may contribute to the productivity and competitiveness of the host economy. Moreover the greater the number and extent of the MNCs ownership advantages relative to those of its indigenous competitors, and the more countries in which MNCs operate, the more pronounced its impact (good or bad) is likely to be on the host economy (Dunning 1993).

MNCs are disproportionately well represented in the high value-added, technology and marketing-intensive industries which are characterized by strong ownership-specific assets (Dunning 1993). Their managerial and training resources, R&D activities, marketing skills and brand names can improve the human resources and intangible assets available in the host country. Besides the direct effects, FDI may improve the host country's resource base indirectly through the competitive stimulus, improved working ethos and organizational innovations that they bring to national resource creation and accumulation processes.

International trade shapes the national production resources through exports and imports. The clearest contribution of exports to the national resources relates to the financial reserves earned abroad. Besides the effect of a positive balance of payments, export receipts are often an important source of finance for national economies. However it is conceivable that some economic systems can also lose scarce human capital and raw materials. Thus an increasing number of countries are concerned about the 'brain drain', or exports of high quality human resources. On the other hand many developing countries are still quite willing to deplete their natural resource in an attempt to earn more export revenue.

Raw materials and other resources have become increasingly well available in the global factor markets. These markets allow firms and nations to outsource those basic resources which are more efficiently supplied by other economic systems. Japan, for example, imports large quantities of foodstuffs which it could also produce domestically but not only at prohibitive cost. Importing basic resources which could also be produced at home saves scarce domestic resources for those activities and industries in which the home country has a competitive advantage (Hämäläinen 2003, p 103).

3.7.2 Technology and Human Resources

Technology is affected heavily by human resources. The adoption of technology requires skilled human resources. The gaining of competitiveness in most new technologies requires a more highly skilled workforce at all levels of enterprise. What is more, it requires different kinds of skills and work attitudes: multi-skills, teamwork and flexibility, rather than simply people trained in traditional ways to do routine production line tasks. The pace of technological change also raises the need for a constant retraining of the workforce, and many developed countries are now emphasizing the central role of "lifetime education" to maintain an efficiency and innovation edge. Of course, different economies have different skill needs. However, all economies constantly need to upgrade their human capital stock to sustain industrial competitiveness.

3.7.3   Influences on Market Condition

Domestic demand conditions reflect many national attributes such as the standard of living, income, population, climate, social norms, and a mix of other factors in the economy.

Perhaps the most important influence is again *domestic competition*. A group of local competitors invests in marketing, driven by an intense commitment and attention to the domestic market that I have described. Pricing is aggressive to gain or hold local market share. Products are introduced earlier at home, and the available product variety is greater. The very presence of competitive local rivals builds an awareness of the industry. Primary demand in the home market is stimulated. Not only is home demand expanded, but saturation occurs sooner and leads to more aggressive efforts to internationalize. A good example is the wine industry, where high per capita consumption in wine-producing countries such as Italy and France is due in large part to the presence of local production that is associated with wide local availability of wine and greater product awareness by local consumers.

Active domestic competition also upgrades domestic demand. The presence of a number of aggressive local competitors works to educate local buyers, make them more sophisticated, and make them more demanding because they come to expect a lot of attention. In furniture and shoes, for example, Italian demand has been upgraded by the rapid pace of new product introduction in the home markets by hundreds of Italian companies. (Porter 1990, pp 133-134).

Robust domestic competition can also enhance *foreign demand*. A group of domestic rivals builds a national image in the industry. Foreign buyers take notice and include the nation in their review of potential sources. Their perceived risk in sourcing from the nation is reduced by the availability of alternative suppliers.

The presence of clusters can also enhance international demand for an industry's products. One way is through transferability of reputation such as the image of Swiss watch or consumer electronics of "Made in Japan".

Internationalization of home demand is also affected by factor conditions, especially factor-creating mechanisms. A nation with sophisticated factor-creating mechanisms connected to a particular industry will attract foreign students and firms, who will learn and observe. These students and firms often provide foreign demand for a nation's goods and services.

Domestic competition structure is also influenced by other determinants. The role of other determinants in affecting the number, skills, and strategies of local rivals is particularly important.

Demand conditions enhance domestic rivalry when demanding home buyers seek multiple sources and encourage entry. Highly sophisticated buyers based in a nation may also themselves enter the industry. This is particularly significant when they have relevant skills and view the upstream industry as strategic. A good example is the Japanese robotics industry. Many of the early and leading robotics competitors, such as Matsushita and Kawasaki, are major robot users. They initially designed robotics for internal consumption but then began to sell to others. This example illustrates how sophisticated users who enter an industry can bring an acute understanding of buyer needs as well as pool of expertise and thus enhance the prospects for competitiveness. The response of other industrial participants to their entry further upgrades the entire domestic industry. Early market penetration by a product in a nation also stimulates entry, not only by users but from other industries and via start-ups.

New entry into an industry is also encouraged directly or indirectly by strong national position in related and supporting industries. Entry by established firms in downstream or related industries, which often occurs along with start-ups, produces a domestic industry structure that can be especially conducive to investment and innovation. Suppliers, particularly those that are internationally successful, often enter user industries. Entrants from supplier industries bring them skills and resources from their core businesses that can reshape competition in the new industry, providing the foundation for competitiveness. They can frequently share brand names, distribution channels and technological knowledge.

Entry by suppliers into downstream industries provides a ready means for transmitting information and skills and thus supports the sort of vertical interchange so important to competitiveness. Entrants from supplier industries in a nation also have a level of commitment to new industry that may be unmatched by start-up entrants in other nations. Suppliers view the new industries as strategic because they are interrelated with their base business, and their brand reputations may well be at stake. The time horizon for decisions is lengthened, and short-term profitability diminishes in importance. Supplier employees frequently leave to enter the industries they serve when they perceive an opportunity to transfer skills and relationships that can be an important advantage. A well-developed suppliers industry also lowers barriers to entry into downstream industries by firms. The presence of many parts suppliers, for example, facilitated new entries into the Japanese sewing machine and car audio equipment industries.

Many of the same reasons explain why competitiveness in a related industry leads to entry into an industry. A high-profile industry often draws attention to industries that are related to it. And the timing of entry from one national industry into related industries is not random. Often related diversification takes place when the base industry either becomes saturated or declines. This often leads to a number of local companies simultaneously diversifying into a related industry. Imitation merely compounds this process.

Entrants from related industries, like entrants from buyers and supplier industries, are particularly desirable types of entrants for the purposes of upgrading competitiveness in a nation. They often possess transferable strengths that lead to higher-order competitiveness. Many Japanese competitors in personal computers, for example, began as consumer electronics companies. While Japan's overall international position in personal computers is modest, strength is now growing in laptops where compact size and liquid crystal display technology are essential to competitive success. These are areas where Japanese firms bring unique and transferable strengths not present in America and European competitors.

The most vibrant competitiveness often comes when entrants from a number of different supplier and related industries converge in a new industry (Ibid., pp 147) . Here a variety of competing approaches are brought to bear and innovation often flourishes. Entrants from related industries also have the same high stakes on succeeding in the new industry as was the case with entry by suppliers. Japanese office machine companies who entered facsimile production, for example, had a brand reputation to protect and were anxious to have a full line of products to gain greater clout with distribution channels.

3.7.4   International Business and Economic Activities and Technology

The main benefit that host developing countries expect from International business economic activities (IBEAs) is access to technology and their ability to implement new technology effectively.

In the rapidly integrating world and regional economies where technological capacity is spread among an increasing number of countries, most economies must import the bulk of their new technology. Since IBEAs provide important mechanisms of international technology transfer, they play a central role in the technology development and diffusion processes of national economies. Besides their direct impact IBEAs shape the national technology base indirectly through the other parts of economic system which are closely linked to the domestic technology transfer and development processes: human resources, technological infrastructure, demand patterns, competitive environment and the institutional and policy frameworks. As a result IBEAs are a significant determinant of a nation's technology transfer and capacity.

In the following we examine the impact of different forms of IBEAs (FDI and International Trade) on the determinants of technology transfer and innovation identified previously.

IBEAs and technology transfer: the rate of technology transfer is shaped by international business and economic activities. As we noted above, FDI (inward and outward) can provide indigenous firms with a better access to global markets. The larger demand of global markets not only favours technology innovation but also the transfer of technologies, particularly if they are characterized by large fixed costs. FDI also shapes the rate and extent of technology transfer by increasing the pressures of international competition. International competition tends to reduce the prices of technology-intensive inputs and thus improves the incentives for adopting new technologies. International competition also puts pressure on firms to use the most technologically advanced inputs and equipment.

In a national economy, the speed and extent of technology transfer depends on the systemic characteristics of technologies. Individual technologies cannot transfer efficiently if other parts of the interdependent technology system remain unchanged. The development and transfer of technologies also requires coordination. MNCs are in a unique position to coordinate complex technology development and transfer processes because such coordination cannot take place efficiently through the market mechanism.

Technology transfer also relies on the absorptive capacity of firms and nations (Cohen and D. Levinthal 1989). The lack of complementary assets, skilled human resources, and especially organizational capabilities can lead to counterproductive results in both firms and nations. Their productivity and competitiveness can be reduced. As we mentioned earlier, MNCs may be able to help their host countries by providing and upgrading the necessary absorptive capacity.

The pace and extent of technology transfer is shaped by the adaptation needs of specific technologies for the characteristics of particular socio-economic systems. As a result, a large part of the R&D conducted by foreign affiliates of MNCs goes into the adaptation of particular products, processes, functions and procedures of firms rather than to basic or fundamental research. Moreover, the fact that so much cross-border technology transfer takes place within MNCs hierarchies rather than through arm's-length markets is a sign of the tacit and complex nature of the transferred technology. MNCs networks and related FDI are often the most efficient and least costly way to transfer such technologies.

As we noted previously, the cross-border transfer of disembodied technology is facilitated by the geographical proximity of MNCs and indigenous firms. On the other hand, a greater geographical dispersion of inward FDI could have a positive impact on technology transfer within host countries. Outward FDI, in turn, may have an adverse effect on the strength of local industrial clusters and hence on the national transfer of disembodied technology.

In general, FDI provides the fastest and most effective way to deploy new technologies in host developing countries. As the number of MNCs grows and their origins diversity, the range of technologies offered also increases. Emerging competition among MNCs can improve the terms on which host countries can obtain technology, potentially strengthening the advantage of FDI as a source of technology transfer, if Governments use their bargaining effectively (UNCTAD 2000).

International trade also has an impact on the transfer of technology (World Bank 1993). Increasing import competition may reduce the price of technology which facilitates its transfer. Exports, in turn, may provide important financial resources for the acquisition of newly transferred technologies. Exports may also help cross-border technology transfer by providing the competitiveness of domestic firms' technologies and capabilities to prospective foreign partners. Exports also may attract inward FDI and hence facilitate technology transfer by signalling the good quality of national framework conditions for industry. In addition foreign buyers may give exporters technological information acquired from their other suppliers. Finally, both exports and imports expose domestic firms to more intensive competition which pressures them to adopt new technologies gradually.

IBEAs and Technology Innovation: IBEAs influence technology innovation processes through identified contents in the section of technology innovation[28]:
Foreign direct investment (Inward and outward) can provide MNCs' local affiliates and suppliers a ready access to global markets (UNCTAD 1995). The importance of MNCs' global marketing and distribution networks for their host countries has often been demonstrated when they have acquired a foreign company with strong technological advantage but weak international marketing capabilities. The improved access to global markets, in turn, provides better incentives for technology innovation. Moreover foreign demand patterns are likely to be somewhat different from those at home which provides new incentives for innovative activities.

---

28 Market potential, technological opportunities, appropriability regime, organizational resources and capabilities, incentive mechanism and the geographical concentration of firms (Hämäläinen, 2003)

FDI can also contribute to local innovation processes by widening the scope of technological opportunities available to a national economy. MNCs account for around three-quarters of civilian R&D undertaken in market economies and as much as 90 per cent of the trade in technology or technology-intensive products (Dunning 1993). Moreover, in a world where technologies have become more systemic and independent, foreign MNCs often possess technologies which are complementary to those of domestic firms and thus create totally new technological opportunities in their host countries. The fact that MNCs provide crucial complementary resources to domestic firms may also be a drawback for the innovation of their host economies. The local appropriability of innovations may suffer if the MNCs can leverage their strategic position to appropriate the rents from local innovations. FDI can also make local markets more competitive which tends to decrease the approvability of innovations. However, in the longer term, the opposite result is also possible if the MNCs are able to conquer the host country market and thus improve the appropriability.

The international integration of markets and production and the tendency for technologies to become more systemic have increased the organizational advantages of large MNCs in innovatory activities. The commercialization of new technologies increasingly requires a network of organizational resources and capabilities which global companies are best equipped to supply (Dunning 1993). The countries which can offer the best framework conditions for innovatory activities are most likely to benefit from the MNCs' technological capabilities.

The increasing competition related to inward and outward direct investment can increase the innovatory activities of indigenous firms (Porter 1990). With regard to inward FDI, the positive impact of competition on technology innovation is likely to be greater than the negative effect of decreasing due to the weakening appropriability regime. In a similar vein market-seeking outward FDI can expose home country firms to more intensive competition. On the other hand, resource-seeking outward FDI may be motivated by the cheaper input (such as labor and materials) costs in foreign countries. If such FDI is used as an alternative to innovative upgrading in response to the competitive pressure, it is likely to have detrimental effects on the long-term technological competitiveness of the home country (Hämäläinen 2003).

Finally, MNCs may sometimes be able to fill in the gaps or reduce the weakness of geographically concentrated user-producer networks. By locating close to domestic firms, MNCs can strengthen the agglomeration economies of geographically concentrated industries.

International trade can also have an impact on the technological innovation of an economic system. Similar to FDI, exports increase the size of potential markets and thus provide additional incentives for innovation. Exports may also provide better information about foreign buyers' preferences which improves the probability of successful innovation (World Bank 1993). Imports, in turn, may have a negative effect on the market potential of domestic firms by reducing their market shares. However imports may also introduce new technological opportunities to a national economy and thus increase the innovative potential of domestic firms. International trade may also affect the appropriability of domestic innovations. Both exports and imports can decrease the appropriability of domestic innovations by increasing foreign competition. On the other hand, the more intensive international competition can also improve the firms' innovation. It may do this directly through increasing the opportunity costs of not being innovative, or indirectly by forcing the firms to develop the organizational resources and capabilities required for successful innovation.

Exporting to foreign markets exposes firms to new demand patterns which may work as incentives to technological innovation. Finally, imports may increase the number of possible sources of crucial complementary inputs and hence increase the appropriability of firms' innovations.

3.7.5 Effect of IBEAs on Human Resources

The contribution of MNCs to human capital (skill) is potentially large. Many foreign affiliates in developing countries pay higher wages to employees than local counterparts, and invest more in training. They tend to be more aware of emerging trends in training and the need for new forms of skill creation; they are able to use state-of-the-art training materials and techniques; and their training is oriented to global markets (UNCTAD, 1994, 1999). Several MNCs have set up training facilities to ensure that their need for specialized skills is fully met. Furthermore, the presence of advanced manufacturing MNCs also can attract a host of foreign investors in modern services, which create valuable new skills in finance, marketing, insurance, accounting and so on.

However, host countries cannot rely on MNCs to meet their broader or emerging skill needs. MNCs use the technologies that are appropriate to local education levels and train mainly to create efficient operators of such technologies. They tend not to invest in creating the skills needed for higher levels of technologies because of the high cost and long-term nature of the training required. In other words, the upgrading of the general skill level and provision of high level specialized training is something that host countries have to do for themselves. Indeed, such upgrading itself can be used to attract higher-quality inward FDI and to include existing investors to move into more complex activities. Moreover, MNCs from developed countries tend to concentrate in advanced technology industries, leaving a wide range of simpler activities in which skill creation has to depend on local firms. MNCs from other developing countries do enter into simply labor-intensive activities, but these tend not to invest heavily in training. In essence, MNCs cannot replace the education and training provided by the national education system, and this remains a vital area of host government policy (UNCTAD, 2000).

MNCs can make a valuable contribution to the upgrading of management and organization systems in host countries, with beneficial spillover effects on local firms. Nevertheless, the introduction of new organizational techniques has a life of its own.

3.7.6 Government's Influence on all other Determinants

Government can affect (and be affected by) each of the six determinants either positively or negatively. Production resources are influenced by government through subsidies, policies toward the capital markets, education and training, and infrastructure. Government affect technology via science and technology policies. Market and demand conditions are influenced by government through antitrust law and expenditure. Government can create environment in which clusters are formed. Government plays significant role in international business and economic activities through investment attractive policy and exchange rate policy. Government policy also influences firm's strategy and operation through such devices as capital market regulations, tax policy.

3.7.6.1 Government's Effect on Production Resources

Government has critical responsibilities for fundamentals like the primary and secondary education systems, basic national infrastructure, research, and efficiently exploiting natural resources in areas of broad social concern such as health care. The government's effect on production resources is justified by externalities or benefits to the economy that exceed those to any individual participant, and is especially significant where resources can be deployed in a range of industries. A nation's industry will not be competitive if the government does not meet these responsibilities well.

Education and training Achieving greater competitiveness demands human resources with improving skills and competences. The quality of human resources depends on quality of education and training system. Education and training constitute perhaps the single greatest long-term leverage point available to all levels of government in upgrading industry. Improving the general education system is an essential priority of government, and a matter of economic and not just social policy. The effectiveness of an educational system is partly a function of the rate of spending. The appropriate government policies toward education and training must reflect each nation's particular circumstances.

Infrastructure Improving the competitiveness of a nation depends on enhancing national infrastructure. The improvement of national infrastructure is influenced strongly by government investments. Both firms and government have a role in creating and upgrading infrastructure. Governments have historically played a major role in most nations. Japan, Korea, and Singapore, for example, have adopted the most aggressive posture toward infrastructure investments and they have reaped significant benefits in improving competitiveness and economic growth.

Capital Raising the competitiveness of an economy requires that ample capital is available at low real cost and is allocated efficiently through the banking system and other capital markets to investments with the highest productivity. Government has a role in affecting both the supply and cost of capital as well as the markets through which it is allocated. A nation's supply of capital is most influenced by the personal savings rate, the size of the government surpluses or deficits, and foreign capital flows. Government policy can affect all three. In Singapore, for example, there is a program of forced savings tied to the social security system. This has generated an enormous pool of capital that is beyond the ability of the Singaporean economy. Tax policy is another prominent tool for encouraging or retarding savings (Porter 1990).

Natural resources have been contributing to national competitiveness as an available element. The more natural resources are exploited efficiently the more sustainable competition an economy remains. Government policy affects the processing exploiting of natural resources through structure policy and scheme policy within the nation. If government policy of natural resources is efficient, it takes advantage of natural resources to gain competitiveness, especially in early phase of economic development.

3.7.6.2 Government's Effect on Technology

An upgrading economy demands a steadily rising level of technology. Improvements in technology, broadly defined, are integral to improving efficiency, commanding higher prices through better quality, and penetrating new industries and segments, the underpinnings of productivity growth. Stimulating improvement in science and technology is a widely acknowledged role of government. Research and development cannot be left solely to firms because the benefits to the national economy exceed those to individual firms due to spillovers. Technological progress not only benefits a firm but often raises the rate of advancement in the entire national industry as well as linked industries. This is particularly true in basic research and in fields with applications in numerous industries such as advanced materials, information technology, flexible manufacturing systems, health science, environmental sciences, and energy. At different degrees, government also participate directly in conducting research in government laboratories (Porter 1990).

The exhaustive principle in addressing science and technology should be to create an innovation-enhanced policy and not just a science and technology policy. Science and technology cannot be decoupled from its commercial application in seeking to enhance national competitiveness. Policies to stimulate commercial innovation must go beyond science and technology and include competition, regulation and other policies. In general, the effects of government policy on technology are via such policies as the match between science and technology policy and the patterns of competitiveness; principal emphasis on commercially relevant technologies; strong links between research institutions and industry; encouragement of research activity within firms; and primary emphasis on speeding the rate of innovation.

3.7.6.3 Government's Effect on Market Conditions

Few roles of government are more important to the improving an economy than ensuring vigorous domestic competition. Competition at home is not only uniquely important to fostering innovation, but also benefits the national industry and cluster in many other ways. Maintaining vigorous domestic competition is also important to ensure that a nation's firms gain competitiveness. Governments influence domestic competition through policies and regulation such as antitrust law and regulation competition and protection.

Antitrust policy The importance of domestic competition for competitiveness has heavy implications for antitrust policy, particular policy toward mergers and alliances. So far the need for antitrust has been questioned because of the globalization of industries and the view that domestic firms must merge to gain economies of scale.

A strong antitrust policy, especially in the area of horizontal mergers, alliances, and collusive behaviour, is essential to the rate of improving in an economy. Mergers, acquisitions, and alliances involving industry leaders should be disallowed. Acquisition of smaller domestic rivals by a firm in related industry seeking to transfer skills are more potentially beneficial to competitiveness and should be permissible. The similar standards toward mergers and alliances should apply to domestic and foreign firms in order to prohibit acquisitions that significantly threaten domestic competition. A strong policy bias should favour internal entry, both domestically and abroad, instead of acquisition. Antitrust laws must also not be a barrier to vertical collaboration between suppliers and buyers that is so integral to the innovation process.

Regulation of competition Regulation of competition via such policies as maintaining a state monopoly, controlling entry, or fixing prices, usually works against the improving of competitiveness in an economy. It has double negative consequences. Firstly, the regulation of competition frequently makes the industry a less desirable buyer or supplier. Secondly, it produces a lack of dynamism and innovation which undermines the competitiveness of firms, industry and the nation.

In contrast, deregulation of competition, openness, and privatization of state monopolies are usually spurs to national competitiveness. They will encourage competition and have ripple effects on linked industries.

3.7.6.4 Government's Effect on IBEAs

Governments influence international business and economic activities (IBEAs) via investment attracting policy and trade policy.

Foreign direct investment Policy toward foreign investment in a nation has long been an issue for governments. It raises concerns about national sovereignty and the effects on a nation's industry. Foreign investment is a manifestation of global competition and the need for global strategies; it raises national productivity by stimulating improvements by domestic firms and supplanting the less efficient competitors. Government policy that creates a favourable business environment to attract foreign investment is extremely significant.

Trade policy National competitiveness will not be fully reflected in rising productivity unless a nation's firms have access to foreign markets. Government trade policy should pursue open market access in every foreign nation. To be effective, trade policy should not be a passive instrument; it cannot respond only to complaints or work only for those industries that can muster enough political clout; it should not require a long history of injury or serve only distressed industries. Trade policy should seek to open markets wherever a nation is competitive and should actively address emerging industries and incipient problems.

Where a government finds a trade barrier in another nation, it should concentrate its remedies on dismantling barriers, not on regulating imports or exports. Orderly marketing or voluntary restraint agreements, which divide up and often effectively cartelize markets, are dangerous, ineffective, and often enormously costly to consumers. So are other specific quantitative targets for exports or imports, which have the effect of guaranteeing a market for inefficient firms rather than promoting innovation in a nation's industries (Hasse 1988). Dumping remedies are also fraught with danger. However, compensatory tariffs than punish companies from the offending nation, no matter where goods are actually produced, are a far better remedy for unfair trade practices than quantitative restrictions. Another remedy is restricting firms from the offending nation from investing in the nation either in the form of acquisitions or production facilities.

Any of these remedies from government, however, can backfire. It is virtually impossible to craft remedies to unfair trade practises that avoid both reducing incentives for domestic companies to innovate and export and harming domestic buyers. The aim of remedies should be adjustments that allow the remedy to disappear.

Chapter 4: Empirical Study of Determinants Driving Vietnam's National Competitiveness

In chapter 3, determinants of national competitiveness were examined based on Porter's theoretical frameworks. They are namely production resources, technology development, market conditions, international economic and business activities, government role, and company's strategy and structure. These determinants will provide most of the independent variables for our empirical study in the second section of chapter 4.

In the first section of this chapter, we will discuss the economic development in Vietnam since its reform. This section shows us an outlook of the expressive economic performance of Vietnam as well as its background and integration into the regional and global economy in two decades. In the second section, we empirically test all of the determinants presented in the previous chapter and the abovementioned summary. We conduct this by using the model of multiple linear regression. Models 1-3 will be conducted using hard data of time series from 1990-2005 with GDP per capita as the dependent variable. Models 4-6 will be done using survey data from 154 respondents with VNC[29] as the dependent variable. In addition, we use human resources (HR), infrastructure resources (IR), capital resources (CR) and natural resources (NR) as independent variables when testing the impact of them on Vietnam's national competitiveness (model 7 and model 8). These results of the regression will provide empirical evidence which determines the drive of national competitiveness in Vietnam. The result is also a base for analyzing the competitiveness of the Vietnamese economy in the following chapter.

4.1 Overall Economic Development of Vietnam in the Last Two Decades

4.1.1 Background

By the end of the 1980's, the legacy of the wars and the centrally planed mechanism had left Vietnam one of the poorest countries in the world with a severe macroeconomic imbalance, widespread rural hunger and underdevelopment in almost all fields of the economy. The GDP per capita was approximately US$

---

29   VNC, standing for Vietnam national competitiveness, is identified by each respondent (see Appendix 5)

129.7[30] in 1989, and the GDP growth rate was around 2-3% while inflation was at the record level of 275.14 % annually during the period 1985-1989[31]. Seven out of every ten Vietnamese citizens were estimated to be living in poverty[32]. These results stem directly from the centrally planned mechanism. Under the mechanism, the private sector was prohibited, and trading was restricted. State-owned enterprises, playing the sole role in the market, were characterized by high inefficiency. The banking system simply responded passively to politically driven investment decisions while prices of products were imposed by the state. Meanwhile, the international context was characterized by rapid changes of the technological revolution, growing globalization, stagnating signals of the East European countries, and the development miracle of East Asian[33] and then Southeast Asian countries[34], that were at the similar stage of development like Vietnam in the 1960s. China, especially, "a big brother of Vietnam", has reformed its economy since 1978 and it has gained striking achievements in economic growth. These internal and external factors motivated the Government of Vietnam to carry out a comprehensive reform of the economy (Doi Moi), including promoting the domestic and foreign private sectors, liberalizing prices and trading, transforming agriculture collectives, developing a two-tier banking system, improving fiscal and monetary policies to curb inflation, and reforming the legal system.

4.1.2 Economic Performance

Economic growth and productivity Vietnam has been one of the world's fastest-growing developing economies since its "Doi moi" reform policy was established by the 6th Party Congress in 1986 its transition from a planned to market oriented economy with an extremely low level of development and high poverty rate. It has the potential to be one of the great success stories in development. Since the 1990s, the economy experienced high economic growth, an average of 9%[35], until 1997. Economic growth then noticeably slowed, partly due to the onset of the financial and economic crisis to afflict the region in 1997-98, and partly due to a disconcerting, and related, decline in foreign direct investment flows. However, the GDP growth remained at the average annual rate of 6.8% from 1997 to 2004[36] and growth hit 8.4%[37] in 2005 and 8.2%[38] in 2007. The GDP per capita (PPP-

---

30   IMF, World Economic Outlook Database, September 2005
31   Ibid
32   World Bank, 1999, pii
33   South of Korea, Taiwan province of China
34   Singapore, Thailand, Philippines and Indonesia
35   CIA – The World Factbook-Vietnam, 2006
36   Ibid
37   WB, World Development Report, 2000-2005

Purchasing Power Parity) rose from 942.4 current international dollar (1990) to 3716 (2007)[39] (Figure 4.1).

In line with economic growth, labor productivity (defined and measured as output per employee) has improved over time, with an increase in the GDP (PPP) from current international dollar 2116 (1990) to 6614 (2006) per employee. Labor productivity growth gained an annual average of 7.3% between 1990 and 2006, which is lower than economic growth (7.5%) in the same period. As compared with the labor productivity level in 1990, the productivity level in 2006 is three times as high (Figure 4:2). However, labor productivity performance in Vietnam still lags behind neighboring countries, especially China and Thailand (Figure 1.2).

As a result, the poverty rate (defined as a percent of the population living under $1 per day) has declined significantly and is now smaller than that of China, India and the Philippines[40]. According to the World Bank's report in 2006, the rate of the poor declined from 51% of the population in 1990 to 8% in 2005. Vietnam can reach most of the Millennium Development Goals.[41]

Figure 4. 1: Labor Productivity and GDP Growth Rate (1990-2006)

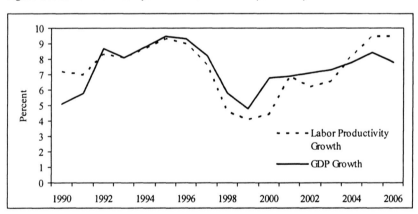

Source: ADB, IMF and own calculation by using data from ADB and IMF 2007

38   ADB, Key Indicators 2007, available at
      http://www.adb.org/Documents/Books/Key_Indicators/2007/pdf/Key-Indicators-2007.pdf
39   IMF, World Economic Outlook Database, October 2007
40   CIA - The World Factbook-Vietnam, 2006
41   WB, IDA, Vietnam: Laying the Foundation for Steady Growth, 2007

Figure 4. 2: Labor Productivity and GDP per Capita Performance (1990-2006)

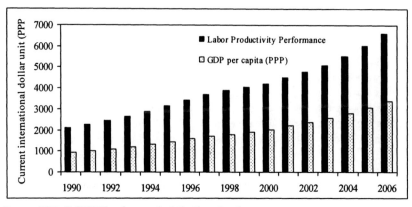

Source: ADB, IMF 2007 and own calculation by using data

Structure of the Economy During this period of rapid economic growth, the structure of the economy has been changing significantly, with the contribution of the agriculture sector to the GDP declining from 38.7 percent in 1990 to 20.9 in 2005, the GDP share of the industry sector increasing from 22.7 percent to 41.6 percent by 2006, and the share of the service sector increasing from 38.6 percent of the GDP in 1990 to 44.1 percent in 1995 then declining to 38.1 by 2006 (Figure 4.3). The economic growth has been led by the industrial sector, where value added increased at an average annual rate of 10.5 and 10.21 percent from 1990 to 1999 and from 2000 to 2006 respectively. However, Vietnam is still predominantly an agricultural society. Over 65% of population lives in rural areas, and two-thirds of employment is in agriculture.

Figure 4. 3: Sector Share of Total Product

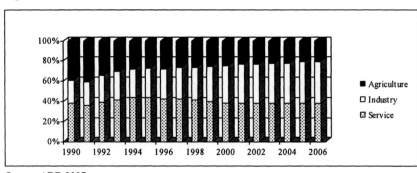

Source: ADB 2007

International Trade A salient feature of Vietnam' economic development process has been the increasing significance of international trade. Vietnam has performed impressive international trade in past the 15 years. Total value of imports and exports reached US $84,2 billion in 2006 or 140 % GDP, compared to $5.156 billion in 1990 or 80% GDP. The ratio of exports to GDP increased from 37.1% in 1990 to 65.3% in 2006, indicating the openness of the economy even before Vietnam joined the WTO in January 2007. Exports have been the main engine of economic growth, an annual average growth of 19.94% during the period 1990-2006. The principal export commodities include crude oil, textile and sewing products, apparel, marine, rice, coffee, wood and wood products, rubber and coal. Remarkable is the strong rise in the value of agriculture export, mainly reflecting the spectacular take-off in rice and coffee production. In only a few years, Vietnam returned from being a net rice importer into the world's second largest exporter, behind Thailand, with over 3.5 million tons in 2005. Vietnam's largest single export market is now the US, which absorbs 21% of Vietnam's exports. Exports to the US have grown exponentially, from a base of zero in 1994. Japan also has 12% share in 2006. Other Asia Pacific markets dominate the country's export trade with Australia (9%), China (6%), Singapore (4%) and other key export markets. European markets are also important, with Germany's 4% share making it the most significant. The UK (3%), France (2%) are the other major European markets (Figure 4.5)

Figure 4. 4: Total Imports, Exports and GDP (US million)

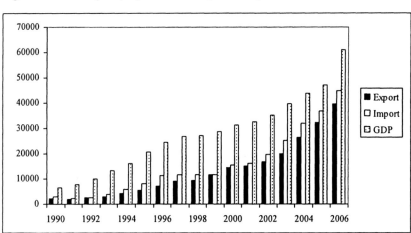

Source: ADB and IMF 2007

Figure 4. 5: Share of Export and Imports by Countries (2006)

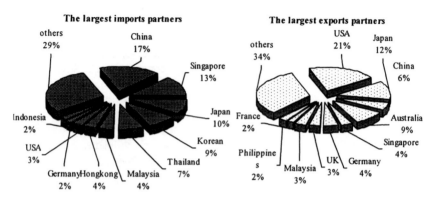

Source: ADB 2007

Foreign Direct Investment has played a key role in the process of the Vietnamese economy's transition. The opening of the Vietnamese economy in 1987[42] and subsequent measures to liberalize the FDI regime, together with the fast economic growth, have led to a rapid increase in FDI stocks since the 1990s, with the FDI stock of 31.135 billion US dollar in 2005, compared to 1.650 billion in 1990 (Figure 4.6).

FDI stock as percentage of GDP rose dramatically from 1990 (25.5%) to 2002 (74.3%) and declined to 61.2% by 2005[43]. By 2006, although foreign invested companies employed 18.11% of the total workforce in Vietnam, they accumulatively accounted for around 57.8%(2006) of the country's exports, 43.7% of the country's total industrial output, almost 17.% of Vietnam's GDP, but contributed around 8% of total tax revenues[44].

Vietnam has been one of the most attractive destinations of FDI inflow in the Asia region. The government generally welcomes foreign investors and has made the effort to create a more attractive investment environment. Nevertheless, Vietnam's investment environment remains weak compared to neighboring countries and raises some issues. These issues will be explored in the next chapter.

---

42   The initial FDI law was issued
43   UNCTAD 2006, available at:
      http://www.unctad.org/Templates/Page.asp?intItemID=3277&lang=1
44   www.gso.gov.vn/statistics

Figure 4. 6: Total FDI Stock and GDP

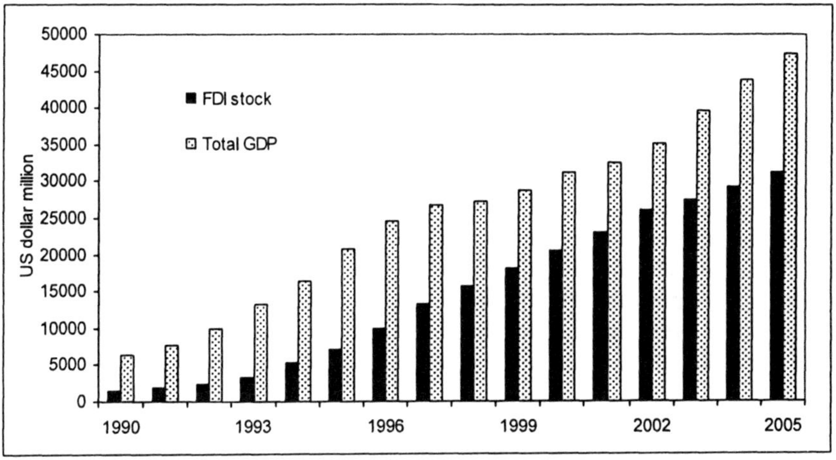

Source: UNCTAD 2006

4.1.3 International and Regional Economic Integration

Vietnam has strongly reaffirmed its commitment to economic liberalization and international integration. It has enacted structural reforms needed to modernize the economy and to produce more competitive, export-driven industries.

In 1995, Vietnam joined the Association of Southeast Asian Nations (ASEAN) and committed itself to implement the necessary requirements resulting from the different ASEAN integration projects. At that time, Vietnam had committed itself to fulfilling the implementation of the Common Effective Preferential Tariff (CEPT) under a framework of ASEAN Free Trade Area (AFTA)[45] by 2006.

Vietnam also became a member of the Asia Pacific Economic Co-operation (APEC)[46] in 1998, committing to liberalize its trade with APEC countries by

---

45   At the 4th ASEAN Summit in Singapore 1992, the ASEAN leaders had agreed to form an ASEAN Free Trade Area (AFTA) within a 15-year period, however, this was later reduced to a 10-year period, ending January 2003. AFTA is flexible by providing the option to exclude goods temporarily or permanently from obligation to tariff reduction and allowing new members to meet the obligations at the later date (Vietnam by 2006, Lao PDR and Myanmar by 2008, Cambodia by 2010)

46   The Asia-Pacific Economic Co-operation Forum (APEC) was formally established in 1989, including 21 member countries with Pacific shores, aiming at achieving free trade among

103

2020. So far, Vietnam has presented four Individual Action Plans (IAPs). The one presented in 2001 is the most precise including the commitment to liberalize the conditions for joint ventures and to streamline the customs system. Although the commitments are not as biding as AFTA-requirements and lack concrete implementation plans, they are also a step toward liberalizing the economic system (Wienmann 2006, pp. 65).

Entry into the US-Vietnam Bilateral Trade Agreement (US BTA) in December 2001 has led to even more rapid changes in Vietnam's trade and economic regime. Vietnam's exports to the US doubled in 2002 and again in 2003. In view of the WTO accession process, it is important to mention that many legal and technical commitments of the US BTA are identical or even stricter than WTO requirements. Therefore, implementing US BTA means anticipating most of the WTO requirements and should facilitate WTO accession.

Vietnam joined the WTO in January 2007, following an over-a-decade long negotiation process. This should provide an important boost to the economy and should help to ensure the continuation of liberalizing reforms. Among other benefits, accession allows Vietnam to take advantage of the phase-out of the Agreement on Textiles and Clothing, which eliminated quotas on textile and clothing for WTO partners on January 1st 2005.

4.2 Testing Determinants Driving Vietnam's National Competitiveness

In this research framework, in order to test determinants of the national competitiveness of Vietnam empirically, we treat collected hard data and survey data separately. The hard data and survey data were collected and designed to correspond to the determinants of national competitiveness. Due to poor statistical data in some areas and requirements of theoretical framework, we were forced to use many unconventional data sources and conduct survey data to support further the outcome of the study. The conclusions as to which determinants drive the national competitiveness of Vietnam will be drawn from the separate regression results of the hard data and survey data.

---

developed member countries by 2010 and for developing countries by 2020. Each member country has to present Individual Action Plan (IAPs), which describe voluntary and non-binding liberalization measures.

4.2.1 Nature of Competitiveness Indices

The independent variables of our study consist of six indices, which measure national competitiveness. The competitiveness components correspond to six the determinants of national competitiveness: production resources, technology development, market conditions, international business and economic activities, government role and company's strategy and operation. The indices include sub-indices that more specifically define the significance of the index. Each of the sub-indices, in turn, consists of several competitiveness indicators, which are qualified by both hard data and survey data. We could possibly not present all indicators reflecting every index and sub-index due to a limitation of statistical data. The different competitiveness indices, sub-indices and indicators are presented in the benchmarking tables of Appendix 2 (hard data)[47] and Appendix 3[48]. They provide a database for testing determinants of Vietnam's productivity and national competitiveness.

Production resources (PR) remains an important determinant of national competitiveness (see chapter 3, section 3). They are nothing more than the necessary inputs for competition in any firm and nation such as human capital, capital, infrastructure and natural resources.

Human resources (HR) have played a significant role in improving productivity, economic growth, and living standard (see chapter 3). It includes the quantity, skills, and personnel costs, and takes into account standard working hours and work ethic. Human resources can be divided into unskilled, semiskilled and skilled labor, of which skilled labor is the most important. In recent decades, economists have been specially interested in skilled labor. To improve human resources, labor forces need to be educated. Education has become the prerequisite for any nation aiming the development of technology, productivity, competitiveness and economic growth. Thus, the human resources sub-index includes several from indicators both hard and survey data. The hard data consists of (i)total population, (ii)primary enrollment, (iii)secondary enrollment, and (iv)tertiary enrollment. The survey data contains (iv) the quality of the education system reflecting whether the system meets the needs of a competitive economy, (v)the quality of public schools, and (vi) brain drain reflecting whether the most talented people remain in Vietnam.

Infrastructure resources (IR) An efficient and cost-competitive infrastructure is closely associated with productivity and competitiveness. In the context of rapid

---

47   We could not possibly present survey data in an appendix due to the abundance of the data
48   Appendix 3 presents standardized competitiveness indicators

economic growth in Vietnam, the demand for electricity, transportation and communication increases rapidly over time. Hence, infrastructure resources are represented (hard data) by (i)the number of telephone subscribers (landline and cell) per 100 people and (ii)electricity production, kWh per head. The infrastructure resources are also measured (survey data) by (iii) the quality of the general infrastructure, (iv)the quality of land and ship transportation, (v)the quality of the telephone services, and (vi)the quality of the electricity supply.

Capital resources (CR) refer to the amount and cost of capital available to finance firms and industries. Capital is not homogeneous, but comes in various forms such as unsecured debt, secured debt, bonds, equity, and venture capital. There are varying terms and conditions attached to each form. The total stock of capital resources in a country, and the forms in which it is deployed, are affected by the national rate of savings and by the structure of national capital markets. Bank and organized capital markets currently play an important role in financing enterprise (see chapter 3). In Vietnam, banks are still the major source of external capital for large as well as small enterprises and, indeed, for the private sector and the economy as a whole. Capital resources hence are represented (hard data) by (i)capital formation and (ii) national saving rate. It is also measured (survey) by (iii)financial market sophistication, (iv)the soundness of the banking system, and(v) ease of access to loans.

Natural resources (NR) was neglected by Porter in improving economic growth and competitiveness (see chapter 3). However, it is an important factor in developing economies, especially in the early stages of economic development. Natural resources are represented by exports of raw materials such as oil, coal, wood or food without processing etc. Natural resources thus are proxied (hard data) by (i)natural resources based products contributions to GDP. It is represented (survey data) by (ii)a resource rich country, (iii)the location of the country, (iv)the country's land, and (v)the greatest resource advantages.

Technology development (TD) is widely accepted in the economics literature that technology plays a significant role in productivity, competitiveness and economic growth. Partly due to its own fast changing nature and partly because of the increasingly integrated world economies, technology per se has moved to the centre stage in economic analyses. Rapid technological advancement is shifting fast the frontiers of technology and thus raising the scope for tremendous improvement in the competitive strength of a nation. Increased globalization of economies is necessitating further improvements in the competitiveness of firms and industries by intensifying international competitive pressures. The competitiveness of a firm can be taken as its ability to do better than comparable firms in sales, markets shares, or profitability (see chapter 3). To achieve this, developing countries (including Vietnam) import new technologies, equipments, patents and so on from developed countries. In addition, firms have applied information and communication technology to management. Hence, technology development is represented (hard data) by (i) imports of means of production, (ii)personal computers, and (iii)internet users. It is also proxied (survey data) by (iv)technology development level in the region, (v)the quality of scientific research institutions, (vi)firm-level technology absorption, and (vii)information and communication technology (ICT) development.

Market conditions (MC) are frameworks that create a competitive environment in which firms can compete and operate to attain their goals. Market conditions have played a critical, if not decisive, role in improving a firm's competitiveness as well as a nation's one. (see chapter 3). Vietnam does not remain competitive unless it creates good market conditions. Traditional mass markets are divided into a myriad of differentiated niche markets where demand will push firms to innovation success. At the same time, market regulations and user-producer relationships have become increasingly important for firms' innovation processes and international competitiveness. The market conditions hence form the fourth competitiveness index. This index is measured (hard data) by (i)newly established private enterprises. It is also captured (survey data) by (ii)the intensity of local competition,(iii)the demand seeks the latest products and technology, (iv)the effectiveness of anti-trust policy.

International business and economic activities (IBEA), a crucial determinant of national competitiveness, refers to the international integration of the Vietnamese economy through inward foreign direct investment and international trade.

Inward foreign direct investment (FDI) Attracting FDI is viewed by economists as a shortcut method for entering the production of manufactures for export and for technologically upgrading competitiveness over time in Vietnam. Among other reasons, FDI facilitates technology transfer from abroad, inflows of managerial and technical skills, access to marketing connections and linkage with international capital markets. It can also promote local technological development via subcontracting and supplier relationships between foreign and locally owned firms. FDI is captured (hard data) by (i)inward FDI stock, (ii)inward FDI stock as % of the GDP. It is also proxied (survey data) by (iii)FDI attracting environment and (iv) FDI and technology transfer.

International trade (IT) Both economic theory and countries' experience show that international trade (import and export) has been a major driving force of the improvement of the national productivity and competitiveness. As trade has been expanded, income has grown. Income growth depends heavily on a country's capacity to raise its productivity. Open economies have been able to harness the power to boost productivity and competitiveness, helping to improve living standards and sustain economic growth. (see chapter 3, section 3). Openness to trade (imports and exports) strengthens the driving force of productivity and competitiveness. Therefore, international trade activity is represented (hard data) by (i)openness of the economy and (ii)total exports. It is also captured (survey data) by (iii) hidden trade barriers and (iv) the openness of customs regime.

Openness of economy is calculated simply by imports plus exports divided by total GDP.

$$\text{Openness index} = \frac{\text{Imports} + \text{Exports}}{\text{Total GDP}}$$

Company's strategy and operation (CSO) Companies directly create productivity and sustain competitiveness and wealth of a nation. The important factors in doing so are the companies' strategies, structures and sizes. The strategies, structure and size of firms in industries vary widely among nations. It depends on the context and circumstances in which firms are created and organized. (see chapter 3). In Vietnam, private companies play an increasing role in the economy. The contribution of the private sector to GDP has increased over time. At the same time, the privatization process of a large number of state-owed enterprises has sped up. Companies build up their strategies such as ownership structure, technology innovation, personnel management, penetrating international and domestic markets and international brands. Company's strategy and structure thus is proxied (hard data) by (i)the contribution of the private sector to the GDP. It is also captured (survey data) by (ii) effectiveness of state-owned firms, (iii) the nature of competitive advantage, (iv) the company - local research institutions/universities collaboration, (v) recruiting and retaining qualified engineers, (vi) the ability to develop new products, and (vii) the extent of international branding and distribution channel.

Government role (GR) plays a crucial part in enhancing the national competitiveness in Vietnam. In fact, it depends on the stage of the development and the country's particular circumstances. Porter argued that government role reduces gradually through each stage of development. In the early phase, i.e. resources-driven development, government intervention is significant to improve the competitiveness of infant firms and industries. In the following frameworks, government role is represented by two areas: Institution and Government Policy (see chapter 3).

Government policy (GP) The central goal of government policy toward the competitiveness of the Vietnamese economy is to deploy the nation's resources with high and rising levels of productivity. Government policies that succeed are those that create an environment in which companies can gain competitiveness rather than those that involve government policies directly in the process, except in nations in the early development processes such as Vietnam and China. A Government's proper policies are to encourage, or even push, companies to raise their aspirations and move to higher levels of competitive performance, even though this process may be inherently unpleasant and difficult (see chapter 3). Thus government policy is proxied (hard data) by (i)government revenue and (ii)expenditure. It is also measured (survey data) by (iii)how the government treats all economic sectors (private, state-owned, FDI-invested), (iv)the competence of local and government officials and (v) the independence of policymaking and (vi)the burden of government regulations.

Public institutions (PI) have been playing a significant role in a market-oriented economy like Vietnam. Institutions are shaped by the judicial and legislative processes of the society, rent-seeking activities of special interest groups, collective bargaining between labor unions and employers, private bargaining between buyers and sellers, and other regulatory processes in the private sector (see chapter 3).

An efficient institutional framework directs productive resources to their socially most productive uses. Efficient institutions also facilitate rapid structural adjustment by speeding up the withdrawal of resources from uncompetitive and unproductive sectors and stimulating the investments into new and more promising sectors. An efficient institutional framework restrains corruption and creates a sound environment, which attracts inward FDI flows. In addition, an efficient institution framework stimulates technology transfer and innovation by which productivity and competitiveness are improved. Therefore our institution competitiveness index includes indicators (hard data) involving (i)total taxes (Bn Dong) and (ii)taxes as % of the budget revenue. It is also proxied (survey data) by (iii)the effectiveness of the legal system, (iv) the property rights regime, (v)the effectiveness of the law-making bodies, and (vi)the corruption situation.

4.2.2 Data Resources

Hard data: in the selection of the hard data sources, we have tried to rely on international and regional statistical organizations such as the ADB-Asia Development Bank, WB-World Bank, IMF-International Monetary Fund, UNCTAD-United Nations Conference on Trade and Development, GSO-Vietnam General Statistic Office etc. Each statistics organization supplies datasets involving some indicators, for example, the WB supplies data of human resources or the data of exports and imports is collected from the ADB. We try to collect data from the above –mentioned sources to form the database which covers the time period of our study, the 16 years, from 1990 to 2005 (see Appendix 2) However, due to systemic and interdisciplinary nature of the theoretical framework and poor statistics on Vietnam, we could not rely on conventional statistical data sources alone. We were forced to use unconventional data sources and conduct the survey in order to match the wide variety of the theoretical frameworks.

Data collection from the Global Competitiveness Report, World Economic Forum is significant to analyze the state of national competitiveness of Vietnam and to compare its competitiveness with some selected regional countries.

Survey data is another important source that supports further empirical study of national competitiveness. Surveys cover many important areas of competitiveness, especially in quality, which was poorly represented or not at all in conventional statistics.

The survey is structured in two parts: the first part, the determinants of national competitiveness, is depicted in the following areas: Production Resources, Technology Development, Market Conditions, International Business and Economic Activities, Company's Strategy and Operation, Government Role. The second one includes the most concerning problems of companies, priorities for the government in the next five years and top priorities for the companies (Appendix 5). The second section is one of the bases to propose recommendations for enhancing the competitiveness of Vietnam in next few years. The survey was conducted for a sample of respondents from business leaders, scholars, and local and government officials across the country. Their responses were be aggregated to produce a database, which is used to test the determinants of Vietnam's national competitiveness, and to analyze further featuring of the emerging key issues and perspectives of Vietnam's national competitiveness in the context of international economic integration.

The survey comprises a total of 44 questions. These survey questions were based on those used by the Global Competitiveness Report 2000 and 2004-05 and Vu, Minh Khuong and Johnathan Haughton (2003). The sample of survey questionnaire is reproduced in Appendix 5. All the questions in the questionnaire were adapted to the regional and Vietnamese conditions.

The questions asked for responses on a scale of 1 to 7 and 1 to 5. The answer of 1 and 7 are at least and at highest value respectively. The answer of 1 means complete disagreement and the answer of 7 means complete agreement. Similar to scale 1 to 5, the answer of 1 (at least value) means not important at all and the answer of 5 means extremely important (Appendix 5).

110

The difference in designing the survey questionnaire of the global competitiveness report and ours is the superlative level of each question. While the former is world-class, the latter is regional class-ASEAN. We compare Vietnam's relative competitiveness with some selected ASEAN economies' competitiveness to deeper understand the competitiveness of Vietnam. Therefore, all respondents who responded the questionnaire have experience in ASEAN countries and China.

The survey data used in the GCR[49] and WCY[50] are limited to business leaders, while this research includes surveys from experts in academia, business and government. This therefore provides a better understanding and broader basis to evaluate the national competitiveness of Vietnam.

The survey questionnaire was sent to a total of 300 respondents including firms, scholars and local and government officials across the country. These surveys were distributed equally to three types of respondents: *Business leaders* from Steel, Electricity, Coal, Textile, Footwear, Food, Coffee, Tea, Rice, Motorcycle, Cycle, Ship, Tobacco industries; *Scholars* from Hanoi National Economics University, Hanoi University of Finance and Accountancy, Hanoi University of Commerce, University of Foreign Trade, Hanoi University of Technology, University of Natural Science, Hanoi University of Communications and Transports, Ho Chi Minh University of Economics, Ho Chi Minh University of Technology, and *Local and Government Officials* from Ministry of Trade, Ministry of Finance, State Bank, Ministry of Industry, Ministry of Science and Technology, Ministry of Posts and Telematics and Ministry of Education and Training; Hanoi city, Ho Chi Minh city, Da Nang city, Hai Phong city, Thanh Hoa province, Nghe An province.

We obtained 154 valid responses, representing a respectable overall response rate of 51.3%. The response rates for each of the objects were: 43% (43 out of 100) for local and government officials; 57% (57 out of 100) for firms and 52% (52 out of 100) for scholars (Appendix 6).

4.2.3 Construction of Competitiveness Indices

In order to construct six competitiveness indices from raw hard data with various competitiveness indicators, we first make them comparable to facilitate their comparison and combination. To do so, all competitiveness indicators need to be

---

49 The GCR stands for Global Competitiveness Report, issued annually by World EconomicForum (WEF). Vietnam is included in this report.

50 The WCY stands for World Competitiveness Yearbook, issued by Institute of Management Development (IMD). Vietnam is not included in this report.

standardized[51]. The standardized competitiveness indicators are presented in Appendix 3. We could now combine and group the comparable indicators to form the sub-indices and then combine the sub-indices to create the six competitiveness indices shown below. We used weighted averages for the combination. The equal weight of indicator and sub-indices follows measurement of HDI by the UN[52] and the competitiveness index by the WEF (World Economic Forum) and the IMD (Institute of Management and Development). The weights of individual indicators and sub-indices under which they were grouped are shown in Appendix 3.

The construction of six competitiveness indices from soft data is composed similarly. All indicators were comparable[53], thus we can group indicators into sub-indices and then combine the sub-indices to form six competitiveness indices under soft data.

The competitiveness indices, in general, are calculated as below:

$$PR_{n4}\ index = W_1 \sum_{j=1}^{n_1} w_{1j} HR_j + W_2 \sum_{j=1}^{n_2} w_{2j} CR_j + W_3 \sum_{j=1}^{n_3} w_{3j} IR_j + W_4 \sum_{j=1}^{n_4} w_{4j} NR_j$$

PR *index is* index of production resources
W_i is the weigh of the ith sub-indices (i=1,2,3 and 4)
w_{ij} is the weigh of the jth indicator (j= 1,2,3..., n_i)
HR_j is the value of the jth indicator of human resource sub-index,
CR_j is the value of the jth indicator of capital resources sub-index,
IR_j is the value of the jth indicator of infrastructure sub-index,
NR_j is the value of the jth indicator of natural resources sub-index.

$$TD\ index = \sum_{j=1}^{n} w_j TD_j$$

TD *index* is index of technology development
w_j is the weigh of the jth indicator (j= 1,2,3..., n_i)

$$MC\ index = \sum_{j=1}^{n} w_j MC_j$$

MC *index* is index of market condition
w_j is the weigh of the jth indicator (j= 1,2,3..., n_i)

---

51   We use SPSS software to conduct this standardization procedure.
52   HDI-Human Development Index, annual publication by the United Nations
53   All indicators (survey data) were scaled from 1 to 7, hence, they don't need to be standardized.

112

$$\text{IBEA index} = W_1 \sum_{j=1}^{n_1} w_{1j} FDI_j + W_2 \sum_{j=1}^{n_2} w_{2j} IT_j$$

IBEA index is index of international business and economic activities
W_i is the weigh of the ith sub-indices (i=1 and 2)
w_{ij} is the weigh of the jth indicator (j= 1,2,3..., n_i)
FDI_j is the value of the jth indicator of foreign direct investment sub-index,
IT_j is the value of the jth indicator of international trade sub-index,

$$CSO\ index = \sum_{j=1}^{n} w_j\ CSO_j$$

CSO index is index of company's strategy and structure
w_j is the weigh of the jth indicator (j= 1,2,3..., n_i)

$$\text{GR index} = W_1 \sum_{j=1}^{n_1} w_{1j} PI_j + W_2 \sum_{j=1}^{n_2} w_{2j} GP_j$$

GR index is index of government role
W_i is the weigh of the ith sub-indices (i=1 and 2)
w_{ij} is the weigh of the jth indicator (j= 1,2,3..., n_i)
PI_j is the value of the jth indicator of public institution sub-index,
GP_j is the value of the jth indicator of government policy sub-index.
Source: Asia Pacific Management Review (2004) 9(20)

4.3 Summary of Regression Analysis Result

4.3.1 Model of Multiple Linear Regression

In order to test whether which factors influence the national competitiveness of Vietnam, we use a multiple linear regression model to conduct. The type of the model follows:
$Y_i = b_c + b_1 X_1 + b_2 X_2 + ... + b_r X_r + u_i$
Where: Y_i is a dependent variable (GDP per capita and VNC),
X_r is independent variables (competitiveness indices),
b_r are coefficients,
n is the number of independent variables in the model (six independent variable in this research), and
u_i is random disturbance.

In models 1-3 *(regression result from hard data)*, the dependent variable was operationalized by GDP per capita (GDPPC). As mentioned in the second chapter, the competitiveness at national level is meaningful at national productivity. National productivity is measured broadly by GDP per capita and is strongly linked over time to a nation's standard of living (Porter 2004, p 27)[54].

The independent variables consist of production resources (PR), technology development (TD), market conditions (MC), international business and economic activities (IBEA), company's strategy and operation (CSO), and government role (GR). Each independent variable corresponds to one determinant of national competitiveness.

In models 4-6 *(regression result from survey data)*, the independent variables are similar to models 1-3. The differences between models 1-3 and models 4-6 are the dependent variable and number of observations. While the dependent variable in models 1-3 is GDP per capita, the dependent variable in models 4-6 is VNC[55]. In the former, there are 16 observations corresponding to 16 years, whereas 154 observations correspond to 154 respondents in the latter.

In addition, we use human resources (HR), infrastructure resources (IR), capital resources (CR) and natural resources (NR) as independent variables when testing the impact of them on Vietnam's national competitiveness (table 4.2 of model 7 and model 8).

4.3.2 The Result of the Regression Models

We present the key results in table format[56](table 4.1 and 4.2). The table include: independent variables and their coefficients, dependent variable, number of observations (n), R square, t-statistics and significance level for coefficients (*** denotes $p < = 0.01$; ** denotes $0.01 < p < = 0.05$; * denotes $0.05 < p < = 0.10$).

Our regression results were quite interesting. In models 3 and model 6, all independent variables were statistically significant at 1 or 5 percent level and had the expected positive sign (except market condition-MC in model 3). Another exciting result, in six the models, is that PR is highly statistically significant and has the strongest influence on productivity and competitiveness. That means thus production resources (PR) was proved to be the most important determinant of Vietnam's productivity and competitiveness. However, R square and coefficients in

---

54   GDP per worker is employed as a productivity measure in some studies. Here is the broader measure because GDP per worker can be increased by high unemployment or low workforce participation, which do not increase wealth. Also, holder of capital, not only workers, contribute to national productivity.

55   The VNC which stands for Vietnam National Competitiveness is identified by each respondents about overall Vietnam national competitiveness (see Appendix 5)

56   The regression results in detail are presented in Appendix 4.

the models are different. Values of the coefficients and R square in models 1 to 3 are higher than that in models 4 to 6.

Results from hard data – Models 1-3 (Table 4.1), we tested all six competitiveness indices with the full data set (16 observations with hard data for all variables) and GDP per capita as the dependent variable (model 1). Several interesting results emerged. The share of explained variation in the dependent variable (R square) was extremely high, 99.8 percent. That means 99.8 percent of the change in one independent variable is due to a change in the dependent variable. Half of independent variables were significant at least on the 10 percent level including: production resources (PR), market condition (MC), and international business and economic activities (IBEA). In model 2, the company's strategy and operation (CSO) variable was excluded. The result was stronger and the three independent variables were very highly significant (at 1 percent level). the two variables (CSO and GR) were excluded. The regression result of model 3[57] was very interesting. All the rest of independent variables were significant at least on 5 percent level and had positive sign (except market condition-MC). The strongest result obtained was PR with highly significant *(sig 0.000)[58]* and highest coefficient *(0,651)*. This coefficient doubles the TD's and IBEA's. Production resources have had a critical influence on competitiveness and productivity in Vietnam. Specifically speaking, infrastructure, human resource, capital and natural resources have significantly contributed to improving competitiveness, productivity and living standard in Vietnam. The negative sign of the market conditions (MC) variables is a bit surprising. Perhaps it is a limitation of the hard data of these variables in conventional statistic resources. It would be explained that due to a lack of the law framework for fair competition. This calls for further research.

Results from survey data – models 4-6 (Table 4.1), all six competitiveness determinants with full data set (154 observations with survey data for all variables) are tested with dependent variable (VNC). The regression fits of model 4 were generally somewhat weaker than that in models 1 but the statistical significance of the independent variables is stronger. Four of the six independent variables were significant at 1 percent and 5 percent (model 4). In model 5, the TD variable was excluded, the regression result is a little stronger. The statistical significance of the independent variables is higher. Similar to model 3, the regression result of model 6[59] was exciting. All four independent variables were highly significant. The strongest result was PR with an extremerly statistical significance (0.000) and the highest coefficient (0.387) (Table 4.1). The coefficient of the PR variable is

---

57   The two variables (CSO and GR) were excluded.

58   See Appendix 4: table A 4.2

59   The TD and IBEA variables were excluded

twice as high as the coefficient of the CSO and MC variables. The interesting difference is that in model 3, the company's strategy and operation (CSO) and government role (GR) variables were excluded, but highly significant in model 6. In contrast, the international business and economic activities (IBEA) and technology development (TD) variables were excluded in model 6, but very statistically significant in model 3.

Results with sub-indices of PR as independent variables (Table 4.2) The results of the above models indicate the dominance of the production resources (PR) determinant in Vietnam's national competitiveness. In order to further understand the impact of production resources on Vietnam's national competitiveness and productivity, we also use HR, IR, CR and NR[60] as independent variables to test the impact of them on the national competitiveness and productivity in Vietnam.

The regression results were also quite interesting. In both the models (model 7 and model 8), all four independent variables except human resources (HR) were very highly statistically significant at least on 1 percent and had the positive sign. Infrastructure resource (IR) and human resources (HR) with highest and lowest statistical significance obtained highest and lowest coefficients in both models respectively (table 4.2). This result indicates that infrastructure strongly influences the national competitiveness in Vietnam. Similar to models 1-3 and 4-6, the regression fits of model 8 were somewhat weaker than that of model 7, but the statistical significances were still extremely strong. R square in model 7 (99.8 percent) was higher than the one in model 8 (43.5 percent).

The key results of the empirical study can be summarized as follows: Firstly, they strongly support our theoretical analysis of the determinants of national competitiveness. The regression results with survey data supplemented the results with hard data. This was consistent with the requirements of the theoretical frameworks.

Secondly, our results also suggest that the production resources (PR) have played the most significant role in improving productivity, competitiveness and living standards in Vietnam since its reform process. In other words, it can be as a decisive factor of Vietnam's productivity and competitiveness. This is very compatible with Porter's theoretical frameworks. Vietnam has stood in the initial stage of the development processes. Thus, its production resources have become a competitive advantage. In this regard, Vietnam should pay more attention to developing and deploying production resources efficiently.

---

60   HR, IR, CR and NR are sub-indices of PR and stand for human resource, infrastructure resource, capital resource and natural resource respectively.

Thirdly, the results strongly emphasize the importance of infrastructure for the productivity, competitiveness and living standard in Vietnam. The infrastructure factor was very statistically significant in both the models (model 7 and 8) with hard and survey data. It is also important to note that the infrastructure's influence on Vietnam's productivity and competitiveness is higher than any other factors of production resources.

Finally, it is also important to note some variables, which did not gain statistical significance in the separate models (models 1-3 and 4-6). The statistical weakness of these variables was particularly critical since the competitiveness literature has strongly emphasized their importance. Some reasons for their apparent insignificance may be the high multicollinearity among the variables, poor statistical resources and the requirements of comprehensive theoretical frameworks. These may seriously distort the significance and even the signs of the independent variables and hence call for further research.

Table 4. 1: Summary of regression results[61] of hard data (1990–2005) and survey data

Model	Model 1	Model 2	Model 3	Model 4	Model 5	Model 6
Dependent Variables	GDPPC	GDPPC	GDPPC	VNC	VNC	VNC
Number of Obervations	16	16	16	154	154	154
Independent Variables						
Production Resources (PR)	0,706**	0,663***	0,651***	0,336***	0,375***	0,387***
	(3,221)	(5,003)	(4,96)	(4,323)	(5,452)	(5,634)
Technology Development(TD)	0,218	0,226	0,312**	0,082		
	(1,427)	(1,595)	(2,881)	(1,1)		
Market Condition (MC)	-0,267*	-,294***	-0,286***	0,154**	0,157**	0,157**
	(-1,914)	(-3,419)	(-3,360)	(2,424)	(2,47)	(2,453)
International Business and Economic Activities (IBEA)	0,362**	0,368***	0,320***	0,089	0,093	
	(3,273)	(3,553)	(3,555)	(1,493)	(1,565)	
Company's Strategy and Operation (CSO)	-0,059			0,196**	0,203***	0,242***
	(-,256)			(2,566)	(2,669)	(3,349)
Government Role (GR)	0,04	0,037		0,152**	0,168**	0,158**
	(0,935)	(0,947)		(2,058)	(2,317)	(2,167)
R square	0,999	0,999	0.998	0,573	0,570	0,562

Note: *** denotes $p <= 0.01$; ** denotes $0.01 < p <= 0.05$; * denotes $0.05 < p <= 0.10$, Dependent variables: GDPPC – GDP per capita; VNC - Vietnam National Competitiveness is identified by each respondent (see Appendix 5). t-statistics is given in the parentheses. The regression results of model 1, model 2 and model 3 from hard data, 1990-2005 The regression results of model 4, model 5 and model 6 from survey data, 154 respondents.

---

61   Seeing in detail in Appendix 4: Table A4.1, 4.2, 4.3 and 4.4

Table 4-2: The regression results[62] of hard and survey data (with independent variables of production resources -PR)

Model	Model 7	Model 8
Dependent Variables	GDPPC	VNC
Number of Obervations	16	154
Independent Variables		
Human Resource (HR)	0,14**	0,181**
	(2,97)	(2,509)
Infrastructure Resource (IR)	0,519***	0,257***
	(16,428)	(3,197)
Capital Resource (CR)	0,205***	0,213***
	(4,98)	(2,761)
Natural Resource (NR)	0,197***	0,291***
	(3,929)	(4,349)
R square	0,998	0,435

Note: *** denotes $p <= 0.01$; ** denotes $0.01 < p <= 0.05$; * denotes $0.05 < p <= 0.10$

Dependent variables: GDPPC – GDP per capita; VNC – Vietnam National Competitiveness

The regression result of model 3 from hard data, 1990-2005

The regression result of model 4 from survey data, 154 respondent

---

62   Seeing in detail in Appendix 4: Table A 4.5, 4.6, 4.7 and 4.8

Chapter 5: National Competitiveness of Vietnam

In the previous chapter, we empirically tested the determinants driving national competitiveness of Vietnam, including production resources, technology development, market conditions, international economic and business activities, government role, and company's strategy and operation.

In this chapter, we will analyze the state of Vietnam's competitiveness relying on six above identified determinants by a combination of hard and survey data. We also evaluate Vietnam's national competitiveness progress in the last two decades and the remaining weaknesses compared to some other selected regional countries[63]. Some main indicators are used to illustrate this analysis and assessment. This chapter is fundamental to point out some emerging key issues and to propose some solutions enhancing Vietnam's national competitiveness in coming years in the next chapter.

In order to understand the competitiveness of the Vietnamese economy, we analyze in this section the determinants of national competitiveness and compare its determinants with selected regional countries, particularly China and Thailand. This analysis is argued by collected hard data and survey data. The analysis result shows the competitiveness's assessment and the remaining weaknesses as well as its causes in Vietnam.

5.1 Production Resource and Competitiveness

5.1.1 Infrastructure Development and Competitiveness

Infrastructure development considered as a critical part of the economic growth has been invested at a high level in Vietnam over the last decade. Around 9-10% of the GDP has been invested on transport, energy, telecommunications, water, and sanitation in recent years (World Bank 2006a). Microeconomic studies provide evidence of a strong link between this investment and Vietnam's productivity, competitiveness and growth (Ibid, pp xvii). Our study shows that infrastructure is the most crucial factor which determines Vietnam's productivity and competitiveness[64].

---

63 Some selected regional countries include China, Thailand, Malaysia, The Philippines, Indonesia.

64 See section 2 chapter 4

The road network has more than doubled in length, from 96,100km in 1990 to 205,782 km in 2002, and its quality has improved substantially. National level roads expanded from 15,100 km with 36,6% in good condition in 1997 to 17,300 km with 44,8% in good condition in 2002 (Ibid, pp xviii). All urban areas in Vietnam are electrified. In the rural areas, electrification grew from 51% in 1996 to 88% in 2004. The number of fixed and mobile phones per 1000 people have multiplied eighteenth-fold, from 10.3 in 1990 to 183.6 in 2004. Access to improved water grew from 26% of the population to 85% between 1993 and 2004. During the same time access to hygienic latrines grew from 10% to 31% of the population, with rural access at 16% and urban access at 76% of the population in 2004. Vietnam's performance of improved sanitation and water was higher than China's, with 92% and 85%, compared to 69% and 77% respectively. However, the infrastructure has not yet met needs of the current and future economic growth, and it lags behind China and Thailand. For example, in 2004 Vietnam had 183.59 fixed line and mobile phone subscribers per 1000 inhabitants, compared to 536.79 in Thailand and 498.84 in China; in Vietnam 19% of the roads were paved, compared to 98% and 81% in Thailand and China respectively (Table 5. 1)

Table 5. 1: Access to Infrastructure Services (2004)

	Telephone (1)	Electricity (2)	Sanitation (3)	Water (4)	Road (5)
Vietnam	183.60	501.45	92	85	19
Thailand	536.79	1864.58	98	99	98.5
China	498.84	1585.12	69	77	81.03
Malaysia	765.56	3165.52	95	99	81.32
Philippines	445.66	597.06	80	85	21.64
Indonesia	185.34	478.20	73	77	58
World	468.84	2522.04	79.63	82.75	n.a

Note: (1) Fixed line and mobile phone subscribers (per 1,000 people)
(2) Electric power consumption (kWh per capita)
(3) Improved sanitation facilities, urban (% of urban population with access)
(4) Improved water source (% of population with access)
(5) Roads, paved (% of total roads); data of the year 2002 for Indonesia, and 2003 for the Philippines
Source: World Bank, World Development Indicator, 2007 and CIA, The World Factbook, 2007

Some costs of infrastructure services were high, compared to some regional countries. The study of the JETRO (Japan) showed that the costs in Vietnam, in general, were higher than the costs in ASEAN-4 countries and China, while income in Vietnam is lower than in those countries, especially the costs of an international telephone call, office rent and transportation Almost all prices of infrastructure service are regulated by the government. In fact, infrastructure enterprises have no right to set price themselves. They propose tariffs of infrastructure service and the government decides the prices.

5.1.2 Human Resource and Competitiveness

Vietnam has abundant human resources as compared to its neighbors. This advantage has attracted FDI inflow in the last decades. By 2005, Vietnam's population was estimated at 83.12 million, an average annual increase of 1.57% between 1990 and 2005. 43.6 million people joining the labor force accounted for 52.45% of the population. Labor force grew at an annual average rate of 2.4% in the duration between 1998 and 2005, compared to 2.24% in China and 1.05% in Thailand (Table 5. 3). The table indicates that the average unemployment rate in Vietnam was the lowest among selected countries (except Thailand) in the last decade, at rate 2.83%. With such labor force, Vietnam avoids the shortage of labor force that is challenging some developed and fast-growth developing countries.

Table 5. 2: A Comparison of Infrastructure Service-Related Cost among Asia Cities

	Hanoi	Bangkok	Beijing	K.lump	Jakarta	Manila
Industrial Estate Rent (Monthly per Sq.m)	0,21	4,60	3,62-7,25		3,8-4,1	4,5-5,0
Office Rent (Monthly per Sq.m)	21	10,13	37	15,58-17,00	14-20	7,49
Telephone Installation Fee (US dollar)	84,75	85,16	28,39	48,68	49,94	65,54
Telephone Charge per Minute (US dollar)	0,003-0,008	0,07	0,01	0,01	0,01	0
International Call Charge, 3 Minutes to Japan (US dollar)	6,93	2,07	2,9	1,42	3,76	1,2
Mobile Phone Subscription Fee (US Dollar)	39,11	23,01	9,67	95,53	15,54	0
Mobile Charge per Minute (US dollar)	0,12-0,17	0,07-0,28	0,05	0,08	0,17	0,12-0,13
Electricity Rate for Business Use (Charge per kWh)	0,05-0,07	0,04	0,05-0,09	0,05	0,04	0,03-0,04
Water for Business Use (Charge per Cu.m)	0,08-0,1	0,04-0,07	0,22	0,06	0,07	0,03-0,06
Container Transport (40-foot Container to Yokohama) (US dollar)	1470	1304	734	884	820	700

Source: Jetro Survey 2003

Table 5. 3: Population and Labor Force

Economies	Total population (million)		Average population annual change, %	Labor force (million)		Average labor force annual change, %	Average labor force participation rate, %	Average unemployment rate, %
	1990	2005	1990-2005	1990	2005	1990-2005	1990-2005	1990-2005
Vietnam	66,02	83,12	1,57	36,9*	43,60	2,40**	50,98**	2,83**
China	1143,3	1307,6	0,93	653,23	768,23	2,24	n.a	3,19
Thailand	55,84	64,76	1,00	31,75	36,80	1,05	73,59	1,86
Malaysia	18,10	26,13	2,44	7,04	10,41	2,67	65,11	3,40
Philippines	60,94	85,24	2,24	24,53	36,64	2,73	65,64	9,21
Indonesia	179,38	219,9	1,46	77,8	105,8	2,14	65,63	6,05

Source: ADB, Key Indicator 2006; Note: * Data of the year 1998; ** an average of duration 1998 and 2005

Vietnam's human resources are at relatively high skill, compared with equivalent development level countries (low income), due to its basic educational accomplishments. One rough but ready measure of the stock of human resource is the literacy of the adult population (Table 5. 4). The table reveals, typically more than 90 per cent of the adult populations of Vietnam was literate in 2004. This rate is equivalent to richer neighbors such as Thailand, China and Philippines, and even higher than Malaysia. This progress emanates from high primary school and secondary enrollment rates in Vietnam: by 2004 around 98% of children attended primary schools, compared to 98.5% in Thailand and 117.62% in China. In China the enrollment rate stood at 117.62% which indicates that a number of students were older people returning to school; the enrollment rate at the secondary level of education in Vietnam (74.35%) is higher than that in China (72.53%) and in Indonesia (64.12%), lower than in Thailand (77.34%), and nearly equal to that in Malaysia (75.78%) (Table 5. 4). This is a testament to the government's efforts to provide primary education for Vietnam's children. A recent study assessed the secondary education system of Vietnam against an international benchmark (World Bank 2007a). On most counts, the findings are encouraging. The study found that teachers are well-educated and have at least two years of training. They prepare their lessons and are assiduous in teaching the prescribed curriculum. Textbooks are the most part adequately supplied. Buildings and equipments are not characterized by standards, but most schools have the basics, including libraries and a reasonable range of teaching aids. Class size is well within the normal range.

Table 5. 4 also shows that the enrollment rate for higher education in Vietnam increases sharply from 1.98% in 1990 to 10.16% in 2004. There was an impressive expansion in higher education under way. It reflected the increasing household demand and increasing returns to education, and also a result of the rapid growth in secondary school enrollment. At present, 230 Institutions accommodate more than 1.3 millions higher education standards. This growth in supply has occurred to a large extent through private sector provision and the introduction of cost-recovery mechanism. Not surprisingly, enrollment is highly skewed, with participation by the richest population quintile being four times that of the poorest quintile. The government tries to influence the quality of higher education mainly through administrative means. For instance, it controls the entrance examination and sets admission quotas. However, in-service students are not strictly required to take entrance tests and enrollment above the authorized quotas common among institutions seeking to increase their income.

Table 5. 4: Literacy and Enrollment Rate

Economies	Literacy rate, adult total (% of people 15+)		Gross enroll-ment rate (%), primary, total		Gross en-rollment rate (%), secon-dary, total		Gross enroll-ment rate (%), tertiary, total	
	1990	2004	1990	2004	1990	2004	1990	2004
Vietnam	n.a	90.28	106.9	97.97	32.22	74.35	1.98	10.16
China	78.29	90.92	125.15	117.62	48.69	72.53	2.94	19.1
Thailand	n.a	92.65	98.13	98.51	30.85	77.34	17.68*	40.98
Malaysia	n.a	n.a	93.71	93.48 **	56.33	75.78 **	7.43	32.35 **
Philippines	91.73	92.6	109.46	112.36	70.69	85.86	27.81	28.8
Indonesia	79.51	90.38	114.31	116.96	45.48	64.12	9.46	16.67
World	n.a	n.a	n.a	106.76	n.a	65.06	n.a	23.68

Source: Edstats Data Query, WB, 2006; Note: * Data of the year 1991; ** Data of the year 2003

5.1.3 Capital Resource and Competitiveness

Vietnam's financial sector has expanded rapidly in recent years, mostly supplying banking loans to the private sector. In the banking sector, the credit to the economy rose from 35% of the GDP in 2000 to 66% of the GDP in 2006. The ratio of bank deposits to GDP stands at 57%. The extension has taken place at an even faster pace in the case of joint stock banks, whose total charter capital has almost tripled over the last years. Access to finance has increased substantially, with the number of savings accounts standing close to 25 millions. So far, there are more than 1,100 ATMs in Vietnam and 2.1 million credits and debit cards in circulation. The most spectacular development is the surge of the stock market. With the VN-Index doubling in one year (2006) since its creation at the beginning of the year 2001, the stock market's capitalization reached $4 billion or almost 8% of GDP[65].

Figure 5. 1: Gross Domestic Capital Formation (% of GDP)

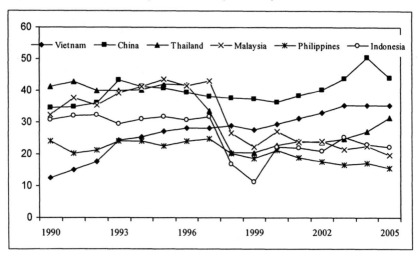

Source: ADB, 2006

State owned commercial banks (SOCBs) dominate Vietnam's financial sector, accounting for approximately 75% total bank credit in the economy and engaging in non-commercial or politically-preferred lending, especially in rural areas. This leads to prevent market-oriented credit allocation as well as equity base reinforcement of Vietnamese industries. Historically, Vietnam's financial system depended heavily on the State Bank of Vietnam (SBV) and SOCBs, for providing almost all services in the country. In 1988, the government set up an additional commercial bank system so that the SBV could specialize in the monetary policy and supervision as a central bank. While allowing the private sector to set up joint-stock commercial banks in 1991 and foreign banks to open local branches in 1992, the Development Assistant Fund (DAF), which was intended solely for pol-

---

65   The above explained data is cited from World Bank 2006b and 2007a

126

icy finance, was added to the state-owned financial facilities in 2000 (WB 2006b, p 18).

The Vietnamese banking system has played a significant role in allocating capital resource. For example, the money supply (M2) of Vietnam has expanded annually, a rise from 27.1% of GDP in 1990 to 82.4% in 2005, higher than that of the Philippines (38.1%) and Indonesia (44.1%). However, the rate is still far lower than China and Malaysia (Figure 5. 2)

Figure 5. 2: M2 as a Percentage of GDP

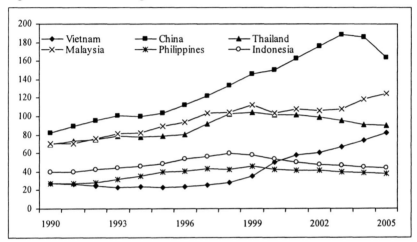

Source: ADB, Key Indicator, 2006

Capital Market The securities market expanded beyond expectations in 2006. The number of listed companies rose to 193 from 41, and total market capitalization increased almost 20 fold from 2005 levels, to $14 billion, or 22.7% of the GDP. The main index of share price soared from 307.5 at the end of 2005 to 751.8 one year later, and climbed further to 1,138 points at the end of February 2007 (ADB 2007, pp 238). There are concerns that speculators using funds borrowed from banks may face repayment difficulties if stock prices dropped precipitously. Big fund flows could cause problems for the implementation of monetary and foreign exchange policies. With this in mind, the central bank warned commercial banks of the risk of increasing securities-backed loans and requested commercial banks to report on such loans. Moves were made to improve corporate governance and market regulation. A law on securities and securities markets was approved, and came into force in January 2007. It provides a legal base for investor protection and market transparency, including disclosure requirements for publicly held companies. The maximum foreign ownership in listed companies was lifted from 30%-49%. The stock market boom also encouraged more state-owned enterprises (SOEs) to issue shares to investors. Subsidiaries of several major SOEs in areas such as hydropower made successful initial public share offerings (IPO). in December 2006, the Prime Minister approved a list of state firms to be equitized during 2007-2010, including major ones such as Vietnam airlines (Ibid., pp 239).

Figure 5. 3: National Saving Rate (% of GDP)

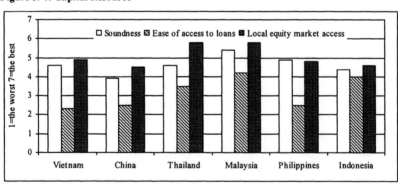

Source: ADB, Key Indicator, 2006

Figure 5. 4: Capital Resource

Source: WEF, Survey 2004-05

Over the last decades Vietnam has expanded its national saving rate and investment to 27% of the GDP in 2004 from -3.5% in 1990 due to sustainable economic

128

growth. Notwithstanding, this rate remains far lower than that in China and Malaysia, and nearly equal to Thailand and the Philippines (Figure 5. 3)

5.1.4 Production Resources' Assessment

Infrastructure An enormous progress has been made in Vietnam's infrastructure over the last decade. Annual investments in order of 9 to 10 per cent of GDP led to a significant increase in paved roads, telephone lines, port capacity and power supply. However, the quality of infrastructure is still poor and its price remains high when compared to neighbors. The survey from WEF also shows that in general, the quality of infrastructure is considered to be poor and not yet satisfied. It marked 2.4, compared to 3.2 for China and Thailand, on a scale that runs from 1 (low satisfaction) to 7 (Figure 5. 5). Our survey conducted in early 2007 indicates that the quality of land and ship transportation in Vietnam is considered to be poorest with 2.26 points, on the same scale from 1 to 7, while the telephone system and power supply is considered to be more reliable and better. The details are revealing, and are described in Appendix 6. The significant point here is that there is considerable room for improvement in creating an infrastructure that is favorable to business growth. We have interpreted this as reflecting poorer services in Vietnam, but it is also possible that firms there are more demanding, and expect better service than is considered adequate elsewhere in the region. Thus it leads to increase business cost, reduce competitiveness and attract less foreign direct investment.

Human resource Over the last decade, Vietnam has enjoyed relatively high skilled and abundant human resources thanks to initial reform of the education system, particularly primary and secondary education. In order to fill the demand for higher-quality education, the government introduced full-day schooling at the primary level. Pupils in full-day classes received 35 periods of instruction per week, compared to 23 periods in half-day classes. In fact, the 20% of Vietnamese teachers who are already in full-day schools have a similar workload to that of their Korean counterparts (around 820 hours of teaching per year). The additional instruction is not financed by the government, but through parents' contributions. This arrangement allows for better quality of primary education, but only for children whose families can afford it. This system therefore put children from poorer families at a disadvantage in accessing quality education. To ease the burden of schooling for the most needful households, Vietnam implements a fee exemption policy.

Figure 5. 5: Quality of Production Resources

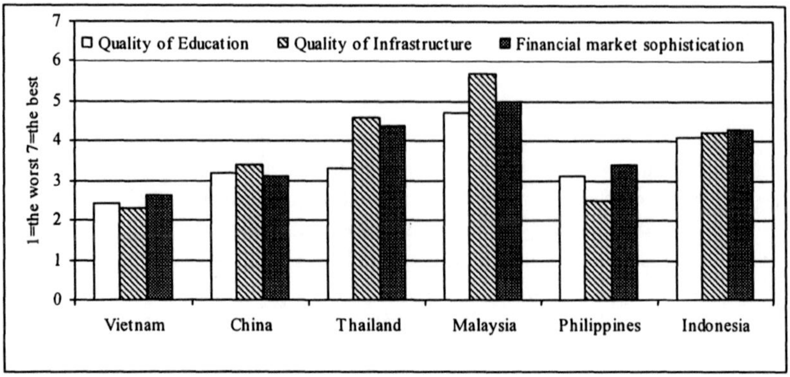

Source: WEF, survey 2004-05

For higher levels of education, the main challenge facing Vietnam is to balance the competing demands of enrolling a larger number of students and achieving a better quality than in the past. Vietnam's tertiary rate (10.16%) was far lower than that of Thailand (40.98%) and China (19.1%) in 2004 (Table 5. 4). Additionally, the quality of higher education remains a great concern to the public. The quality of the education remains lower compared to neighbors and the country's economic development. The survey we conducted shows most respondents stated that the education system has not yet met the needs of a competitive economy and they complain about the shortage of a skilled work force, especially business leaders (Appendix 6). Hence they stated that investing and improving in vocational education and training programs are urgent priorities (Appendix 6). However, some respondents expressed a relatively high degree of satisfaction with the overall quality of the education system from kindergarten through to the end of high school.

Similar findings were reported by WEF survey conducted in 2004-5. This survey indicated that meeting the needs of a competitive economy in Vietnam was lacking compared to that in China and Thailand (Figure 5. 5). This means that Vietnam will need to pay more attention to reforming and improving education system in a new context.

5.2 Technology Development

Vietnamese government has affirmed that Science and Technology development (S&T) in line with education and training development are the national policy

130

priorities and foundation and motivation for speeding up the country's industrialization and modernization process. Although the country is still poor, in recent time, Vietnam has especially improved efforts and endeavors of S&T professional personnel nationwide, S&T potentials have been strengthened, and S&T have had significant contributions to improve national productivity and competitiveness.

5.2.1 Technology Progress

Technology transfer and diffusion by import and FDI has operated strongly. Specifically, the technology transfer through FDI has had an increasing role in the improving of national productivity, competitiveness and living standards of citizens. In line with policy on building an open market economy, Vietnam has eliminated unnecessary regulations to facilitate technology transfer process from foreign countries under foreign direct investment (FDI). In fact, the foreign investment sector has not only contributed to technology development and management skill, but also created pressures on domestic companies that have been forced to apply advanced technology in production to maintain their market share.

The Figure 5. 6 indicates that FDI has been playing a significant role in technology transfer in Vietnam, ASEAN countries and China as well. However, Vietnam obtained a relatively low mark against China and Thailand. It is possible that Vietnam has not taken advantages of FDI. Our survey also shows that most respondents do agree FDI has been playing a significant role in technology transfer and diffusion, by which productivity and competitiveness have improved (Appendix 6).

Technology diffusion and computer use have improved rapidly in recent years. For example, year 2004 the number of personal computers per 1000 people reached 12.7, compared with 0.14 in 1992[66]. Nevertheless, the computerization has been solely concentrated on some areas of the economy such as Banking, Telecommunication and Aviation. Internet users have increased sharply, from 2.55 per 1000 people in 2000 to 128.86 in 2005[67]. This rate is higher than in any ASEAN-4 countries and China (except Malaysia). The rapid increase in internet users facilitates process of technology diffusion and transfer.

---

66   World Bank, Edstats Data Query, Oct 2006

67   World Bank, country data, 2006

Figure 5. 6: FDI and Technology Transfer

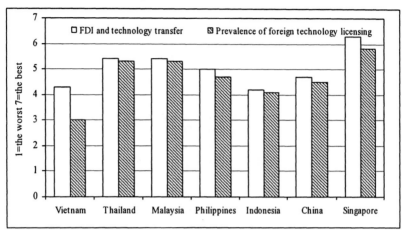

Source: WEF, survey 2004-05

Technology development potentials have been strengthened and developed. In the past decades Vietnam has trained more than 1.8 million in the workforce from college and tertiary levels with more than 30 thousands personnel of post-graduate level (over 14 thousand doctors and 16 thousand masters) and about 2 million technical workers; of these, around 34 thousands work directly in S&T fields under the State-owned sector[68]. This is an important human resource for the country's technology development. The reality shows that this group is able to catch up relatively quickly and master the knowledge and modern technologies in some branches and fields[69].

In addition, a network of S&T organizations has been set up with more than 1,100 S&T organizations under every economic sector, of which nearly 500 are non-State organizations; 197 are universities and colleges, including 30 non-public schools[70]. Infrastructure of institutions, research centers, laboratories, S&T information centers and libraries have been strengthened and upgraded. Some good associations between scientific research, technology development and production – business have appeared.

Policy on technology development Vietnam has made effort to strengthen technology development by issuing different policies such as policy on eliminating the

---

68   Ministry of Science and Technology
69   Vietnam science and technology development strategy by 2010, p30
70   Op.cit

monopoly of scientific research; policy on extent right of signing research contracts; policy on diversity of funding S&T investment. The total investment of S&T has increased 16% annually since 1996. The rate of S&T investment as a percentage of the total GDP has increased from 0.41 in 1996 to 0.47 in 2000. Although the State budget is still limited, with the State's great efforts, the State budget allocation for S&T field has reached 2% since 2000,[71] marking an important milestone in the Party and State's implementation process of policies on investing in the S&T development. Additionally, Vietnam has initially formed legal framework, which protects intellectual property right. Specifically, the industrial intellectual department was established and regulations of intellectual rights registration and transfer were carried out. However, the legal system of property right protection remains weak and the enforcement of the legal document has been inefficient.

Technology development policy has contributed an important part in effectively acquiring, mastering, adjusting and exploiting technologies imported from foreign countries. As a result, technology capacities in some production and service branches have been significantly improved and many products and goods have higher competitiveness. Especially, in the agriculture field, S&T development has produced many plants and animals with high quality and productivity, contributing to the shift in agricultural economic mechanisms, changing our country from importing foods to becoming one of the first exporters of rice and the second one of coffee in the world, i.e.

Science and Technology management mechanisms have been step by step renovated The State management mechanism of S&T organized from the central to local level has sped up the S&T development, contributing to the implementation of socio-economic objectives of branches and localities. Operations of S&T organizations have been expanded from research – development to S&T production and service. The autonomy of organizations and individuals in the S&T field has initially strengthened. The autonomy in international cooperation of organizations and individuals working in S&T field has been extended.

The implementation of Law on Science and Technology, programs, themes and projects on S&T has closely focused on the socio-economic development tasks. The mechanism of selecting organizations and individuals to be in charge of S&T tasks has initially been managed with principles of democracy and publicity. In addition, capital sources mobilized for S&T from contracts signed with production – business sectors, bank credits, international funds and other sources have been significantly increased thanks to policies on diversifying capital invested in

---

71   Op.cit

S&T. The budget allocation for scientists has been improved one step by reducing intermediate phases.

The assignment and decentralization in the State management in terms of S&T have gradually improved through regulations on functions, tasks and responsibilities of Ministries, ministerial agencies, the People's Committee of provinces and cities under the Central government.

Figure 5. 7: High-Technology Exports as % of Manufactured Exports

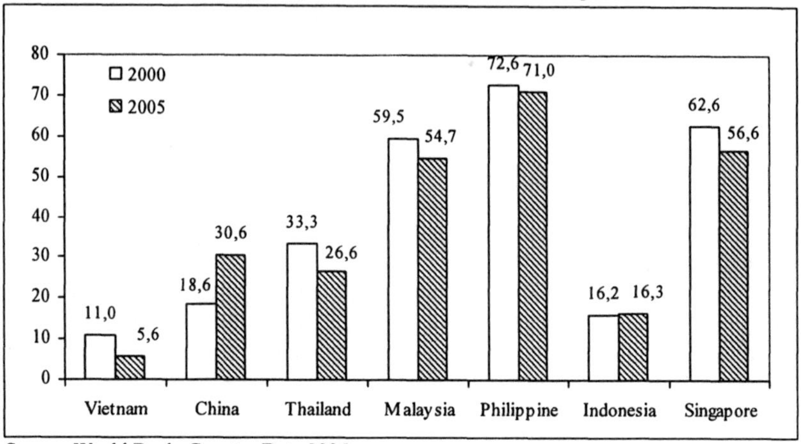

Source: World Bank, Country Data 2006

5.2.2 Technology Development's Assessment

Vietnam has gained significant achievements in technology development in last decades. However, the country's technology development level is generally low as compared with that of other countries in the region. For example, according to US Patent and Trademark Office, the number of US utility patents granted to Vietnam per million population in 2003 is zero, compared to 0.2, 0.4, 0.3, 2.0, 99.3 in China, Thailand, Philippines, Malaysia and Singapore respectively.[72] The high-tech product exports of Vietnam remain far lower than that of the neighboring countries. The high-technology exports of Vietnam accounted for an average 7.7% of the manufactured exports from 2000 to 2005, whereas the rate of China, Thailand, and Philippines is 24.99, 30.4, and 71.17 respectively (Figure 5.7). Notably while China's high-technology exports increased rapidly to 30.6% in 2005 from 18.6% in 2000, Vietnam declined sharply from 11.03% to 5.6% in the same period. These countries have succeeded in taking advantage of technology devel-

---

72   US Patent and Trademark Office, March 2004

134

opment to produce high-tech export products in recent years and now they are among 30 the top high-tech exporters in the world.

5.3 Market Conditions

Market conditions are frameworks that create a competitive environment in which firms can compete and operate to reach their goals. Market conditions have played a critical, if not decisive, role in improving a firm's competitiveness as well as a nation's. A nation does not remain competitive unless it creates good market conditions (Section 3.3 chapter 3).

5.3.1 Competitive Environment

Changes in perception on competition in Vietnam Before the beginning of the reform, competition was thought to be ugly and immoral because it caused economic crisis, bankruptcy, unemployment and so on. It was even criticized by some mass media agencies for causing social evils such as fraud and corruption, although this was not created by competition but rather by humans. Since the opening of the economy, perception of competition has changed positively. The Government, entrepreneurs and citizens have recognized the important role of competition in the economy. Many aspects of a positive impact of competition on the economy such as accelerating the reform, re-allocating resources and selecting viable businesses have been recognized. Companies themselves and the economy in general, are considering competition as a fundamental principle of the market economy.

This change in perception has also had a positive impact on the enterprises' performance and the content of the Government policy in laying the foundation for a healthy competitive environment in Vietnam. Many firms have invested in new technology to improve their productivity and competitiveness. The Government has made efforts to build a framework of market-oriented economy. Many policies and legal documents as well as regulations have been issued to create a legal framework conducive to the setting up of a competitive environment such as the Enterprise Law, the Anti-Trust Law etc.

Monopoly and regulating monopolies in Vietnam monopoly goes closely with the issue of the definition of the role of State in the economy and this definition clearly affects the state intervention with in it. The monopolistic companies were set up via administrative decisions rather than through competition. Hence, there were sole state monopolies and no private or foreign invested monopolies. Many industries have a status of monopoly artificially because they are regarded as natural monopolies. For instance, electricity and water production and distribution are currently essentially state monopolies although they can be contracted out to the private sector. While a market-oriented economy has been officially introduced into Vietnam over the past decades, the monopoly and oligopoly of SOEs still exist in almost all industries such as coal mining, metal production, electricity, water, telecommunication, finance, railway, airline, banking and so on.

Due to limitation of competition, the above industries have not provided good services to customers, but usually high price. Therefore, the Government must supervise and regulate monopolistic companies to prevent them from abusing their monopoly power and harming the benefits of customers. The remedy includes the supervision of prices and quality of goods and services. However, capability to supervise prices is weak and ineffective due to poor and undeveloped information systems. As a result, the effectiveness of anti-trust policy in Vietnam remains much lower compared to China and Thailand (Figure 5.8).
It appears that the Chinese Government has made progress against state monopoly power during this transition period.

Unhealthy and unfair competition The survey we conducted indicates that competition is unfair and unhealthy. The indicator scored an average of 2.7 point, on a scale from 1 to 7 where 7 is equivalent to the best. It means that most respondents did not agree that competition in Vietnam is fair and healthy (Appendix 6). It appears there is a lack of an appropriate legal framework for healthy competition and a dominance of state monopolistic companies in Vietnam. Unhealthy competition is, generally speaking, an action which competes by using illegal tools or immoral measures (Tran 2003). Recently, these unhealthy competitive actions have appeared more frequently with increasingly sophisticated tricks used by the companies concerning fake goods, dishonest advertisement, fake promotion, slandering to damage images of rivals and dumping.

Unfair competition (in this case) is understood to be unequal chances to access the market and resources by SOEs, and private and foreign invested firms. In recent years, the Government has made efforts to build a level playing field such as eliminating dual-price regime and issuing the Unified Enterprise Law[73] and the Common Investment[74]. However, in fact, SOEs receive preferential treatment and have advantages compared to all other firms such as access to land, capital, human resources, and even to the market. Many governmental agencies regard private firms as dishonest businesses. This attitude possibly explains why government inspection agencies visit private firms more frequently than the state ones.

---

73   A combination of the Enterprise Law and the SOE Law
74   A combination of the Domestic Investment Law and the Foreign Investment Law

Moreover, banks also hesitate in lending to private firms because they think there is a probability of being tracked down. The discrimination has negatively affected the competitive environment, and more importantly, it affects the people's confidence in the policy of the reform.

Startups and bankruptcy The Enterprise Law, which promulgated in 1999, and came into effect on January 1st 2000, was a breakthrough for eliminating almost all administrative barriers to market entry, and has created a new atmosphere for the business community. For the first time, the rights of the people in doing business, which were regulated in the Constitution, were institutionalized. People can do business in all fields that are not legally prohibited. As a result of the law, in 2000, 14,400 new firms were established, an increase of 350 percent from 1999 (Tran 2003). The survey result of WEF also indicates that starting a new business in Vietnam is quite easy and not time consuming. It appears that the reform of administrative registration has succeeded (Figure 5.8). As a result, during the period 2000-2005, 72,337[75] new firms were set up, an increase of 500% compared to 2000. In contrast with easy startup, bankruptcy[76] (an elimination process of the free market) is difficult, complicated, and time consuming. Although the Bankruptcy Law was issued in 1993, due to many different reasons, the Law has not yet been effectively implemented. The weak effectiveness of the Bankruptcy Law has had a negative impact on the competitive environment and the economy. It has been claimed that the Law maintains viable firms, hence slowing down the process of re-allocation and economic restructuring. At the moment, many "dead" firms are still "fed" by the banks with the hope that these banks can collect their loan repayments. This leads to reduce the efficiency of the economy by which the competitiveness of the economy is weakened.

5.3.2 Assessment of Competitive Environment

In line with the reform process, a competitive mechanism has been set up and has been operated in Vietnam in the sense that the number of firms in the market has increased, prices of goods and services are set through the demand and supply conditions in the market, the rights of doing business have been expanded, and so on. Competition has positively impacted the economic reform in accelerating economic restructuring, pressuring firms to innovate to increase their competitiveness, and increasing economic growth and living standard of the country's population.

---

75   Data was collected from Vietnam General Statistics Office (GSO)

76   Bankruptcy is in fact a factor to speed up economic restructuring, to re-allocate efficiently resources, and to increase the competitiveness of the economy as a whole

In addition to the Anti-Trust Law being promulgated in January 2005, a number of regulations have been issued to regulate activities relating to competition, such as the Common Investment Law, the Unified Enterprise Law, the Commercial Law. Nevertheless, enforcement of these laws still remains weak. This causes unhealthy and unfair competition. Moreover, attitudes toward the non-state sector have been an obstacle for creating a healthy and fair competitive environment.

Figure 5. 8: Competitive Environment

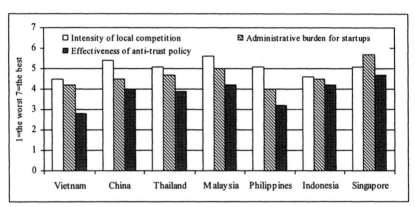

Source: WEF Survey, 2004-05

5.4 International Business and Economic Activities (IBEA)

The impressive economic growth of Vietnam over the last fifteen years has been due in part to considerable international business and economic activities. Through international trade and FDI activity, the IBEA has brought new technology (technology transfer), design and management skill, skilled employment, capital, foreign currency and so on by which national productivity and competitiveness as well as living standard have been improved.

5.4.1 Foreign Direct Investment (FDI) Activity and Competitiveness

Vietnam has been successful in attracting inward FDI since it began economic reforms. FDI has been an important part of the economic transition, business liberalization and improvement of the national productivity as well as economic growth and living standard in Vietnam over the last decades. From the early years of the reform, Vietnam's leadership attached prime importance to FDI as a way to

138

mobilize external resources for achieving national development objectives[77]. The Law on Foreign Investment, passed in 1987[78], formed legal frameworks and facilitated a foreign investment wave to Vietnam from developed and NICs countries in 1990s. A number of positive attributes were recognized in Vietnam, including the abundant cheap labor force, the relatively high levels of education, plentiful resources, and so on. Waves of foreign investors entered Vietnam, seeking to harness different areas of business potential (Figure 5. 9). The figure shows that Vietnam has been one of the most attractive destinations of inward FDI in the region.

Figure 5. 9: Inward FDI (% of GDP)

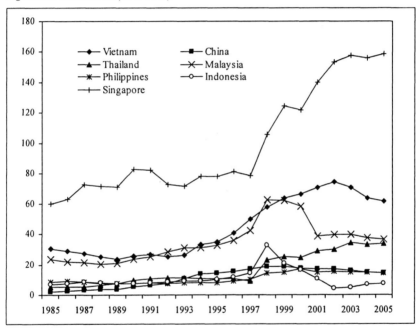

Source: UNCTAD 2006

FDI has played an important role in restructuring the economy. At the same time, there have been significant shifts in the destination of FDI by sector. Be-

---

77 The emphasis was partly a result of Vietnam's recognition that it had been left further behind from other fast-growth economies in the region, which had been using FDI successfully for their development objectives (Le Dang Doanh, 1996)

78 Its later amendments in November 1996 and 2000

tween 1988 and 1992, oil and gas and real estate accounted for more than half of actual inflows, while the share of the manufacturing sector was only about 15% (Jenskins 2006). However, over time, the share of manufacturing has risen significantly. At the end of 2006, the manufacturing sector accounted for 69% of the total registered capital. As a result, the manufacturing by the foreign-invested sector accounted for 37.5% of total manufacturing value, an increase from 18.1%[79] in 1995, while the share of oil and gas and real estate has fallen to between a quarter and a third of the total. Agriculture, which provides the bulk of employment in Vietnam, has not attracted much FDI and accounted for only 1.41% of total investment registered capital in 2006. There has also been a shift in the motivation behind manufacturing FDI. In the early years of Vietnam's reform, almost all of the projects were oriented toward the domestic market. Between 1991 and 1997, there was a significantly higher share of export-oriented projects but their share fluctuated from year to year. By 2006, the majority of new projects were export-oriented due to the Government's export-oriented policy.

Foreign-invested sector has been considered a major source of technology transfer and R&D in Vietnam in recent years. To improve technology transfer through FDI, Vietnam has been trying to attract FDI into high-technology sectors and to promote foreign investors to bring state-of-the-art technology by using tax incentives. For example, FDI in new materials, high technology and R&D fields will be granted a preferential corporate income tax rate of 10% for a ten-year period; a four-year tax holiday of corporate income tax from their profitable operation and 50% reduction of corporate income tax for the following four years shall be applicable[80].

In Vietnam, technology transfer differs among sectors and industries (Nguyen 2004, p112). In services (such as banking, insurance, tourism etc.), technology transfer is the clearest. Foreign investors in finance area, in hotels and restaurants have brought and used their managerial skills in conducting service activities which are similar to that in their home countries. In the manufacturing area, technology transfer does occur, as there is a gap in technology brought by foreign investors and that is currently used in Vietnam. Generally speaking, most technology used in foreign-invested firms is at the medium level of the world (Bui 2000, pp. 63). In agriculture, fishery and forestry areas, technology transfer has been under the form of demonstrating and diffusing new seeds, new cultivation and production methods and new kinds of activities (Nguyen 2004, pp. 114).

---

79   Own calculation using statistics data from GOS, Vietnam
80   Decree 24/2000/ND-CP dated July 31, 2000.

In general, the technology level in foreign-invested firms is higher than that in domestic companies and its level is equal to regional average level. The presence of foreign investors has brought the spillover of the economy such as increasing productivity and competitiveness, learning management experiences, designing products, marketing strategy, etc. The current survey of 154 respondents we conducted early in 2007 also indicates that FDI has been a significant source of new technology in Vietnam (Annex 6)

FDI has contributed to expanding export markets. FDI has been playing a leading role in bringing rapid export-based growth. Strongly rising exports have fuelled the region's highest growth of the Vietnamese economy. The correlation between export growth and FDI inflows is often relatively strong (Figure 5. 10). Vietnam would probably not have experienced the rapid acceleration of exports in the past decade without the presence of foreign investors. Through export-oriented FDI, Vietnam has been shifting toward a manufacturing-based economy in which economic growth has been driven by rapidly expanding exports.

Figure 5. 10: Export Growth and Inward FDI Inflows

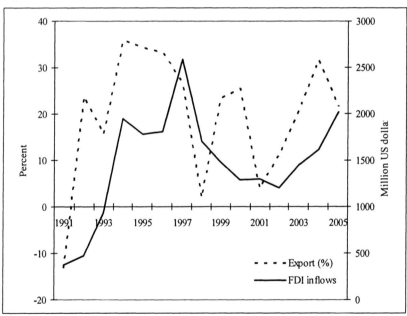

Source: ADB and UNCTAD 2006

141

Figure 5. 11: FDI Inflow as a Percentage of Fixed Capital Formation

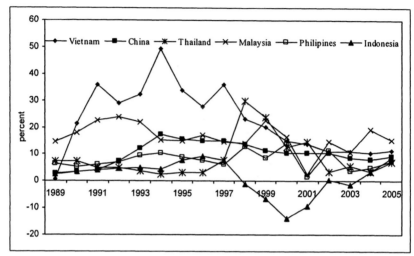

Source: UNCTAD and IMF

Figure 5. 12: Inward FDI Stock (US dollar million)

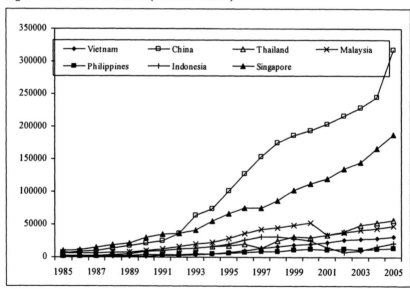

Source: UNCTAD 2006

FDI inflow has become a significant capital resource of economic growth in Vietnam in the beginning period of the reform process. In the early 1990s, the FDI inflow share of fixed capital formation increased sharply from 0.64 % in 1989 to 49.22% in 1994. The FDI share accounted for an average 30.8% of the fixed capital formation in the period 1990-1999 and declined only to an average 12.06% of the capital formation in the period 2000 and 2005. The share reached to the highest, 49.22%, in 1994 (Figure 5. 11). The declined trend of FDI capital can be explained by strongly increasing domestic capital resource due to a high national saving rate.

5.4.2 International Trade Activity and Competitiveness

Over the past 15 years, international trade of Vietnam has been liberalized. Although the foreign trade is still considered to be restrictive to protect specific industries, almost all companies have rights to carry international trade activities[81]. Non-tariff import restrictions which create trade distortions have been gradually abolished. The most favorable mechanism has been applied to exports. Various export promotion measures have been introduced such as allowing private rice exports, the auctioning of garment export quotas, the provision of financial incentives to exporters, the removal of restrictions on foreign invested enterprises to export, the elimination of many export taxes, and the establishment of the Trade Promotion Department, etc. Trade reform helps the private sector by enhancing its access to imported inputs and to export outlets. Liberalized trade, as well as easier domestic and foreign private entry, would increase competitiveness and create incentives for increasing efficiency. Obviously trade reform not only increases competitiveness and transparency, but also raises returns to export agriculture products and encourages investors to move into more productive areas in Vietnam. As a result, Vietnam has performed well in international trade. Total value of imports and exports reached $84.2 billion in 2006, compared with $5.15 billion in 1990. Exports increased from $US2.4 to $US39.8 billion between 1990 and 2006. An average growth of exports and imports between 1990 and 2006 was highest among ASEAN-4 countries and China, 20.2% in export and 19.8% in import, compared to 14.6% and 12.9% for Thailand, and 19.2% and 17.3% for China respectively (Table 5.5). Vietnam has been considered one of the most open economies in the region. The openness of the Vietnamese economy[82] increased steadily from 0.5 to 1.39 between 1990 and 2006 (Figure 5. 13). The openness in

---

81   Circular No 57/CP 31.7.1998 and amendment 46/2001 turned point foreign trading rights, under the Circular all firms have rights to implement international trade activity following listed areas

82   The openness of economy (simple method) is calculated as the ratio of the total value of exports and imports to Gross Domestic Product (GDP)

Vietnam is far higher than in China, in Indonesia and in the Philippines. It figures that the Vietnamese economy become more open and more liberal over time.

Figure 5. 13: Openness of Economy

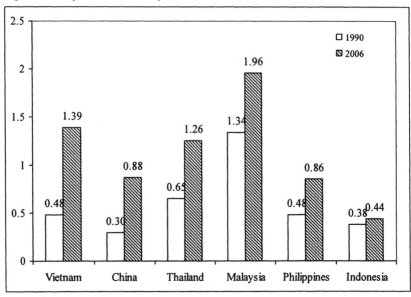

Source: Own calculation using data from ADB and IMF 2007

Table 5. 5: Growth of Foreign Trade in Selected Countries, 1990-2006

	Average Growth Export	Average Growth Import	Export as % of GDP		Import as % of GDP	
	(1990-2006)	(1990-2006)	1990	2006	1990	2006
Vietnam	20.15	19.76	37.15	65.30	42.52	73.59
Thailand	14.57	12.94	27.96	63.28	38.53	62.32
China	19.2	17.3	16.01	48.2	13.76	39.3
Malaysia	13.91	13.56	69.04	107.80	68.59	87.99
Philippines	11.57	10.24	18.53	39.97	29.53	45.70
Indonesia	9.72	9.80	20.42	27.64	17.36	16.77

Source: Own calculation using data from ADB, Key Indicators (2007) and IMF (2007)

Figure 5. 14: Annual Export Growth Rate

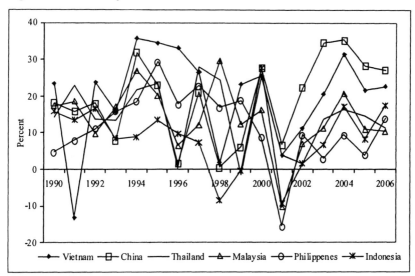

Source: ADB 2007

Trading rights before 1989 were essentially characterized by the state monopoly in foreign trade. Since 1989, in line with the market oriented reforms, the entry into trading activities has been gradually relaxed. However, up to 1997 the conditions for entry were still very restrictive. In 1992, for example, firms were required to have foreign contract, shipment license, sufficient working capital, business license, and trade experience. In 1997, the conditions were reduced to having sufficient working capital, business license, and trade experience. The monopoly position of the SOEs in foreign trading activities has been gradually weakened and the abolishment of trade license in 1998 was a most significant step forward in trade liberalization. Further relaxation can be observed in 2001 (Decision 46/2001/QD-TTg). Under the decision all domestic enterprises have been allowed to trade commodities or items freely, except those prohibited or under specialized management. The number of enterprises registered for trading activities increased from 2,400 in early 1998 to about 18,000 in early 2004[83]. Since 2002, the foreign invested enterprises have also been granted the right to export goods other than those they produce.

Tariff and non-tariff system The import tariffs were first implemented in 1988, but with the simple duties system covering only 130 commodity categories with the

---

83   Ministry of Trade and Industry (formerly Ministry of Trade)

tariff rates of 0 per cent to 60 per cent. Since then, frequent changes in the tariff system have been taking place. In 1989, the maximum tariff increased to 120 per cent for some luxury goods and tariff coverage was reduced to eighty commodities. In December 1991, the (new) Law on Export and Import Duties was approved. The new law distinguishes the normal tariffs from the preferential ones. The preferential rates with lower tariff levels (50 per cent of normal rates) have been applied to exported or imported goods to or from countries that have signed trade agreements with Vietnam[84].

In recent years, while the trading rights have been liberalized to a very significant extent and the coverage of non-tariff barriers (NTBs) has been reduced substantially, the tariff structure has not changed significantly (Table 5. 6). Since 2000 there has been an increase in the average tariff rate due to the tariff rate of some goods that had been subject to quantitative restrictions (Vo 2005, pp. 76). Though the average rate of all tariff lines is not high compared to China and Thailand, and the low tariffs cover a big share of imported items, the imported items and the state budget revenue from tariffs have been mainly concentrated in the items with the rates of 20 per cent or more (Ibid., pp. 77). Moreover, the tariff structure has been characterized by the heterogeneity and high dispersion, in which the high tariffs have been generally applied on several finished or consumer goods.

In order to promote exports, Vietnam has implemented several measures such as zero export duty, tax exemption, export credit, and especially the duty draw back scheme. Under the duty drawback scheme, exporters pay duty on their inputs and are reimbursed for the share of imports used to produce exported goods.

Table 5. 6: Nominal Tariffs Rates and Dispersion in Selected Asia Countries

	Total lines	Tariff bands	Range tariff	Average tariff	Dispersion rate (CV)
Vietnam (Sep 2003)	10,689	16	0-150	18.53	120.78
China (2001)	5,098	57	1-122	17.48	71.3
Thailand (2002)	5,110	45	0-80	18.48	84.4
Malaysia (2001)	5,106	45	0-1195	10.2	340.3
Philippines (2001)	5,112	38	0-60	7.6	93.9
Indonesia (2001)	5,056	56	0-170	8.42	127.8

Source: Jurgen Wiemann, 2006, p177

---

84   The preferential rates are applied for about eighty countries that cover about 75 percent of Vietnam's total imports

146

Non-Tariff barriers to trade (NTBs) exist in Vietnam in the following categories: *Quantitative restrictions (QRs)* Import quotas and licenses Vietnam has reduced the use of QRs substantially. At present, only petroleum products and sugar are still subject to licensing while the government has committed itself to lifting quotas on sugar imports by 2005. SOE dominate in imports that are regulated by QRs due to only a few private enterprises which are able to pass the strict procedures.

Foreign exchange regulations: Foreign exchange control has been loosed in recent years. The foreign exchange surrender requirement for trading businesses came down from 80% in 1998 to 40% in 2001. Foreign investment enterprises now can purchase foreign currency from domestic banks to repay loans obtained from offshore banks. Notwithstanding, although officially all firms are enabled to buy foreign currency from banks, in fact, only large companies, most SOEs, receive foreign exchange from state-owned commercial banks.

De-facto NTBs: Vietnam has made the first steps through the new Law on Customs Valuation. It introduces the internationally required Transaction Value as a basis for the valuation of imported items according to WTO law. So far, the new law lacks some important specifications. Since six additional valuation categories have been introduced as alternative means of valuation instead of valuation standards with different priorities, the Vietnamese valuation system has not yet complied with WTO standards. As necessary transparent valuation rules and procedures have not yet been implemented, customs offices still provide fertile ground for arbitrary classifications. In theory, the Law on Customs Valuation sets solely one tariff rate for a certain item. But in practice, different tariff levels are applied to the same product in different provinces due to the fact that customs offices in the provinces work rather "independently". The problems of customs valuation were discussed at length at the meetings of the Working Party on Vietnam's access to the WTO. Some members noted that Vietnam's customs procedures have been complicated and at times unpredictable depending on the discretion of customs officials[85]. Therefore, a predictable environment for investment in international trade activities is missing (Wienmann 2006, pp. 75). However, Vietnam has applied for an extended transitional period to fully implement the Custom Valuation Agreement (CAV) due to the required experience, expertise, knowledge, technical facilities, and equipment.

---

85   WTO 2006 Accession of Vietnam, Report of the Working Party on the Accession of Vietnam, WT/ACC/VNM/48, Geneva, 63, para. 245.

5.4.3 Assessment of International Business and Economic Activities

Inward FDI attracting activities Vietnam has performed well in attracting FDI inflow since 1990. The FDI inflow to the country has been higher than the Philippines and Indonesia due to the abundant low-cost labor and the reform policy of the economy. Nevertheless, the strategy to rely solely on low-cost labor is risky and fleeting. Investors are likely to shift their production sites to other destinations as their wages become higher compared to other countries. This is especially likely if the host country lacks other factors that are particularly attractive to foreign investors, such as a huge market potential, good infrastructure, as in the case of China, or solid domestic industrial base, which would offer the advantage of agglomeration for foreign investors.

In practice, the investment environment in Vietnam has been less attractive than in China and Thailand. The Figure 5.12 shows clearly that FDI inflow to China and Thailand has been far higher than that to Vietnam over time. Undoubtedly China has been the most attractive destination because of the huge market potential and low-cost labor. Notwithstanding, Vietnam is still attractive for locating skill-incentive processes. The skill-incentive processes seem to be the most plausible way for Vietnam to take part in the division of labor in East and Southeast Asia, which is emerging in some of the most dynamic industries (Ohno and Nguyen 2005).

International trade activities In recent years, the government has acted to codify practices in law and greatly supported increased transparency of the trade regime. Only fifteen years ago it could be said that there was virtually no trade regime in Vietnam, as most trade decisions were centrally determined. Incentives, taxes and conditions for trade such as licenses and quotas were irrelevant in shaping responses because individuals and firms had no capacity to respond. In recent years, Vietnam's trade regime has been completed as a basis for trade activity needs. It could be argued that conventional trade barriers as they are understood in a modern economy now exist and are relevant as an indication of just how far Vietnam has come in liberalizing trade. The Government has implemented its commitments to push the scheme of trade policy reform and liberalization further. First, as trading rights are further liberalized and private firms get a larger share of export quotas, there has been greater competition among trading firms and much greater access to the domestic private small and medium-sized enterprises (SMEs) to imported inputs and to export outlets. Second, as non-tariff import barriers, like import-licensing, are improved, the import regime has been more transparent, access to imports by firms more equal, and tradable goods more price-responsive. Third, state-owned enterprises have been exposed to more discipline and competitiveness. Fourth, lower import protection and lower implicit and explicit taxes on exports have improved incentives for investors to move toward processed agriculture and manufactured exports. These steps have improved transparency, reduced rents to state enterprises, expanded access to international markets from all importers and exporters, as well as increased competitiveness of the firms and the economy. Nevertheless, Vietnam's trade regime has still operated within a rather comprehensive framework of trade barriers with efforts to promote exports as well as to protect import-substitution products. This kind of trade regime has some problems associated with the efficiency in resource allocation. Administrative rigidities and delays in the customs administration have continued to remain an important de-facto NTBs. It takes time to do customs procedures and hence raise transaction costs of enterprises. These costs arise not only through delayed customs procedures but also through unofficially required extra payments, which seem to be a common practice (Wienmann 2006, pp. 70). Cumbersome customs procedures have been an obstacle for doing international trade in Vietnam. High administrative costs for delayed and opaque certification and licensing procedures are still a difficulty, especially for private and foreign invested firms. The survey conducted by WEF shows that the customs regime in Vietnam lags behind Thailand and China (Figure 5. 15). The indicator, Vietnam's openness of customs regime, scores 2.6 compared to 4.0, 3.9 and 4.7 in China, Thailand and Malaysia respectively. The survey we conducted indicates a consistent result that customs procedures are emerging as an obstacle in international trade activities (Appendix 6). These restraints represent a considerable disadvantage for Vietnamese firms in term of competitiveness on international markets and hinder the development of the private business sector (Ibid., pp 73).

Figure 5. 15: Customs and Hidden Barriers

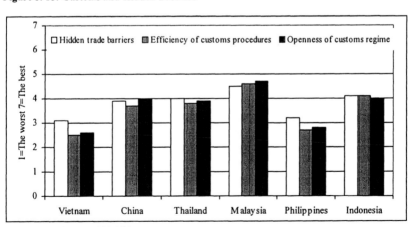

Source: WEF Survey, 2004-05

5.5 Company's Strategy and Operation (Competitiveness)

An economy cannot maintain competitiveness unless companies operating there are competitive, whether they are domestic firms or affiliates of foreign companies (Porter 2004, pp. 21). Since Vietnam began its reform process, its economy has become a multi-stakeholder one, from the entire dominance of SOEs to the emerging of private and foreign invested firms. In line with the decline of inefficient SOEs, private and foreign invested firms have been playing an increased role in improving productivity and competitiveness because of their efficient operation. As a result, they have been as an engine of economic growth and living standards.

5.5.1 Company's Development and Contribution

Private Enterprise The reform process in Vietnam has provided its private companies a robust energy. Private firms started expanding and formalizing, and the process has accelerated in recent years. As of December 2005, there were about 105,169 private firms, accounting for 18.6% percent of total value of production in manufacturing and 24.94 percent of total capital in all enterprises. Between 2000 and 2005 private investment increased from 12 percent of GDP to over 17 percent, with the domestic private sector being specially buoyant in recent years. As a result, it has created a massive amount of jobs, allowing for the absorption of 1.4 to 1.5 million entrants to the labor market every year, accounting for 47.74% of the total labor force in enterprises (an increase from 29.42% in 2000)[86].

The implementation of WTO commitments, as well as greater integration into ASEAN, will bring domestic firms on increasingly equal footing with foreign firms. Because domestic firms differ in their ability to withstand and benefit from greater competition, the gradual leveling of the playing field will have different consequences across sectors. The government is only now starting to build a capacity to analyze industrial linkages and value chains within Vietnam, and across national borders, in order to identify the influences on various industries and strategize the liberalization process and steps.

The impressive performance of private enterprises is partly due to a radical simplification of bureaucratic procedures. The Enterprise Law 2000 (now Unified Enterprise Law) has been protecting the right of citizens to establish and operate private businesses without needless official intervention. Notwithstanding, admin-

---

86   The above collected data is available at
      http://www.gso.gov.vn/default_en.aspx?tabid=491

istrative procedures at both national and local levels still leave inconsistencies, gaps and overlaps in authorizing an investment and a new business.

The weak legal framework for bankruptcy and insolvency does not promote the restructuring of the SOEs and SOCBs and prevents valuable resources such as land from being released for use by other businesses. A typical bankruptcy process in Vietnam take five years, costs up to 15 percent of the property value and has a recovery rate of only 18 percent of the redeemable value. The Civil Law permits creditors to foreclose on debtor's collateral as it has an event of default. As a result, there have been very few cases of formal bankruptcy brought to court (World Bank 2007b, pp. 74-77).

The development of long-term capital markets possibly does not do much to improve the access to finance by small and medium enterprises (SMEs). One of the distinctive features of Vietnam's business activity is precisely its "missing middle", meaning that the overall distribution of enterprise by size is skewed toward either very large ones (mainly SOEs and foreign firms) or very small ones. Nevertheless, the missing middle is being filled through entry of bigger enterprises and growth of existing small ones (World Bank 2006c, p.15-17).

State-Owned Enterprises (SOEs) In hand with the reform process in 1986, autonomy was given to SOEs to formulate and implement their own long-term, medium-term and short-term operating plans. In 1991, SOEs deemed inefficient or lacking capital and technology or not having sufficient demand for their products were forced to dissolve or merge with other units and the number of SOEs had been reduced to 6,264 by 1994 (Ibid., pp. 9). By 2005, Vietnam still had an unusually large number of SOEs compared to other countries in the region (except China), around 4,086 firms[87] and these enterprises account for 54.96% of total capital in all enterprises (a slight reduction from 67.13% in 2000).

From an initially slow start, ownership transformations sped up in 2003. The reduction of SOEs has been mainly through equitization[88] by which the SOEs after IPO (initial public offer) operate under the Enterprise Law rather than the SOE law. The equitization of larger companies and the auctioning of their shares have succeeded in attracting outside investors. On average, the state holds roughly 46 percent of capital in equitized firms, employees own 30 percent, and outsiders 24 percent (World Bank 2007a).

---

87   General Statistics Office (GSO), Enterprise Survey
88   Equitization is, in the case of Vietnam, understood to be privatization.

151

SOEs enterprises have made progress compared to the previous phase as they are given more autonomy to decide their business activities. Empirical evidences show that equitized SOEs have been doing business better than before they were equitized[89]. It appears that SOEs have operated inefficiently. Not surprisingly, when we conducted our survey in early 2007, most of the respondents stated that SOEs' performance is poor. That is somewhat surprising that respondents from enterprises are evaluating lower compared to officials and scholars. Perhaps they have recognized their weaknesses of business activity in new context (Appendix 6).

Many of the SOE managers gaining control through this process are engineers by training with a specialization in their particular industry. This professional background enables them to master new technology as transferred by foreign investors to a joint venture and to implement it in production processes. Notwithstanding, they often lack business education and management skills, which limit their capacity to engage in fundamental management change, including the reorganization of work processes and the delegation of decision-making authority.

Due to political patronage from their respective authority, SOEs tend to be exposed to conflicting interests, including those of the state in general, their direct authority and their employees. This conflict leads them to pursue not only profits, but also a broader set of objectives, reflecting the interests of their various stakeholders. Obviously, there are crucial weaknesses hidden behind the relatively solid performance of SOEs in Vietnam. The most obvious one is the implicit transfer many of them receive from the rest of the society, by operating in sectors sheltered by tariffs and barriers to competition, by getting access to considerable amounts of land at low cost, and also by getting their bad debts rolled over or even written off. The profitability of SOEs would be lower if these costs, which are very real to society, were factored in.

Foreign invested enterprises By 2005, there were about 3,697 foreign firms, accounting for a large share of the value of production in some industries, including oil and gas (almost 100 percent), automobile assembling (84 percent), electronics (45 percent), textile and garments (41 percent), chemicals (38 percent), steel (32 percent) cement (30 percent). They accumulatively accounted for around 57.8% (2006) of the country's exports, 43.7% of the country's total industrial output and 20.10% (2005) of total capital in all enterprises, and they constituted almost 17.02% of Vietnam's GDP.

---

89   A survey of 550 equitized SOEs conducted by World Bank in 2005, following a similar one undertaken two years earlier indicates that almost 90% of those sampled reported an improvement in their financial performance.

The size of FDI enterprises have also changed over time. In 1996, the average size was about 23 millions dollars. But it declined to 5 millions in 2000, and to 2.5 millions in 2003. This said the size of FDI projects in Vietnam were relatively small by international standards. It is worth noting that only about 80 of the 500 biggest multinational corporations in the world have established a presence in Vietnam, compared to roughly 400 in China (World Bank 2006c).

Up to 1998, roughly two thirds of total FDI commitments were under joint venture, often with an SOE as the Vietnamese partner. There are several reasons for this bias. In the early years of the economic reform, SOEs were the only possible legal partners for foreign investors. And domestic private firms were still very weak anyway. Moreover, the privileged position of SOEs also made the joint venture modality more attractive, compared to green-field investments. SOEs have better access to commercial land, as well as good political contacts, which are essential in areas where the rule of the law is not fully established.

5.5.2 Assessment of Company's Competitiveness

In order to assess the companies' competitiveness, we can evaluate some indicators such as the company's competitive advantage, value chain, and capacity of innovation.

Competitive advantage Companies are on the front line of international and domestic competition. They must increasingly compete regionally and globally. In Vietnam firms' competitive advantage is based on business costs due to taking advantage of low price labor and natural resources. Export of seven principle commodities accounting for 40% of total exports (non-oil) are extracted mostly from natural resources and uses abundant labor force (Figure 5. 16). The survey of WEF indicates that enterprises' competitiveness in Vietnam is far lower than that in China and any other ASEAN-4 countries (Figure 5. 17). A relatively similar finding we conducted shows that most respondents stated that Competitiveness of Vietnam's firms in international markets is not primarily due to unique products and processes. The indicator scored an average of 2.95, on a scale from 1 to 7 where 7 is equivalent to the best (Appendix 6). Obviously, Vietnam's companies need a strategy to compete in the long term as its economy is moving to the next stage of competitive development because low labor and natural resources based on competitiveness is fleeting.

Value chain system The value system is the entire array of activities involved in a product's creation and use, encompassing the value chains of companies, suppliers, channels and buyers. Close and ongoing interchange with suppliers and channels is integral to the process of creating and sustaining competitiveness. Competitiveness frequently comes from perceiving new ways to configure and manage the entire value system. Companies restructure or integrate their activities with suppliers, modify the strategies of channels, and recombine or integrate activities with buyers[90].

Figure 5. 16: Export by Principle Commodities (2006)

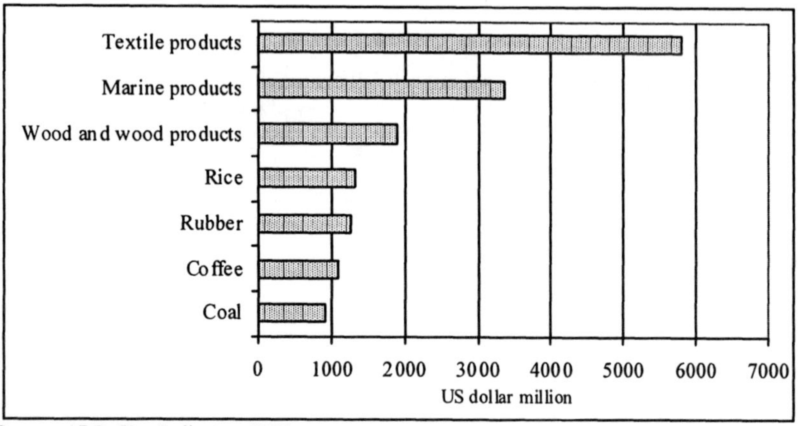

Source: ADB, Key Indicators 2007

Deeper insights can be gained by analyzing the way in which Vietnam's companies actually operate and participate in the global and regional economy, either directly and indirectly. Those analyses show that Vietnam's pattern of integration in world trade is faster than that of China and ASEAN-4 countries. But they also reveal a still insufficient integration of domestic companies in global and regional value chains (Ibid., pp. 29). Being consistent with the result by the World Bank, the outcome conducted by WEF indicates that value chain employing by enterprises in Vietnam is lower than China and any ASEAN-4 countries (Figure 5. 17). It appears that exporting companies in Vietnam primarily is involved in resource extraction and assembling, and less in designing, producing and marketing sale as well as after-sale service.

One relevant question is whether Vietnamese enterprises can compete in global and regional markets or not while the vast majority of them is not directly involved in international trade. If it does not, then it would be difficult to claim that the Vietnamese economy as a whole is competitive. The emerging private sector is still, to a large extent, inward-oriented; only 9 percent of the sales correspond to direct exports (Ibid., pp. 34). This inward orientation is worrisome, given that the

---

90   See section 3.5 chapter 3

154

labor productivity of the average exporting enterprise is nearly twice as high as the average productivity of SMEs.

Figure 5. 17: Company's Strategy and Operation

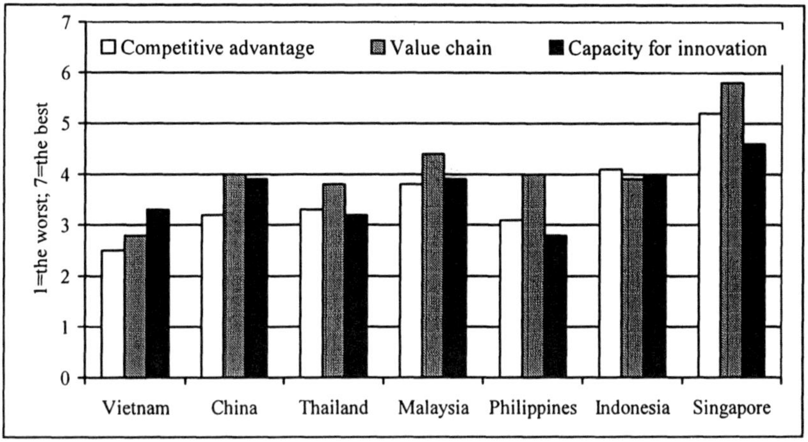

Source: WEF Survey, 2004-05

A stronger involvement of private sector in the supply chains could help identify new overseas partners and establish higher quality standards. A small survey of enterprises conducted by the World Bank shed some light on the relationship between contractors and suppliers in Vietnam. The result shows that for a third of the contractors, the value of the inputs purchased was equivalent to more than half of their total revenue. The process typically involved a large number of subcontracts with many different parties. The commercial relationship was even more important when seen from the suppliers' end. On average, suppliers generated two thirds of their total turnover out of the business-to-business transaction (Ibid., pp 35).

Capacity for innovation Companies gain competitiveness over international competitors because they perceive a new basis for competing, or find new and better means to compete in old ways. It means that they must recognize the central role of innovation (Porter 1990). Innovation, in strategic terms, is defined in its broadest sense. It includes not only new technologies but also new methods or ways of doing things, which sometimes appear quite mundane. Innovation can be manifested in a new products design, a new production process, a new approach to marketing, or a new way of training or organizing. It can involve virtually any activity in the value chain. In a comparison with other indicators, the indicator of capacity for innovation was evaluated relatively high. In this regards, Vietnam's

155

capacity for innovation was higher than that of Thailand and the Philippines, but still lower than China. Undoubtedly, Vietnam lags behind China in innovation, not only in technological innovation but also management and process innovation (see further in section technology development).

5.6 Government Role and Competitiveness

The Vietnamese government has been playing a significant role in robust economic growth as well as improvement of productivity and competitiveness through its policies since its beginning of the economy reform.

5.6.1 Development of Institution and Government Policies

Legal System Framework In line with economic growth and productivity, Vietnam has been also going through a process of wider and deeper social and institutional transformation. Supporting this high-pace change demands adjustments in the legal framework and the judicial system. Over the two decades since the beginning of "Doi moi" process, Vietnam has made enormous progress in terms of developing its legal framework. Economic and civil relations have gradually become regulated by law and market practices instead of the administrative orders and disciplines of the former centrally planed economy. International commitments such as the US Bilateral Trade Agreement (BTA) and accession to the WTO, as well as the signing of numerous international conventions and agreements, have resulted in the accelerated issuance of the most important legal normative documents needed for the conduct of business. The currently promulgated new Unified Enterprise Law, Law on Common Investment, Law on Accession, Completion and Implementation of International Treaties have made a positive contribution in this respect, by establishing a procedure for the transformation of commitments into legislation. The last few years have been a particularly intensive legislative agenda. The number of laws passed by National Assembly increased from 8 in 2004 to 22 in 2005. Also, much has been accomplished in terms of increasing legal transparency. However, the progress in filling legal gaps remains uneven. The current legal framework reflects to a large extent Vietnam's transition from plan to a market-oriented economy, less so the ongoing changes in relationship between state and society. On the positive side, there are now clear guidelines for the collection of comments from stakeholders directly affected by legal normative documents. On the negative side, the legal framework for activities of civil society organizations, including their involvement in the delivery of social services, can not be considered satisfactory.

Figure 5. 18: Public Institution

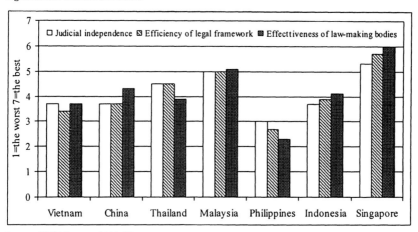

Source: WEF Survey, 2004-05

In spite of carrying out later economic reform, Vietnam has had significant progresses in changing public institution. The survey conducted by WEF in 2005 indicates that public institution in Vietnam is relatively higher than the Philippines, equal to China and Indonesia, and somewhat lower than Thailand (Figure 5. 18). It reflects the improvement of efficiency of legal system and the independence of judicial system as well as the effectiveness of law-making bodies in Vietnam in recent years.

Public Financial Management Over the past decades Vietnam has made sustained efforts to establish a sound public financial management system. A first organic budget law was passed in 1996 and revised in 2002. A centralized treasury system was set up, with branches extending in 2002 from the central to all provinces and districts, to provide basic essential financial services to all government agencies. Steady progress was achieved in making the budget more predictable and the budgeting process more transparent. There is increased disclosure of information on detailed government spending as well as on expenditure policies, regulations and procedures. And a relatively prudent fiscal policy has been maintained throughout.

The implementation of the revised Law on the State Budget, which became effective in 2004, was one of the cornerstones of this reform process. The law clearly delineated the roles of the National Assembly and Provincial People's Councils in budgets approvals and supervision. It also assigned the Treasury Department as the agency responsible for budget execution and for financial management information. In 2005 the entire State Budget Plan was disclosed for the first time, including an aggregate amount for defense expenditures. The trend toward disclosure was reinforced by Prime Minister's Decision 192, which mandates that details of budgets at all levels of government be published within a stipulated time period, for all units using budgetary resources. Importantly, this decision introduces financial transparency in public investment projects. Allocation of funds to such projects must be based on approved investment plans, and details of the bidding process need to be made publicly available. Decision 192 also covers the disclosure of information on the financial situation of SOEs. The more recent Decision 232 extends disclosure to external debt levels twice a year.

Another important development was the transformation of the State Audit of Vietnam (SAV) into an independent institution reporting to the National Assembly. The Auditor General is now appointed and dismissed by the National Assembly and the audit report has to be made public. Annual auditing and the disclosure of the audit reports will also apply to SBV. The SAV audit reports were made public for the first time recently, triggering serious debates on the use of public resources. Auditing capacity remains weak, however, which makes it difficult to manage the increased scope of its tasks, including the compulsory audit of all SOEs, and precludes checking value for money.

The integration of capital and recurrent expenditures into a single budget, one of the main weaknesses of Vietnamese public financial management, has gradually improved. These two components of the budget are prepared by MPI and MOF respectively. The collaboration between these two ministries has been strengthened recently. The introduction of forward-looking budget plans as the background for annual submission to the National Assembly, together with the adoption of budget allocation norms for both capital and recurrent expenditures, have also led to greater coherence. But the separate preparation of the two components still hampers the effective management of resources. As a result, the composition of public expenditure remains unbalanced; in some sectors it could be argued that the share devoted to capital accumulation is too high. Processes for prioritizing expenditures remain ineffective, as they are conducted for capital and recurrent spending.

Figure 5. 19: Budget's Revenue and Expenditure

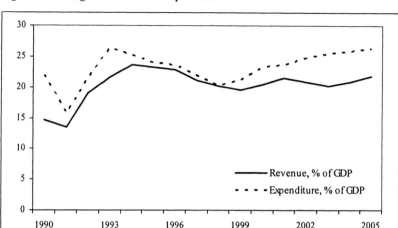

Source: GSO, MOF and ADB

Administration Reform Vietnam has been implementing public administration reform (PAR). The PAR refers to improving the ways in which the civil service works, by better delineating the competencies and responsibilities of various government agencies, streamlining the steps and procedures required to make decisions, improving the mechanism by which the individuals in charge are selected, promoted and remunerated, and improving the relationship between government agencies and the rest of society (World Bank 2007a). Such is the meaning given to a better business climate by which the productivity and competitiveness of the country are enhanced.

The process of fundamental economic renewal has been carried out in Vietnam. Public administration under the new orientation is bound to differ considerably from the central planning model and consequently, its roles and functions need to be redefined. PAR, as an integrating concept, started to become prominent in the early 1990s; it was officially endorsed in 1995 at the Eighth Plenum of the Party Central Committee. The Master Program further specified its objective as building an effective and efficient public administration system in which cadres and civil servants have capacity to contribute to the country and to meet requirements of managing a market economy.

Figure 5. 20: Efficiency of Public Financial Management

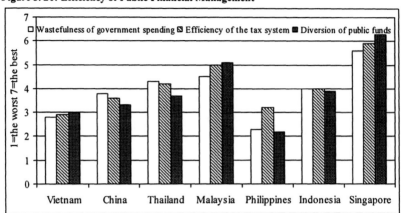

Source: WEF Survey, 2004-05

Since then, action has been taken to reorganize government functions, streamline administrative processes and strengthen accountability. Because these reforms are necessarily gradual, and nationwide implementation is still ongoing, actual impacts are still limited. But there have been incremental improvements in important aspects of public administration and public service delivery, and very negative developments.

Considering functional reorganization, several ministries and agencies have undertaken a comprehensive overhaul of their internal structure, adapting it to their new roles in the steering of a market economy. Importantly, service delivery units that have been separated from administrative reform, have increased the efficiency of limits such as hospitals. It has also made it possible to formalize and to some extent monitor undocumented payment. At the same time, this reform has led to some neglects of the services to be provided for free, and it may have resulted in excessively high fees where public providers do not face competition. Both developments have impacted negatively on the poor.

There has been clear progress in relation to the streamlining of government processes. The adoption of the one-door model has reduced red-taped and enhanced transparency. The intention is for the one-door model to be the main mechanism for citizens and business to interact with the public administration. As a result, transparency of the Vietnamese government is equal to Thailand and Indonesia, and still lower than China (Figure 5.21). In general, they have provided an accessible and recognizable entry point for people in need for administrative services. Procedures have been published and fees have been made more transparent. So

160

far, all 64 provinces have established the one-door model in at least one of their departments, as have 98 percent of all districts and 88 percent of all communes (Ibid., pp. 161-163). However, many locations or units that reported implementation are in fact only partially operational or apply the model in a perfunctory manner. There are also issues of financial viability and budgets, organization affiliation, and staff status and remuneration.

Better policies relating to government employment and pay have been developed, with the aim of providing adequate incentives while keeping the payroll affordable. The size of the administrative civil service in Vietnam is not particularly large. In spite of the limited size of the administrative civil service, a downsizing initiative was introduced by the PAR Master Program. Its objective was to remove poor performers and those who would become redundant as a result of functional reorganization. Retrenchment was accompanied by a severance package, but its design was not based on an assessment of earnings alternatives of the retrenched staff. In practice, the package did not seem attractive enough, judging by the reluctance of civil servants to leave. The dominant mechanisms for retrenchment became early retirement and reassignment to other non-civil service units promotions remain to a large extent based on seniority[91]. But a rotation policy was introduced for leaders, with a successful public management experience in the provinces becoming an important step toward advancement to positions of senior leadership.

Several measures have been undertaken to increase government accountability. Administrative courts, introduced in 1996, represent a major effort to protect the rights of citizens and businesses in relation to administration. However, after a decade in existence, their impact is well below expectations. Barely one thousand cases are processed every year, compared to more than one hundred thousands complaints submitted. The promotion of grassroots democracy was another important step toward increased government accountability at the commune level. The corresponding decree moved the reform focus away from the internal workings of the administration itself to involving the general population, as summarized in the slogan "The people know, the people discuss, the people implement, and the people monitor". The decree is quite specific on the rights and responsibilities of citizens and officials, as it clarifies the areas and context where "knowing", "discussing", "implementing" and "monitoring" are to be a significant change in the way public administration relates to the public. But there is substantial variation in the actual implementation of the grassroots democracy decree.

---

91 Vietnam economy-Thoi Bao Kinh Te Vietnam (2007), "Public Administration Reform:Three Priorities" available (26/04/2007) at *http://www.vneconomy.vn/cai cach hanh chinh.htm* in Vietnamese

The recent decree 43 aims at making service delivery units, for example hospitals, more accountable. One of the measures it introduces is the administrative monitoring of the services provided, so as to make sure that those supposedly free of charge are indeed delivered. The decree also reduces the incentive to charge excessively high fees, by capping the salaries of personal working for these units. Importantly, the decree introduces the notion of mandatory user feedback as a tool to access the performance of service delivery units. In principle, citizens and businesses should be consulted in relation to their satisfaction with services provided, including timeliness, quality, cost, and, potentially, unofficial payments. How this decree will be implemented in practice remains to be seen.

Figure 5. 21: Government Transparency and Burden of Regulation

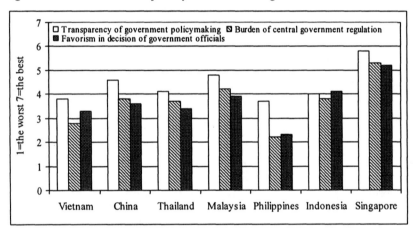

Source: WEF Survey, 2004-05

5.6.2 Government Role's Assessment

The Vietnamese government has been playing a crucial role in enhancing its national competitiveness. The central goal of government policy toward the competitiveness of the Vietnamese economy is to deploy the nation's resources with high and rising levels of productivity. It is not surprising when the government policies and forming public institution influence strongly on productivity and competitiveness within firms and industries because Vietnam still stands in the initial stage of economic development. In the last fifteen years, Vietnamese government has reached some remarkable achievements in establishing legal frameworks and public financial management as well as administration procedure reform. Nevertheless, the Vietnamese government management continues to have many problems which create obstacles for economic development, especially for doing business.

Legal system Despite the significant progress of the legal framework, the legal system is still complex and inconsistent. Admittedly, the situation is nearly similar to most developing countries. But in Vietnam there is a clear need to improve the enforceability and the consistency of legal documents. Legal documents issued at different stages in the transition process coexist and in some cases overlap. The intense legislative activity of the last few years has resulted in the promulgation of around 200 implementation decrees, which in turn has led to a large number of guiding circulars, decisions and other regulations being issued by line ministries and local governments (Ibid., pp. 110).

Limited consideration of how legal provision will be implemented has also re-sulted in unrealistic laws and over-burdened service delivery. In this respect, there is a need for improved dissemination of laws to the lower levels of government, along with clearer guidelines on the interpretation, application and enforcement. This need is made even more pressing by the accession to the WTO, which will confront local authorities with a much changed environment for the product of business.

Public financial management Vietnamese government has made its efforts to manage its public financial system efficiently. Notwithstanding, there are many existing weaknesses. The lack of a fully consolidated budget makes it difficult to monitor total revenues and expenditures, as well as the true fiscal position. Extra-budgetary funds, on-lent official development assistance are not consolidated into the budget. Financial reporting with lacking and inaccurate data contributes to the poor flow of budgetary information between ministries, provinces, donors and the public.

The stability of government revenue has become an important concern, as a result of the trade liberalization commitments made to accede to the WTO. However, the impacts of these commitments will not be felt in the immediate future, as they do not entail the dramatic reductions in tariffs that could actually lead to increased revenue through a surge in imported volumes. Moreover, WTO commitments allow imposing low tariffs on a range of goods which are duty-free at present. With the emergence of small and medium enterprises, which are more difficult to tax, sustaining the same ratio of revenue to GDP will require increased efficiency in tax administration. The efficiency of tax system in Vietnam remains lower than in neighbors, scored 2.9 compared to 3.6 (China), 4.2 (Thailand) and 5.0 (Malay-sia) (Figure 5.20).

Administration reform In practice, progress on the narrower civil service reform agenda has been considerable. But it needs to be taken forward. Functional reorganization has allowed various ministries and agencies to adapt their structure to their new stewardship role in a market economy; it has also led to the separation of administrative bodies from service delivery units. In the future it could move in the direction of better coordinating policy making across ministries and agencies. Simplification of procedures has relied, to a large extent, on the introduction of the one-door model, which has proven successful. Looking forward, the introduction of common standards for information technology (IT) applications within the government should facilitate the introduction of e-government, and help move in the direction of a single identification number for enterprises and a single social insurance number for individuals. Pay policies have brought remuneration in the civil service closer to the relevant market alternatives; overall, civil sector salaries have caught up and have been decompressed. The next step should be to de-link the civil service remuneration scale from minimum wage applying to the business sector. The current link may result in unwarranted adjustments to government pay, especially at a time when the minimum wage must increase rapidly, due to WTO commitment. Progress in term of increasing accountability has been more limited. Both the introduction of administrative courts and grassroots democracy decree were promising steps.

Chapter 6:   Emerging Issues and Recommendations

In chapter 5, we analyzed the state of Vietnam's competitiveness and growth through six determinants and point out its progresses as well as existing weaknesses compared to some selected neighboring countries. This chapter is basic for exploring in the following chapter.

In chapter 6, we first present some emerging key issues of Vietnam's competitiveness growth based on the analyzing of the previous chapter, including production resource shortage and low quality, outdated technology, bureaucratic and corrupt administration, and slow SOEs reform. In the second section of the chapter we propose some recommendations to enhance Vietnam's competitiveness and sustain its growth in coming years such as: address production resources shortage and quality; develop an independent and vibrant domestic private sector; strengthen public institution and government effectiveness. Each above mentioned solution includes some detail recommendations.

6.1   Emerging Issues of Vietnam's Competitiveness

The "Doi moi" policy has brought expressive economic fruits and radical changes within the economy. Physical infrastructure and human resource have been improved compared to the previous phase, and the financial market has been initially set up. International trade and foreign investment activities have become more liberal and open, and as a result they have performed remarkable achievements. The business environment has become more attractive due to simplification of administrative procedures. As a result, investment (both foreign and domestic) has risen over time, by which productivity and competitiveness have been improved. However, the competitiveness of the Vietnamese economy appears to have many weaknesses and causes some concerns, especially compared to some neighboring countries. The emerging key issues are namely: the shortage and low quality of production resources such as inefficient and poor infrastructure, lack of skilled labor and the under-developed financial market; out-dated technology; bureaucracy, red-tape and corruption; and inefficient SOE operation and slow privatization process.

6.1.1   Production Resources Shortage and Low Quality

Over decades Vietnam has gained progress in providing production resources such as infrastructure, human resource, capital resource and natural resource. However, there have been some challenges that Vietnam has had to face: inefficient and poor infrastructure, shortage of skilled labor force and undeveloped financial market.

Inefficient and poor infrastructure system In a comparison with Thailand and China, Vietnam has performed infrastructure services less well than its regional competitors. Among the access indicators presented, Vietnam lags in terms of transportation and teledensity (Table 5. 1).

Telecommunication is considered as the most efficient industry in the infrastructure service sector, but its labor productivity is poor compared to productivity in neighboring countries. Telephone mainlines per employee are 50, compared to 160 and 225 in China and Thailand respectively (World Bank 2006a).

An alternative perspective on what is important for competitiveness can be provided by business perceptions surveys. The World Bank's investment climate surveys asked small, medium and large manufacturing businesses about 18 potential constraints to their businesses. Transport and electricity were ranked the 3rd and 4th most severe constraints. Transport is seen as a major or severe constraint for 24% of manufacturing firms, and electricity is a severe constraint for 19%. Transportation is considered as a greater constraint in Vietnam than in neighboring countries for which these surveys were conducted (World Bank 2006a). For electricity, the main problems are perceived to be the price and the quality. Sixty percent of firms consider the price of electricity to be excessive. In fact, EVN is reasonably efficient in terms of cost, and a requirement for EVN's sustainability is that tariffs cover costs, so that there is little to be done about these concerns in the short term. More significantly, forty-one percent of firms are concerned about the poor quality of electricity services. Power outages and surges are estimated to cost manufacturing firms the equivalent of 3.2% of their sales. Around a third of firms have bought generators to cope with EVN's unreliability. The unreliability imposes substantial costs even for those with generators (about 10cents per kWh or twice EVN's average tariff). These concerns suggest that investments in increased generating, transmission and distribution capacity, as well as reductions of system losses, are the main priorities for electricity.

Losses of electricity in transmission and distribution still perform poorly in comparison with China and Thailand. To some extent this comparison is unfair. For example, China has a higher proportion of businesses receiving high voltage supply, and therefore has lower distribution losses.

At 7.1% of total road expenditure in 2003, Vietnam has the lowest maintenance expenditure in the region and trends downward. Neglect of maintenance is inefficient since it is likely to increase long-term maintenance costs.

Vietnam's trains have low operating speeds of 40 km/h for passenger trains and 22 km/h for freight trains. Due to the lack of maintenance and new investment, the rail network has deteriorated. Labor productivity is low at 124,000 traffic units/employee, compared with 548,000 in Thailand and 610,000 in Indonesian. Accident statistics for Vietnam's railways suggest a neglected network. In 1998 there were 41 deaths per 1000km of track. This figure increased to 271 in 2003. Corresponding figures for Indonesia were 11 in 1998 and 16 in 2003, and for Thailand: 5 and 2 respectively (World Bank 2006a).

Causes of inefficient and poor infrastructure services are provided solely by SOEs and there is little room for competition In Vietnam most infrastructure services are provided by state-owned enterprises. Corporate governance is under the Law on State-Owned Enterprises. SOEs are not subject to the general principles of private sector corporate governance, and are not able to make their own autonomous commercial decisions. To the extent that business strategies exist they are embodied in sector Master Plans prepared by line ministries, personnel policies are controlled by the Ministry of Labor, Invalids and Social Affair, the Ministry of Planning and Investment approves their investment projects and the Ministry of Finance grants fund.

Corporate governance in Vietnam is generally said to be weak. A new Unified Enterprise Law (UEL) was enacted in 2005 for implementation beginning April 1, 2006. It is intended to provide common and improved rules of corporate governance for domestic and foreign private firms. But SOEs will only be subjected to the new UEL if they are specifically converted into either single member limited liability or joint stock companies. Subjecting infrastructure SOEs to the UEL would be a logical element of any corporatization program, but there currently seem to be little impetus in this direction.

Competition is the most powerful mechanism for improving efficiency. Competition provides firms with the incentives to keep costs to a minimum, to offer products that are better adapted to the needs of consumers, and to adapt new technologies as they become available. However, there is no competition in infrastructure (except telecommunication). In other words, state monopoly dominates in supplying infrastructure services. The continuing philosophy is generally one of trust in government planning processes and bureaucratic performance targets rather than market competition. For example, in telecommunications international experience strongly suggests that the speed of network rollout is accelerated by greater competition. Unfortunately, Vietnam is lagging behind in international best practice. Several new entrants have been authorized to compete with VNPT in fixed line and mobile services, but VNPT remains dominant, with a 90-94% share of the entire telecommunications market (including segments such as equipment construction and installation). Vinaphone and Mobilefone, despite a common parent, do seem to compete, perhaps in part because they have business cooperation contracts with foreign partners. Four SOEs have been licensed to enter fixed and cell line markets, because they have traditionally had their own private networks. SPT is present in Ho Chi Minh city; Hanoi Telecom is present only in Hanoi, Viettel is an SOE owned by the military; and Viet Power Telecom is owned by EVN, the electricity utility. Effective regulation, in particular spectrum management and resolution of interconnection disputes, will be important in facilitating the progress that could be made by allowing the entry of foreign firms. In this respect, the United States has obtained an early advantage, obtaining preferential access for its firms under the Bilateral Trade Agreement (BTA). But even these advantages limit foreign ownership to 49% and 45% in the mobile and land line services markets. These limits restrict the potential for competition to drive greater investment and improved services.

At the moment Vietnam's efforts to involve the private sector in infrastructure sectors is largely focused on meeting financing needs through the equitization program and BOTs, rather than improving infrastructure efficiency. But private participation can be introduced as a means of improving efficiency, especially when introduced through competitive bidding for the right to serve a market. Greater use of private participation as a means of improving enterprise efficiency would be encouraged with various institutional reforms.

In telecommunications, the main problems are perceived to be price and quality. The best solution to these problems may be greater competition. Greater competition would help to drive down prices, and would provide consumers with a choice in the event that they had problems with the quality of services from particular providers.

Shortage of Skilled Labor Force Despite rising educational level, 80% of the labor force is considered to be unskilled. Skilled workers are disproportionately concentrated in and around the main cities such as Hanoi or Ho Chi Minh city. There is a shortage of trainers; trainer-student ratio in Vietnam is one to 28, while the world average ratio is one to 15[92].

Adapting content to the needs of a market economy is especially important in the case of vocational training. According to a recent ICA[93] report, the third most important constraint faced by enterprises in manufacturing, after access to finance and access to land and infrastructure, is the shortage of appropriately skilled

---

92   Ministry of Labor, War Invalids and Social Affairs (MOLISA)

93   Investment Climate Assessment

workers. Only 40 per cent of workers in foreign companies operating in Vietnam have received professional training, according to the Ministry of Planning and Investment. To some extent, the severity of this constraint reflects the fast labor turnover characterizing the Vietnamese economy. Workers use the assignment with the best companies (especially, those with foreign technology and management) to learn on the job and then rapidly move on, either to create their own businesses, or to get jobs with bigger responsibilities in domestic private companies. With rapid economic growth, and the change in economic structure toward activities with higher value added and knowledge content, labor skills will have to be upgraded. However, current training programs are often outdated because teaching tools lag far behind the development of technology, particularly technology of FDI enterprises (Mac Van Tien[94]). Additionally Initial training is still input-oriented and follows curricular requirements instead of workplace requirements.

Undeveloped Finance Market This development of financial market is the result of a series of reforms aimed at adapting the banking sector reform accelerated in 2001. It is not quite surprising when the survey result of WEF shows that the soundness of banks is relatively high, compared to neighboring countries, especially China, and equal to Thailand (Figure 5.4). The access to the local equity market of Vietnam scores higher than China, Philippines and Indonesia and just slightly lower than Thailand and Malaysia. However, the capital markets, which aim at supplying the economy with medium-and long-term risk capital, remain underdeveloped. The government debt market and especially the corporate bond markets are still in an early development stage. In addition, the banking sector remains financially weak and may benefit from more competition to accelerate its current reform agenda. The obstacles of access to loans, particularly SMEs, reflect an inefficient and monopolistic bank system. Our survey conducted in early 2007 shows a consistent outcome. Most respondents complain of restrictions of access to loans from SOCBs, especially private enterprises (Appendix 6).

The banking system faces several major difficulties due to its financial support of SOEs and its failure to operate solely on market-based principles. Vietnam's banking system is regulated and controlled by the central government, which set interest rates and attempts to allocate credit to certain Vietnamese firms. The central government has used the banking system to keep money-losing SOEs afloat by pressing state banks to provide low interest rate loans, without which a large number of the SOEs would likely go bankrupt. As a result, Non-Performing Loans (NPLs) of SOCBs were estimated at approximately 15 percent of the total credit as of May 2005, which was around 8% of the GDP (World Bank 2006b, p. 19).

---

94   Director of the Vocational Training Science Research Center

The high volume of bad loans now held by Vietnamese banks poses a serious threat to Vietnam's banking system. Assessment based on International Accounting Standard (IAS) audits suggest that the overall quality of the SOCBs portfolio is not improving (Ibid., pp. 30). On the contrary, according to the judgement of external auditors analyzing the limited information the SOCBs have already suffered from capital shortfall. In addition, the supervisory capacity of the SBV over the banking system is limited, as its methods are still based on compliance with mechanical rules, with little focus on risks. The institutional organization does not, as four simultaneous inspection-related systems co-exist, whereas an extensive provincial branch structure results in overlapping functions and responsibilities. More importantly, the SBV faces an inherent conflict of interest, as the regulator of a banking system that is still dominated by the SOCBs it owns. The SBV must act as the sole shareholder in the SOBCs, which have no independent board members, face serious corporate governance problems, and are subject to interference from various government authorities. Not surprisingly, the incentive structure within the SOCBs is not tied to performance targets and credit risk management practices remain weak.

The capital markets are still in the early stage of development. The securities market has benefited from the increasingly positive assessment of Vietnam's economic potential by the international community, but it still suffers from important shortcomings, including under-developed regulations and supervisory mechanisms, an insufficient trading infrastructure and weak information system. The bond market is hampered by fragmentation. This is due to the multiplicity of channels and methods used for the issuances, and to a pattern of "buy and hold" used by investors, which results in little secondary trading. The corporate bond market remains very small, tapped only by a few large SOEs. The insurance market has been especially dynamic in relation to life, but less so in relation to property. This market suffers from an inadequate regulatory framework in relation to taxes, entrance, investments and exit. Tools such as factoring and leasing could serve to meet the needs of SMEs but are constrained due to the inadequate regulatory framework, limited funding resources, low public awareness and lengthy foreclosure procedures. As a result, the precarious state of the financial markets in general and the banking system in particular has made Vietnamese reformers reluctant to open the banking sector to foreign competition.

6.1.2 Backward Technology

Technology in Vietnam has been improved over time, allowing productivity and competitiveness to progress. However, in fact, technology development in Vietnam still lags behind its neighboring countries. Capacities of creating new technologies are still limited and could not meet requirements of the country's industrialization and modernization process[95]. The growth of production capabilities has not led to a similar deepening of capabilities into design, research and new technology development. Such deepening is an increasingly important part of the development process as the industrial sector diversifies and uses more complex and fast-changing technologies. It is particularly important for export-oriented industries that have to continuously upgrade their processes and products. The technology development has been faced with being far behind in strong technology development tendencies and knowledge-based economy in the world.

The survey we conducted in Vietnam in early 2007 indicates that technology development in Vietnam still lags behind other ASEAN countries (Appendix 6). The other finding conducted by WEF in 2005 was consistent with ours. The figure 6.1 also shows that the relatively weak R&D linkages between university and industry research collaboration stem, in part, from problems of low quality of research institutions and universities. The survey indicates that Vietnam public research institutions and universities are not sufficiently responsive to the needs of industry and company, emphasizing academics over commercial applications in their research orientation. Vietnam receives a low score and tails countries in the region such as Thailand, China, Indonesia and Malaysia. This result roots from main causes as follows:

Low Investment As compared with other countries in the region, the country is still faced with very big gaps in investment in technology development. An average investment of one research program is 5,000 US dollar and that of one researcher per year is 3000 US dollar.

This rate lowers 4th, 7th, 8th, 26th-fold, compared to Thailand, China, Malaysia and Singapore respectively. The share of technology development investment from non-state sector only accounted for 9% of the total investment. This share is far behind, compared to 60% in Malaysia, and 45% in China. The R&D investment from Vietnamese companies accounted 0.01% of their total revenue. It is also very low, compared with 5-6% in NICs and 10% in developed countries.[96] This results, in part, from the financial management mechanism of S&T activities. The mechanism hasn't created favorable conditions for scientists and mobilized many non-State capital sources; the finance autonomy mechanism of S&T organizations hasn't been linked together with the autonomy in the human resource management so the efficiency is limited.

---

95   Vietnam science and technology development strategy by 2010, p10
96   Centre Institute of Economic Management (CIEM)

Figure 6. 1: Survey Technology Development

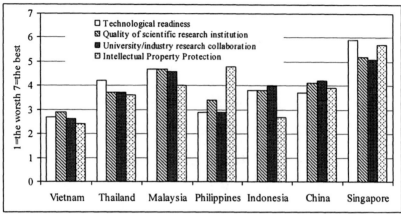

Source: WEF, survey 2004-05

Shortage of scientists There is a lack of planning on training high-level professional workforce in prioritized S&T fields, especially scientists. In fact, Vietnam lacks of the world and regional class researchers. The competence of Vietnamese scientists is still limited, in part, due to low foreign language and computer skills. Therefore it is impossible to update state of the art research in the region and world and joint international conferences.

Poor technology development environment including S&T information, consultancy for technology transfer, intellectual properties, and standard-measures-quality are still poor in terms of both facilities and capacities for providing services which can meet requirements of regional and international integration. For example, in 2004 Vietnam had zero (0) internet hosts per 10,000 inhabitants, compared with 1.3 in China, compared with 16.6 in Thailand and 1,155.3 in Singapore [97]. In the same year Vietnam had 12.7 personal computers per 1000 inhabitants, whereas there were 40.88 for China, 58.34 for Thailand, and 196.83 for Malaysia (Figure 6.2)

---

97   International Telecommunication Union, June 2004

Figure 6. 2: Personal Computer per 1,000 Inhabitants

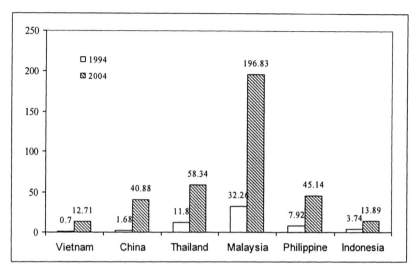

Source: World Bank, country data, 2006

In addition, the intellectual property rights regime remains weak. The legal framework should ideally provide enterprise with a strong incentive to undertake R&D and commercialize innovations. Few private investors would invest on R&D activities in a situation where everybody benefits and few carry the cost. Strong intellectual property rights regimes are therefore a key component of promoting R&D activities in any society since they allow innovators to receive a return on their investment. Vietnam officially adheres to most treaties and international agreements on intellectual property rights. However, some elements of the enforcement regime are still at variance with Vietnam's international obligations. Particularly copyrights protection remains a problem. The Vietnamese government has made few efforts to impose criminal penalties in commercial piracy cases and stop counterfeit importation. Bottlenecks in the judicial system have caused substantial delays in the completion of the criminal and civil infringement cases. Figure 6.1 reveals a low perceived protection of intellectual property rights in Vietnam compared to ASEAN-4 countries and China.

Limited cooperation There is a lack of organic links among S&T research, education–training, production–business, and a lack of close cooperation among research and development organizations, universities and enterprises. The model of R&D organizations and their mechanism have not encouraged research institution, university and company together to collaborate (Figure 6.1).

173

In general, Vietnam's S&T capacities are still weak. Issues that have arisen in the renovation process can't timely be solved and can't closely link with and meet requirements of the socio-economic development.

6.1.3 Bureaucracy, Red Tape and Corruption

Administration reform has brought considerable changes to the procedures and impacted positively social economic development, especially within the business environment. The significant simplifications in business registration introduced by the Enterprise Law of 2000 (now new Unified Enterprise Law) has led to a perceptible reduction in the number of licenses in force. The positive perception on licenses and permits can also be reflecting the success in introducing the one-door model for administrative procedures at the local level. However, administration in Vietnam is still cumbersome, with red tape and much overlapping. In addition, the law system is lax and its enforcement is weak. These salient characteristics of the administration system and institution result in emerging corruption.

Bureaucracy and red tape administration procedures are time consuming and unnecessary. The survey we conducted shows that administrative regulations are burdensome. The indicator represents an average of 2.67 (on a scale from 1 to 7 where 7 corresponds to the highest integrity standards) of which 3.28 was scored by officials, 2.29 scored by executives, and 2.58 scored by scholars. It appears that most respondents, including officials, stated a disagreement with administrative procedures. It is also not surprising that officials mark a higher point compared to executives and scholars (Appendix 6).A previous survey of enterprises jointly conducted by CIEM and GTZ shows that in order to operate a firm, it needs to go through 13 administrative procedures, taking 260 days altogether. Nevertheless, 231 days in this estimate correspond to the time needed to acquire land, under the assumption that the enterprise wants to purchase it from the government and needs to go through land clearance and compensation of resettled populations. Getting land in an industrial zone would reduce the waiting period, on average, from 231 days to 83. And delays possibly can be much shorter if the land was purchased or rented from other enterprises. In contrast, the business registration process is narrower, only 15 days are required by Enterprise Law and the exercise requires fewer days[98]. This obstacle causes the land administration

---

[98] The CIEM-GTZ study found that the deadline was respected in two thirds of the cases, with only 5 percent of firms having to wait for 30 days or more. In many provinces the registration process was actually completed in less than one week. Similarly, 70 percent of the firms surveyed received their tax code within seven days, and solely 6 percent of them had to wait for more than 15 days.

agency to rank first[99] in corruption among administration bodies in Vietnam. Findings were similar in the survey of competitiveness conducted by WEF; the burden of government regulations is higher than in China, Thailand, Indonesia, Malaysia and only lower than in the Philippines (Figure 5.21).

Corruption is a consequence of weak governance and burdensome administration as well as the shortage of a law system and weak law enforcement. It represents a serious threat to development progress as well as undermines productivity and competitiveness because it raises the cost of doing business and reduces confidence of domestic and foreign investors, hence slowing economic growth and job creation. In recent years, Vietnam has made efforts to fight corruption, however, the success of these efforts are still quite limited. The commitments of Vietnam government relating to fighting corruption have translated into a series of important international agreements and legislative undertakings. Vietnam signed the UN convention against corruption in December 2003, with the intention to ratify it in 2006. In 2004 it endorsed the ADB-OECD Anti-Corruption Initiative for Asia and the Pacific. And in 2005 it passed the Law on Anti-Corruption, which by and large covers compliance with the UN convention and takes into account the principles of the ADB-OECD Initiative. In 2006, the Corruption Perceptions Index of Transparency International gave a rating of 2.6 to Vietnam (111th out of 163 countries), compared to 2.5 in 2000[100] (75th out of 77 countries) It appears that there is some progress in fighting corruption in Vietnam although corruption is widespread. In comparison with some selected regional countries, Vietnam got a higher grade, compared to the Philippines and Indonesia, but was lower than China, Thailand and Malaysia (Figure 6.3).

The diagnostic study of corruption conducted by the Central Committee on Internal Affairs (CCIA) was released in 2005. This study used an international methodology, combining surveys and interviews of citizens, public official and enterprises. Its results show that corruption is perceived as common and existing at all levels and in all organizations, although varying to a considerable extent. The respondents thought that land administration, customs, the traffic police, tax administration and construction registers were the most corrupt agencies[101].

---

99   The ranking based on survey conducted by ICCA
100 On a scale of 1 to 10 where 10 corresponds to the highest integrity standards
101 The finding is similar that was investigated by the ICA

175

Figure 6. 3: Corruption Perception Index

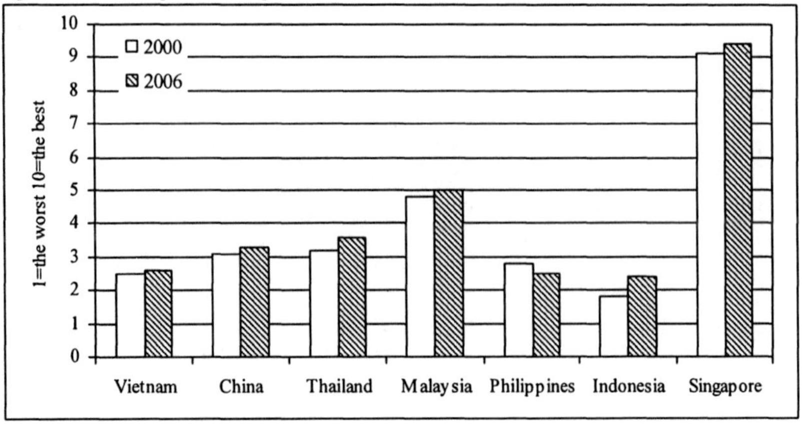

Source: Transparency International

The survey we conducted shows a relatively similar finding. The average score for corruption was 2.01, on a scale from 1 to 7 where 7 corresponds to the best, indicating that most respondents, including officials, business leaders and scholars, find the corruption to be pervasive. However, attitude forward corruption is quite different between officials and business executives. While executives marked an average score of 1.55, officials appreciated a higher average grade of 2.65. (Appendix 6).

The ICA survey[102] reveals that the forms of corruption most commonly mentioned are soliciting bribes by creating obstacles, accepting bribes for favors, and using public means for personal benefit: The "ask-give" mechanism was identified as a major cause of the corruption.

The management of the investment projects appears to be more problematic. The recent PMU 18 scandal served as a warning about the risk of resources being misappropriated. At the same time, several investigations involving contracts under the investment projects showed how challenging it is to uncover corrupt transactions. A culture of "sharing" and "taking turn" somewhat undermines the effectiveness of conventional bidding mechanism. The corruption also takes the form

---

102   The ICA survey is based on a large survey of manufacturing firms in the formal sector, including the domestic private sector, foreign companies and SOEs. The survey was conducted in 2005 in 25 provinces of Vietnam, using a representative sample. A private firm was in charge of the interviews, which were carried out without the presence of government of officials.

of "gift exchange" not to be reciprocated immediately, but when an opportunity arises. Based anecdotal evidence, giving out fat enveloped at wedding and funerals and losing large sums of money in card playing and other games, are among the mechanisms used to channel the "gifts". To add to the murkiness, sometimes the beneficiary is not even the public servants who are supposed to reciprocate, but rather a close relative.

6.1.4 Slow State-Owned Enterprise Reform

Vietnam has undertaken SOEs reform since 1991. Yet, it still has had an unusually large number of SOEs compared to other countries in the region (except China)-around 4,086 firms[103] and these enterprises account for 54.96% of the total capital in all enterprises. The pace of SOE reform has been slow. The survey we conducted shows that one of the priorities of the Government is to speed up the privatization process (equitization)[104].

In the early 1990s, the number of SOEs was halved from about 12,000 to around 6,000. During the time between 1998 and 2002, the transformation process in the forms of equitization, divestiture, and liquidation has reduced the number to about 5,000. In 2003, a new roadmap for SOE reform was put into operation: 55 per cent were due to take place in 2003, but the transformations fell far short of the target (945 enterprises, or 62 per cent, out of a planned 1,459 that had been completed). More importantly, most transformed SOEs have been small and medium enterprises with chartered capital less than 10 billion VND (about 0,7 US$ million); only 23 percent of companies with chartered capital over 10 billion VND have completed the process. And the shares sold for now account for only 14 percent of the total SOE capital. In 2004, despite the efforts to accelerate the transformation process, including the equitization of some General Corporations and State-Owned Commercial Banks (SOCBs), there is still no significant improvement. In the first eight months of 2004, the number of equitized SOEs accounted for 35 per cent of the target, or 350 out of 1,000. Note that the new SOE reform roadmap issued in 2003 identifies the specific names and timetable of SOEs under transformation and annual targets over the period of 2003 and 2005. The reform of the banking system has also been sluggish. Moreover, the SOE reform roadmap seems to seriously not take into account the impacts of integration by economic sector; it largely emphasizes the size of enterprises. The postponement of SOE

---

103   General Statistics Office (GSO), Enterprise Survey
104   In Vietnam, privatization is understood as equitization

and banking reform is not recommendable for many reasons[105]. First, there is substantial welfare cost associated with the provision of fiscal subsidies credits to inefficient SOEs. Second, subsidizing SOEs would de facto lead to a redistribution of resources to the SOEs, thereby reducing resources available to finance poverty-reduction programs. The authorities may also request SOCBs to make loans to failing SOEs. This would only transfer the burden associated with keeping afloat inefficient SOEs to the banking sector, and create difficulty for the restructuring of SOCBs.

In addition, the equitization of SOEs has brought some concerns such as the valuation of SOE assets, state capital representative of equitized SOEs, overstaff and so on. So far, divestiture mechanism, involving public auctions, is considerably more transparent. But SOEs continue to face difficulties in relation to the valuation of their assets. How to appraise landholdings and intangibles remains one of the most contentious issues. Some SOEs are also facing excessive debt levels, which makes their divestiture difficult.

While equitization increases the autonomy of enterprise management to make business decisions, it does not fully remove the distorted incentives faced by supervising line ministries and provincial governments. The latter can want to encourage local SOCB brands to lend to the firms they partly own, whereas the former could be tempted to design sector regulations in a way that favors firms with state capital. Distorted credit allocation at the provincial level and inefficient market regulation at sector level can be more damaging to the economy than the micro-management of firms. Removing the exercise of state ownership rights out of line ministries and provincial government is necessary to address this potential conflict of interest.

The transformation of SOEs has resulted in an increase of unemployment due to the overstaffing of former SOEs. SOEs do not only have an economic function, but also a social function. They were used to generate employment. An empirical study conducted by World Bank shows that roughly 14% of employment is overstaffed after SOEs are equitized. In order to fill in this unemployment, SMEs need to be strengthened, because SMEs create more jobs than any other enterprises.

---

105 Auffret 2002: Trade Reform in Vietnam: Opportunities with Emerging Challenges". Background Paper on Trade for the 2002 Vietnam Development Report by World Bank in Hanoi, November 2002

6.2 Recommendations to Enhance the Competitiveness of Vietnam

As mentioned previously, there are some emerging issues of Vietnam's competitiveness such as production resources shortage, out-dated technology, dominance of SOEs and their slow reform, and red-tape and corrupt administration. These issues impact negatively on productivity and competitiveness as well as sustainable economic growth in the long-term. At the same time, Vietnam cannot do everything at once to improve its competitiveness due to a limitation of resources and competence. Furthermore, national competitiveness is a large scope concept relating to many areas of an economy. In this study framework, we propose some solutions to solve some key issues, which are considered to be the most urgent[106], to enhance the competitiveness of Vietnam in coming years. They are namely: address production resources shortages; develop independent and vibrant private sector; and strengthen public institution and government effectiveness.

6.2.1 Address the Shortage and Quality of Production Resources

Although the fundamental structures in the economy have been changing, production resources have been a decisive determinant of the national competitiveness. As said previously, production resources[107] in Vietnam remain short and low quality. In other words, the supply of inputs for the economy is insufficient in both quantity and quality such as lack of skilled labor, poor infrastructure (transport and electricity supply), and barrier of capital resources. Therefore, some measures are needed to fulfill production resources shortages in Vietnam in coming years.

6.2.1.1 Reform Higher Education and Develop Vocational Education

The quality and cost of human resources are the defining characteristic of competitiveness. Human resources must not only be efficient and asked but also innovative and dynamic to proactively meet the continuous changes required by an ever more competitive market place. The basic skills possessed by human resources need to be further channeled into more specialized areas so as to fulfill specific tasks which require technical skills[108]. The competitive supply of certain products and services require properly trained human resources, and efforts at

---

106 The most urgent issues are based on our analysis and conducted survey

107 Production resources is defined as including human resources, infrastructure, capital and natural resources (see chapter 3)

108 Vietnam economy – Thoi Bao Kinh Te Vietnam (2006), "What need to be done to the integration of the higher education" VN Economy 12/05/2006 in Vietnamese

maintaining a top-class vocational and higher educational system are important components of the country's competitiveness.

As said previously, in order to address the shortage of skilled labor force, we will propose some recommendations to raise higher and vocational education in this framework.

Higher Education to strengthen skilled labor force at present and to reach the long-term objective with 40 percent enrollment in higher education by 2020[109], an appropriate balance of funding mechanisms, autonomy and accountability should be established.

At higher level of education, raising the quality and relevance of the teaching imparted involves both more private sector participation and increased autonomy of publicly-funded institutions. The new Vocational Training Law promotes offers at various levels oriented toward labor market needs and standardization of curricula. It also foresees an increased role of businesses in designing and implementing training offers. More systematic consultation should lead to an upgrade of the curriculum, teaching methods and training places, with the latter including actual workplace. One of the main constraints in this respect is overlap of responsibilities between MOET, MOLISA and other relevant bodies. The respective roles of the main stakeholders should be revised at all levels, from national government to provincial governments to local training centers.

The World Bank suggests that, on the funding side, partnership arrangements between businesses and higher education institutions should be encouraged. But they should not be seen as substitute for government resources, especially in areas related to research. Business sponsorships may lead to a neglecting of research and general knowledge, in favor of the technical skills more urgently needed by enterprises. However, support to research is one of the few tools for industrial policy available to Vietnam, as a latecomer of the WTO. The direct subsidies to industry used by other East Asia countries in their development drive are all but ruled out. Supporting laboratories, libraries and faculty working on basic knowledge would be a way to improve both quality of universities and Vietnam's competitiveness. Grants should be provided through competitive mechanism and open to all higher education institution. A program could also be set up to encourage the return (permanent or temporary) of reputable academics and researchers from the overseas Vietnamese communities.

---

109   This ratio is equal to that of Thailand at present

Delivering on the education agenda requires thorough rethinking of the overall financing frameworks for the sector. On the revenue side, the government strategy envisions an increased reliance on tuition fees but this has to go in parallel with the elimination of all other fees and out-of-pocket payments. For vocational training and higher education, the private sector should become an increasingly important source of funds. The government should encourage the private sector to participate in this area. However, to inhibit disadvantaged students from poor families' subsidies to training facilities or student credit implementation[110], and/or a scholarship program should be considered.

Broader concerns are raised about the relevance of the education imparted. The credibility of the education system, hence social satisfaction with it, will depend on the match between education content and the economic development needs of Vietnam. There is a perception that the education system is functioning quite well but in the pursuit of backward goals. The survey we conducted showed that most respondents complained the education quality has not yet met the needs of the economy. Therefore, the quality debate should be related to the need for an approach to teaching and learning which is better suited to Vietnam's transition to a market economy. Knowing how to learn problem solving, evaluation skills are necessary to deal with the uncertainties and continued changes brought by integration into the global economy.

Vocational Education Vietnam has a huge labor force, but foreign companies still face problems finding skilled labor and competent managers[111]. Vietnam must develop a master plan to expand vocational training schools to ensure a qualified labor force.

In several places, Vietnam needs to pay more attention to being devoted to vocational training with the objective of increasing the pool of skilled labor by which the national competitiveness of Vietnam will be enhanced. There is also recognition of the need for better educated and trained young people, especially in rural areas, to enable them to get jobs. Increased private participation is seen as part of the solution. The Vietnamese government should encourage the establishment of private education and training institutions; encourage more foreign companies to establish training facilities, especially those with a large number of employees; encourage training cooperation with high-quality foreign training institutions; and foster the opening of high quality, accredited and 100 percent foreign-invested

---

110 Banks should join in the education process through supplying preferable long-term loan for poor students, who their family cannot cover their study, but they have competence and want to graduate a university or college

111 Kotaro Uchyama, General Director Staley Electricity Ltd in Vietnam

training institutions in science, technology, techniques and economic management.

Although the government has carried the primary responsibility for vocational education, in a market economy vocational education policy design and delivery should be achieved through a new partnership between the government, employers, professional associations, industries, employees and their representatives, the local community and non-government organizations (NGOs). This partnership must create a coherent legislative framework to enable the launching of a national strategy for change. The government, apart from actually providing the vocational education, can also provide leadership and vision, facilitate, coordinate, establish quality assurance, and ensure that the vocational training is for all by identifying and addressing community service obligations.

The vocational training is best served by a diversity of public and private providers (including foreign investors). The appropriate mix can be found in many ways, with the responsibility of the government being to facilitate choice while ensuring quality. Both the government and private sector should recognize that the vocational training is an investment, not a cost, with significant returns, including the well-being of workers, enhanced national productivity, and competitiveness. Therefore, funding for vocational education should be shared to the maximum extent possible between the government, industry, and the community and learners, with government providing appropriate financial incentives. Moreover the government should seek or encourage the private sector to seek bilateral and multilateral capacity-building cooperation in vocational training.

6.2.1.2 Improve Transport Infrastructure and Strengthen Electricity Supply

As mentioned above, the infrastructure system in Vietnam, in general, is poor and inefficient. The infrastructure system needs to be improved. However, it would be difficult to improve all the infrastructure services simultaneously due to the limitation of resources and regulations. In this study framework, we propose some measures to strengthen the infrastructure services of transport and electricity which was considered to be the top priorities in our conducted survey.

Transport
Financing Transport expenditures reached 4.5% of the GDP in 2002. This expenditure should to be increased substantially, which would correspond to the GDP growth. ODA currently finances 37% of the central transport expenditures. As in other sectors, the expectation that ODA financing will not grow at the same pace as GDP means that the growing sectors expenditure will need to be paid for either by consumers or the Government. To guarantee affordability of transport projects

and to supply relatively sufficiently in this area, the financing burden should be shifted to future generations through government borrowing and direct private investment. The private sector should play an expanded role in financing highways, railways, ports and airports.

Road maintenance should be strengthened. Current maintenance expenditures are at about 50% of the necessary levels. If expenditure on national road maintenance remains at their current levels over the next ten years, the condition of the network will be substantially deteriorated, with 34% of national roads being in poor condition, including 55% of the high traffic volume network (World Bank 2006a). Therefore, the Government should maintain a significant budget for maintenance and call for investments from the private and foreign sector.

Reform the Ministry of Transport's State Owned Enterprises[112] should be a central task to improve outcomes in the sector. Frequently the Ministry's SOEs are over-indebted and deliver low quality and delayed work. Therefore, an equitization program should be designed to close non-viable enterprises, to establish clear lines of accountability and improve commercial incentives for the remaining enterprises, and to provide clear separation between Ministry finances and enterprise finances. A further possibility would be to remove ownership of shares in the SOEs to a separate agency, to ensure no conflict of interest between the Ministry of Transport's policy role and the profit motives of share ownership.

Competition in transport infrastructure service should be introduced gradually. Competition is the most powerful mechanism for improving efficiency. Competition provides firms with incentives to keep costs at a minimum, to offer products that are better adapted to the needs of consumers, and to adapt new technologies as they become available. Competition in the transport infrastructure is used to procure road construction, but the competition is between state-owned companies who use the same norms to prepare their bids, and typically prepare similarly priced bids. This suggests either collusion in their bids or that a greater number of competitors are required to produce vigorous competition.

Electricity
The capacity of Vietnam's electricity system needs to double in just five years, to meet demand growth projected at 16% per year during 2006-2010. While demand-side management must be pushed as hard as possible, the main solution lies

---

112 In the area of infrastructure, increasing investment is indeed one of the top priorities, and evidence from OECD as well as non- OECD countries suggest that privatization has led to substantial increases in investment (OECD, 2000 Privatization, Competition and Regulations, p25-30)

in a large-scale medium-term capacity expansion program. Annual power sector investment requirements during 2005-2010 are expected to cost over US$3 billion per year. The three main financing options for the sector are self-financing by EVN using retained earnings, using different types of borrowing, and independent power producers (Ipps). EVN cannot even come close to meeting this requirement from its own resources or massive borrowings, especially without further increases in unit sales revenue. EVN has maintained profitability each year since its inception in 1995, and has retained a sound financial position. However, the size of the sector investment requirement is no match for the company's borrowing capacity. In addition, the Government is neither willing nor able to pick up the bill (World Bank 2006a, pp. 32). Therefore, IPPs investment needs to be encouraged. One way or anther, directly or indirectly, consumers need to pay the cost of the power system expansion. The task of the Government and power industry is to implement the expansion program as efficiently as possible, to keep the costs as reasonable and affordable as possible for consumers, and stimulate private investments.

The government should diversify electricity supply sources and encourage the establishment of new IPPs from foreign or domestic private firms to meet the huge and rapid increases in power demand. IPP arrangements for new power plants include: BOT ventures wholly owned by other public-owned Vietnamese entities; joint–ventures BOT arrangements, involving EVN investment with other parties (local public or foreign); and BOT arrangements wholly owned by parties, either public or private. In addition, new joint-stock company IPPs are being created from EVN's partial divestiture of existing power plants under its equitization program. This aggressive IPP development runs in parallel with the Government's efforts to gradually restructure the power industry, as dictated in the new Electricity Law. In general, the Government should seek to pursue all types of IPPs, as quickly as possible, in its efforts to get new plants on the system. In addition, the price of electricity should be maintained at a reasonable[113] level, which recovers costs and earns profits, to stimulate further private investment in the period of recent power shortage.

In the electricity sector, the reform of state-owned enterprises is to focus on the transition to a future competitive market for electricity. EVN will need to be broken up into truly separate corporations. Decisions on size, structure and operational scope of newly formed shareholding companies need to ensure adequate

---

113 In China in the late 1980s and early 1990s, the willingness of large consumers to pay higher "second track" prices or make other types of contributions for new power plant investments, in exchange for guaranteed power in time of shortage, was the most important single factor in overcoming national power shortages. (World Bank 2006a)

competition in different market segments as well as adequate resources to ensure financial viability, but should not wield excessive control over the market. As the sector and market structure changes, distribution companies will be drivers in attracting new generation investments and hence protecting end consumers via reliable supply. Distribution companies, in particular, need to have sufficient financial strength and managerial capacity to be perceived as credible and make long-term contracts with generating companies.

The World Bank strongly recommends that competition be used wherever possible in awarding IPP power purchase agreements (Ibid., pp. 36). Through competitive bidding, supply price will be lower than negotiated one. As in Vietnam, power utilities, public officials, and especially potential power providers often argue that there is insufficient time to proceed with competitive bidding. Often, however, this is due to lack of planning and / or lack of proper incentives to minimize costs. Vietnam's power consumers will be the ones to suffer from higher than justifiable costs, unless competitive bidding is strongly favored over negotiated contracting. In cases where negotiated contracts proceed, clear and transparent information should be provided to the public about costs and contract details. If power providers are public entities, detailed and accurate reporting of all aspects of equipment contracting, construction contracting, and power plant operation affecting costs should be openly reported to all relevant government agencies, and made public where possible.

6.2.1.3 Develop Financial Market and Reform Banking System

The government should move forward with concrete actions to open the financial sector further and increase foreign competition. A key milestone in the process was the submission of the Law on the State Bank of Vietnam and the revised Law on Credit Institution to the National Assembly in 2007 that will be passed in 2008. These two Laws should provide a new regulatory environment for the operation of commercial banks and transform SBV into a modern Central Bank for a market economy. The state owned commercial banks[114] (SOCBs) should be equitized. The equitization of Bank for Foreign Trade of Vietnam (Vietcombank) and Mekong Housing Bank was scheduled to be completed in 2007, also when the equitization of the Bank for Investment and Development of Vietnam (BIDV), and Industrial and Commercial Bank of Vietnam (Incombank) is said to start. The Viet-

---

114 Vietnam has 5 large state own commercial banks, accounting 65% of total credit of the economy, including Bank for Foreign Trade of Vietnam (Vietcombank), Bank for Investment and Development of Vietnam (BIDV), Industrial and Commercial Bank of Vietnam (Incombank), Vietnam Bank for Agriculture and Rural Development (VBARD) and Mekong Housing Bank

nam Bank for Agriculture and Rural Development (VBARD) will follow in 2008. However, the equitization process of the SOCBs seems to be slow. So far, there has not been one of them, which has been equitized in time (except Vietcombank). The equitization process of the SOCBs should be implemented through IPO and selling to foreign strategic investors. Only the state should hold the controlling 51% shares of the total shares. The foreign strategic investors should prefer to buy the large remaining shares because they will bring state-of-the art technology and their managerial experiences to change the corporate governance of SOCBs and make the equitized banks more efficient and have a more profitable orientation.

The government needs to focus on cleaning up and restructuring the SOCBs' balance sheet, and enhancing the adequacy of their capital. There is a little doubt whether most of these banks will succeed in attracting private capital. However, a disperse ownership may not fundamentally change the way they are run. Allowing foreign investors to hold a larger share of capital and, especially avoiding the sale of shares in small packages, would help in attracting international banks with a sufficient scale and managerial expertise.

The government, in regards to credit institutions, should aim at establishing a sound regulation framework for commercial banks, which focuses on prudential regulation, provisioning, and risk management requirements. The classification of loans should gradually move from quantitative to qualitative assessments. The new law should contribute to diversification of the types of credit institutions operating in Vietnam and to broaden the scope of their activities.

Other solutions could help to improve the quality of credit and facilitate the recovery of NPLs. The implementation of current plans to develop a private credit bureau and to bolster the SBV Credit Information Center could be continued. The system of registration of mortgage over land-using right certificates (LUCs), to be managed by MONRE at province and district levels, needs to be upgraded.

In fact, the transformation of SBV will require a revision of its structure, and in particular of its organization by provincial branches. Regrouping those branches by regions could help introduce an arms-length relationship with provincial People's Committees (PPCs) and the provincial branches of SOCBs, thus undermining the cozy relationship that there is at present between borrowers, lenders and supervisors. Upgrading the supervision capacity of SBV is another important priority. At presents, this capacity suffers from the duplication and overlaping of functions between departments at headquarters and provincial levels. These respective roles of SBV and other government bodies such as MOF and Deposit Insurance Agency in relation to supervision should also be clarified. Which agency will exercise the state ownership rights in SOCBs, once this function is taken away from SBV, is also unclear.

Equally important, the transformation of SBV will require the strengthening of its capacity to run monetary policy. The increased financial depth of the Vietnamese economy and its growing openness to international capital flows, call for a better understanding of the relationship between external shocks, policy instruments and macroeconomic outcomes. For example, a major stock market correction was almost irrelevant a few years ago, but it could become a major source of instability today. Admittedly, other ongoing trends could actually strengthen financial stability. If the government were to move more fully to non-cash payments there would be greater predictability of the volume of deposits. If the economy was to become less "dollarized", the ability of money demand trends could be enhanced as well. But even in the presence of these trends, the conduct of monetary policy in an open economy will be challenging. Upgrading the human resources of SBV and supporting the development of its in-house expertise should be priorities for technical assistance over the next five years.

The new law on securities could do much for development of capital markets. The law strengthens the authority of state stock company (SSC) over all public offerings. Securities and publicly held companies brokers and intermediaries dealing in securities will need to be licensed by the SSC, which will able to regulate issuers, intermediaries and investors in the over-the-counter market. The law also provides the legal basis for the establishment of the Vietnam Securities Depository, which is expected to become a privately owned entity. However, to make the most of this new law it will be necessary to upgrade the systems supporting trading at stock exchanges, the central securities depository, and information management by SSC. Such an upgrade would involve the introduction of registration systems for securities and individual brokers.

The equitization process should also be more tightly linked to the development of the capital market, with a clear requirement for SOEs to meet the standard that applies to publicly held companies. The equitization of the exchanges should be also considered, as a way to separate the ownership of the markets from their supervision. Consideration should also be given to the establishment of an investor protection fund, as an incentive for investors to trade through regulated brokers. The development of contractual savings policies to expedite the formation and growth of private sector pension funds would generate new demand for securities and the regulations for institutional investors. In terms of the bond market, the government could create a debt management policy that aims to build sizable and predictable debt issuances and an integrated primary market.

The government should provide the issuance of benchmark bonds for the development of the government bond market. The corporate bond market should capitalize on the availability of benchmarks, which should allow banks and enterprises to control the maturity and currency mismatches. This in turn could contribute to reducing NPLs, by helping reduce systemic rollover of short-term loans to infrastructure enterprises. Securitization needs to be made possible in order to provide new means to finance infrastructure projects, SMEs and housing development.

6.2.2 Develop an Independent and Vibrant Domestic Private Sector

The competitiveness of the Vietnamese economy would have a greater achievement if it were supported by a robust private sector, and reform of the inefficient SOE sector and banking system. The reforms and the restructuring of SOEs have meant that there are many entrepreneurial opportunities available to private firms, especially SMEs. The key task for Vietnam is to provide promotion and to create a fair competitive business environment for development of the private sector, which is considered a dynamic force for the competitiveness of the economy. In this section, we propose some recommendations to enhance the reforming of SOEs and to promote the development of private enterprises, especially SMEs, by which domestic private sector is bolstered, and become more independent and vibrant.

6.2.2.1 Strengthen State-Owned Enterprise Reform

As analyzed in the previous sections, SOEs equitilization process has been slow in recent years and there still exist a large number of SOEs in almost all industries of the economy. While both theoretical and empirical studies show that privatization (equitization) of SOEs has brought more efficiency of enterprise operation and its economy, the survey of 550 equitized SOEs conducted in 2005 by World Bank indicates that the diversification of ownership has also contributed to increased efficiency at the enterprise level, by which the national productivity and competitiveness have been increasing. Almost 90 percent of those firms reported an improvement. Turnover has increased by 13 percent on average and on pre-tax profits by 9 percent, which is considerably more than among non-equitized SOEs. Investments and salaries have increased as well. The study also suggests that performance improved faster when the reduction in the state share of capital was larger. This sign shows that it is time for Vietnam to speed up equitization of SOEs.

This improvement is not due to a change in the management team of equitized SOEs. In more than 80 percent of the cases, the chairman of the Managing Board, the director, the deputy directors and the chief accountant remained in their jobs. More importantly, there is a clear concentration of power. It appears that the real change is in the motivation and autonomy of the management team. More than 96 percent of the respondents stated that their managers paid more attention to performance, and enjoyed a higher autonomy to pursue profit objectives (World Bank 2006c).

Box 3 A number of privatization methods (OECD 2000)

Initial public offerings (IPO) in the capital markets is an open competitive procedure that allows for share pricing and company valuations by market. Building competition in offering process itself is important. IPO are highly transparent methods of sale, but to be effective, however it requires a development of capital market, legal framework and large privatization candidates.

Trade sales to strategic investors are especially vulnerable to competition failures. The state is often tempted to sell its controlling stakes to local interests with negative results on the competitiveness of industry, especially the case of the sensitive sector (i.e utilities). The main benefits that trade sales bring are the introduction of considerable managerial and technical know-how and a stable investment environment for economically important firms or sectors. The latter is especially crucial for countries where capital markets are shallow.

Management or employee buy-out is the acquisition of a company by the existing management. It is frequently used as a means of divestment by companies seeking to focus their core activities. The new owner-managers of the buy-out frequently improve its performance as they usually are well aware of any remedial action required and have serious incentive in the form of their stake. Additional capital is provided by financial institutions and venture capitalist and also in many cases by allowing other employees to join in so-called *employee buy-outs[115]*.

Liquidation is the distribution of a company's assets among its creditors and members prior to its dissolution. This brings the life of the company to an end. The liquidation may be voluntary or compulsory[116].

The reduction in SOEs has been mainly through equitization, whereby the SOE after a sale of shares is converted to a joint stock company (JSC) that operates under the Enterprise Law rather than the SOE Law. Other forms of SOE transformation have been mergers, conversions to limited liability companies, and outright sales liquidation. Therefore, in this study framework, we focus on how to speed up the equitilization process of SOEs because empirical evidence shows that the equitization of SOEs is best method than any other ways in the current context of Vietnam. Initially, the focus of equitization had been on smaller SOEs, but since 2004 the average size of SOE transformations has been rising. The eq-

---

115   Dictionary of Business and Management, Oxford University Press 2006, p327
116   Dictionary of Business and Management, Oxford University Press 2006, p 315

uitization process itself has undergone major improvements, with appraisals being conducted by outside evaluators and the sale of shares taking place at market price, via auctions at the Securities Trading Centers.

The restructuring of SOEs should maintain a priority over the next five years but it should involve increasingly large SOEs and lead to divestiture of a larger share of their capital. And it ultimately aims to create companies (both private and state) which can compete domestically and internationally. The Government should make efforts to steadily speed up the reorganization and renovation of state enterprises by diversifying the ownership to improve efficiency and competitiveness and to expand the scope of equitization of state enterprise. In addition, the Government needs to put pressure on SOEs to force them to be IPO under the road map. The World Bank suggests that the State should only hold controlling shares in corporations and joint stock companies (JSCs) in the most important fields or sectors which play key roles in the economy such as petroleum, telecommunication, fertilizer, and so on. The State also should hold 100 percent shares of non-equitizable businesses in the fields of national defence, securities[117], and pure public service provision[118]. The suggestions are in line with economic theory, that stresses that the state should for efficiency reasons, concentrate on the provision of public goods and let private actors be responsible for other products and industries.

The auction mechanism has been implemented to equitize SOEs, accelerate equitization pursuant to market principles, and SOEs equitization must parallel the public offering and listing in the stock market. There is a focus on equitizing large-scale businesses, entire corporations and attracting more capital through their valuation in the stock exchange. The Government should also be required to completely dispose of loss-making state enterprises in a suitable way and to reclaim land and water surface of no or limited use from institutions, organizations or SOEs or provide it to other investors.

The successful equitization process of SOEs requires the development of financial market and competition conditions. The development of a financial market (stock exchange) encourages SOEs to equitize their companies. In order to develop a financial market, Vietnam should prioritize to reform its banking system and set up a regulatory framework of stock market operation (see the previous section).

---

117   No permission of joining of private sector
118   Which private sector does not want to do or do inefficiently

The holding company model is to be used for large-scale corporations which can not be equitized as a whole. In their case, the chosen approach is to equitize their member businesses and transform the remaining ones into the Single-member (state) or limited companies of several state members; at the same time, transforming those corporations into the form of group companies held by a holding company. The management board is reorganized to represent the ownership in the corporation.

The State needs to separate its management functions from owners' management and from business administration functions. The key to accomplish this separation in practice is to gradually narrow and eliminate the function of representatives of line ministries, agencies and provincial city people's committees in the governance and management board of state enterprises. In most cases, the exercise of state ownership rights is to be transferred from line ministries, agencies and provincial governments to the recently created State Capital Investment Corporation (SCIC), a holding company under MOF with a mandate to allocate state capital so as to maximize its returns. Such transfers should increase the incentives to allocate resources or reliable information on the performance of the enterprises in its portfolio. In practice, larger enterprises will need to be listed and smaller ones fully divested or disbanded, so as keep the size of the portfolio manageable.

Some of the most difficult challenges ahead are related to the exercise of enterprise ownership rights on behalf of the government. The current strategy foresees the transfer of the state share of capital from line ministries and province to SCIC. But there seems to be less clarified in relation to the state share of capital in General Corporations 90/ 91[119]. If that share is to remain out of SCIC, other mechanisms will be needed to strengthen their corporation and increase transparency of their operations. Similarly, the experience of the economic groups reporting directly to the Prime Minister will have to be closely monitored and evaluated, so as to develop an appreciate regulatory framework over time.

Effectively running the SCIC for a profit will be technically demanding. Reallocating state capital to the most dynamic enterprises while fully divesting from the worst performers (and possibly liquidating some of them) should increase economic efficiency. But it requires knowing who the good performers really are. Share prices in stock market can help in this respect. One of the priorities of the SCIC should thus be the preparation of large companies for listing. However, for many smaller enterprises this will not be an option thus other performance assessment mechanisms will be needed.

---

119 General Corporations 90/91 were established by the Prime Minister under Decision No 90 and 91 in 1990 and 1991.

6.2.2.2 Promote Development of the Private Sector

In written responses to questions submitted by the Wall Street Journal, September 26th 2007 the Vietnamese PM said:

> "The Vietnamese government is now trying to reduce its role in directing the country's economy and bolster that of the private sector in driving the country forward. The private sector is an important part of the economy, and the government is paying particular attention to how to facilitate private businesses".

Developing a multi-stakeholder economy, one that allows space for the private sector to prosper, requires a level playing field for all enterprises regardless of their ownership. In this respect, the Vietnamese government should issue several policies that encourage the development of the private sector[120]. Vietnam should make the role clear as a driving force of the private sector and create favorable conditions for the development and investment of the private sector without limiting their scale, field and region. The government should eliminate all forms of discrimination, praise good producers and entrepreneurs, and encourage the development of large private enterprises, private economic groups and, enterprises owned by women. This recommendation is to minimize the scope of state monopoly and eliminate business privilege.

Vietnam needs to implement a series of reforms aimed at creating a more conducive business environment. They range from the introduction of new legal frameworks to the simplification of administrative procedures. Urgently the government has to issue the rules and regulations to implement the Unified Enterprise Law and the Common Investment Law (MPI). The Vietnamese government should encourage firms in developing e-commerce, using the internet to search market information advertisement and business opportunities, and continue improving supportive environment to provide favorable conditions for enterprises of different types to develop; focus on a streamlining of administrative procedures, time and cost for all domestic and foreign investors to participate in Vietnamese market; remove limitations of investment and labor scales; remove discrimination in terms of access to opportunities, resources and market information.

As previously mentioned, a major constraint facing private enterprises, especially private SMEs in Vietnam is a shortage of funds. Private SMEs lack access to long-term loans, an equity financing system and access to collateral. The strict collateral requirement by banks and the low incentives for SOCBs to lend to

---

120 Some signs of discrimination and unfair treatment that discourage these economic sectors from investing their capital in business and production development

SMEs, and on the other hand the unwillingness of private SMEs to deal with SOCBs, are serious restrictions. This generates a vicious cycle that prevents many SMEs from entering the formal credit sector, and forces them to rely on informal credit. Thus, local governments should establish credit guarantee companies to support SMEs' access to finance. Financial policies have an important impact on capital mobilization and development of enterprises. Vietnam's banking system reform aims to address the shortages and problems of availability of credit and capital for the economy. However, the impact of these reforms on the domestic private sector will continue to remain limited if the private sector continues to experience difficulties in securing access to land use rights, their potentially most valuable source of collateral. In this respect, Vietnam should also abolish limitations on capital contributions and mobilizations of foreign-invested enterprises and institutionalize the mechanism that allows foreign investors to use as collateral their property, including land and values of land-used rights in accessing loans from credit institutions who are permitted to operate in Vietnam.

The competition law and associated policies should be implemented consistently, to avoid situations of privilege or excessive market power. Similarly, the strategy to create major corporate groups around General Corporations under the PM should not inadvertently create an anti-competitive business environment. The possible combination of multiple commercial and financial interests under the SCIC could also facilitate practices compromising the objective of sound corporate governance, such as transfer pricing and affiliate party transactions.

Through business associations[121], the voice of the business sector should be strengthened. These organizations effectively represent and communicate the interests of the business community to authorities, as an input of policy making. Channels of policy dialogue between government and representatives of the business community should also be strengthened and formalized, so as to benefit from the direct knowledge and perspective of enterprises and to communicate policy orientations more clearly. However, in promoting the role of business associations must also be exercised not to allow them to become an anti-competitive industry Cartel. In addition to playing the role of a lobbying body, the business associations can be a standard setter for business practices and ethics for their industry. This useful function could turn into being a hurdle for potential new entrants if not properly watched from the perspective of competition policy.

---

121   In many countries business associations are playing a crucial role on identifying and advocating the needs and demands of the business community and relevant authorities (Harvie 2003, pp. 199)

The image of the private sector has to be improved in the country. The vital role of private companies for employment generation and modernization of Vietnam should be acknowledged and disseminated through the media and the educational system at all levels. Given the many years of discrimination against private enterprises and private entrepreneurs, stronger and more frequent endorsement of private business by the Vietnamese leadership is required as was the case in China. Regular public exhortations by top leaders of the Party and Government to the bureaucracy to provide support to the private sector under the laws would be extremely helpful. Stories in the media of domestic private business successes and visits by top leaders to successful private exporters would help to reinforce the value of private business in Vietnam's development. The Government should continue to praise successful young private entrepreneurs through awards and public media, by which the image of private businesses is improved and younger Vietnamese generations are encouraged to do business.

6.2.3 Strengthen Public Institution and Government Effectiveness

The pervasive corruption at all levels of government shows the weak public institution and inefficient governance. It reflects the lack and weakness of law system frameworks and its enforcement as well as a red-tape and cumbersome administration. This results in a less attractive business environment in Vietnam and deters domestic and foreign investors. In order to create a better business climate and improve competitiveness, some measures are proposed to fight corruption and strengthen public institution and governance.

6.2.3.1 Launch a Strong and Effective Anti-Corruption Campaign

Despite much talk, often involving grand principles, corruption is an under-researched topic in Vietnam. Country-specific information and data is still limited and scattered, whereas cross-country indicator are not reliable enough.

Deterring of corruption is a top priority because corruption represents a serious threat to development progress. It raises the cost of doing business and undermines the confidence of domestic and foreign investors, thus slowing economic growth and job creation. It drains the capacity of government and deprives vulnerable people of the right to basic services. Importantly, it compromises social values and norms and undermines public confidences in the institutions. But corruption cannot be eliminated overnight. International experiences suggest that there is no quick-fix recipe, and constant and concerted efforts are needed for lasting and sustainable impacts to be achieved (World Bank 2007a).

While far from being perfect, the legal framework to combat corruption is indeed being put in place. The capacity of government agencies to detect and investigate corruption does not seem to be a major limiting factor. However, it is unlikely that the passing of laws and a more active investigative stance will suffice. A combination of powerful forces makes it difficult to achieve a "critical mass" in the fight against corruption. With rapid growth creating temporary rents and leading to dramatic changes in the prices of assets such as land, the opportunities for unlawful gains are widespread. Meanwhile, the collective nature of corruption protects those engaged in wrongdoing. In these circumstances, it is almost impossible for any government agency to cover all fronts. Stakeholders outside government, including the media, civil society organizations and the public at large, have to be engaged.

The role and responsibility of the society in anti-corruption, such as social-political organizations, mass media, enterprises and industrial associations must be strengthened. The media has recently been encouraged by government to write more proactively about corruption and to publicize corruption cases as reported by the police and government agencies. The purpose is to raise awareness about the necessity of fighting corruption, to publicize laws and regulations, to help mobilize public support and hopefully convince potential perpetrators that the risks of detection and severe sanctions are becoming dissuasive enough. In doing so, the media has increasingly assumed a supervisory role over the administration. Journalists should be encouraged further to detect corruption cases on their own and they have indeed done so in a number of highly visible cases. But there is still a tension between policy and reality, due to lack of clarity on where the lines are drawn and fines applied to investigative work. Thus, the adoption of a more determined stance in the fight against corruption and the passing law on Anti-corruption may have encouraged the media of address the issue more openly. The number of articles dealing with corruption has increased by roughly 60 percent between 2005 and 2006, for both types of media, regardless of definition used.

The mechanism to conduct asset declaration of managers, civil servants in administration agencies and organizations, and to monitor the assets of civil servants, introduced by the Law on Anti-Corruption, needs to be implemented urgently. Success in this area will depend on the design of the mechanism. For example, it is clear that monitoring the assets of civil servants in Vietnam is beyond the capacity of any agency. Thus, there is a need to be selective, focusing on positions of responsibility. Also, the diagnostic study on corruption and the CCIA survey both indicate that some agencies are more exposed to corruption than others. Priority should be given to the monitoring of assets of civil servants in such agencies[122] as Tax, Customs, Land, Construction, and Police.

---

122   These agencies are considered to be the most corrupted following the diagnostic study of the CCIA

The responsibilities of heads of agencies in the fight against corruption should be clarified. Their aim is to prevent cases of bureaucracy, harassment and the abuse of power affecting citizens or enterprises. Heads of agencies should be instructed to establish all effective monitoring mechanism in relation to these problems and to introduce hotlines and other entry points to gather comments and complaints.

E-government needs to be implemented to increase efficiency, to boost transparency and to reduce corruption. IT centers have been established in almost all government organizations and much has been done in terms of equipment. Several provinces are setting up their own e-government interfaces. However, business process reengineering has not been given enough emphasis. Introducing IT systems such as e-businesses and citizens, in order to reduce clearance times, minimizes fraud and reduces the scope for abuse. Fragmentation and quality are issues of concern, partly due to the dispersed nature of IT development, which is being conducted by ministries and provinces with limited coordination.

The competence of officials at both local and government levels should be improved and trained. The clearest message from the survey is that business people are concerned about the corruption and lack of professionalism of officials[123]. To effectively tackle corruption, the government needs to make rigorous efforts in recruiting highly motivated and talented people, especially for crucial positions to the quality of business environment. In addition, a practical step forward would be to modernize the curriculum of the government and party schools at both central and local levels (Vu 2003). China and Singapore have successfully designed curricula that effectively enhance the competence and commitment of government officials and staff, who go through mid-career training programs in these schools. The main focus of their training is on economic development strategy, policy analysis, and teamwork.

Reporting by the media is a potentially effective deterrent of corruption. A more active media is bound to lead to increased reporting on corruption. Therefore, reliable mechanisms to collect feedback from citizens and enterprises are needed. Updating the diagnostic study on corruption, and conducting further research on more detained aspects of it, would certainly help. On a more regular basis, a technical agency like GSO should be entrusted to regularly gather the view of households and firms on their experience with corruption in various government agencies.

---

123 Including local and government officials

6.2.3.2 Strengthen Public Administration Reform

The government should continue to strongly implement an administration reform program. There is a clear continuity in the government strategy for public administration reform, with the year 2006 simply marking the beginning of the second phase of the PAR Master Program 2001-2010. Functional reorganization, aimed at focusing the government on a stewardship role, remains the core of the strategy. The scope and content of the state's economic management should be defined more clearly; adjust the functions of the government so that the government, ministries and central branches can concentrate on policy-making and exercise the monitoring and supervision of the implementation of state, plans, policies and legislation.

Focusing government activities on policy making has implication both on decentralization and on the direct provision of services by units with budget funding. In the former, regulations on central-local decentralization and decentralization among different levels of local authorities improve their powers and responsibilities, clearly defining the tasks for which local authorities should have full decision-making power, those that have been wholly decided by the central authorities. As for the latter, state administrative management needs to be separated clearly from management of public services.

Discussing about functional reorganization focuses on simplifying the structure of ministries (and departments at a local level). At present, there are twenty two ministries and they should be reduced further. On the other hand, there is a clear need for better policy coordination across ministries. The OOG (Office of Government) can only partially fulfill the coordination role, as its functions are to a large extent administration. The creation of an empowered technical body above current ministries, which coordinate in making policies among ministries, especially between the Ministry of Finance, State Bank of Vietnam and Ministry of Plan and Investment, could be considered.

In order to simplify administrative procedures, several proposals need to be implemented such as: the widening of the one-door model to different levels of government; decentralizing authority to the lowest level possible together with closing inspection and checking by superiors; preventing the trend of being too bureaucratic in public organizations; continuing to eliminate currently unnecessary business licenses and business conditions to facilitate for all investors.

In addition, it will also be necessary to introduce immediately common standards for IT application and e-government interfaces. The ability of IT systems across government to dialogue with each other will be essential to move in the direction of a single identification number for enterprises and a single social insurance number for individuals. ISO standards in quality management of administrative agencies and procedures should be adopted widely at all levels of government

Strengthening employment and pay policies remain a priority. The objective of the salary and wage policy in the upcoming time is to go against subsidy and privileges, eliminating egalitarianism; implement the principle of distribution on the basis of labor and outcome of production activity of each organization and business; separate salary and wage policy for administrative cadres and civil servants and public employees working in public service delivery organizations based on financial autonomy; and make sure publicity and transparency in income, controlling and legalizing salary-nature earnings so that salary will become the major source of income. An appropriate wage policy will contribute to the improvement of effective governance and reduce the pervasive corruption in Vietnam.

6.2.3.3 Improve Framework and Enforcement of Legal System

The commitment to build a transparent society under the rule of law has been implemented since the last amendment to the constitution in 2001. Therefore, four priorities have been emphasized to reach this objective (The SEDP 2001-2010). The first one is to reform the law-making process, by facilitating greater participation by citizens, enhancing the representative role of legislative bodies, and improving the skills of legal draftsmen. Second is to ensure the constitutional and legal norms, by monitoring administrative regulations and reducing the number of forms of legal documents. The third priority is to strengthen judicial reviews, building independent administrative tribunals to help ensure the citizens' rights to complain. And fourth is to empower district courts with increasing jurisprudence over civil and criminal cases gradually building a system of high courts for appellation and other specialized courts, on intellectual property issues, for instance.

The SEDP emphasizes the social dimensions of legal and judicial reform. Accordingly, Vietnam needs to reform the methodology and process of developing legislations and issuing regulations to ensure effective participation of the people in the development of legislations, effectively organizing the collection of people's comments before the issuance of legal normative documents, specifying that legal normative documents are to be made in mass media. Another objective is to protect people's assets; eliminate unsuitable and unnecessary legal regulations related to business community, citizens' living and working, confiscation or temporary seizure of citizens' property; competent authorities must compensate in money and kind to those people who have suffered from wrongful rules against the Law. Access to justice receives a special attention. Legal consultation service should be extended to the people, especially the poor, ethnic minority people living in remote and isolated areas. And there is explicit reference to the need to encourage social organizations, mass organizations and civil societies to engage in managing and monitoring some public fields.

Improving the process for formulating laws requires ensuring that policy debate precedes the actual writing of normative documents. It also requires the expansion and strengthening of standing technical committees and professionalizing the drafting process. A revision of the Law on Laws could support a more logical sequencing of policy formulation and drafting process. But practice could also change within the existing legal frameworks, as shown by the open and participatory process adopted by the National Assembly. Regardless of whether the Law on Laws is revised, the system of law promulgation needs to be refined to ensure uniformity between legal normative documents.

The judiciary system should be reorganized and needs to be strengthened to become more independent and effective. To gain these objectives, the judiciary system needs to be separated gradually from the existing administrative structure; the jurisprudence of district courts needs to be expanded; appeal courts and specialized courts needs to be established; and judicial support services (such as lawyers, judicial police, notary and other paralegal services) need to be upgraded.

An adequate framework should be provided for civil society organizations and their involvement in service delivery, as well as grassroots democracy. On the judiciary front, improving the quality of court decisions requires the creation of entry points to resolve complex legal issues, either through specialized judges appointed to help tribunals make decisions promptly or through key legal sector specialists who would provide the relevant information. Further professionalizing judges, especially those working at province and district levels, and upgrading their skills, are necessary for the public image of justice. The scope for the creation of specialized courts should be explored as well. Modernizing the administration of the courts could be necessary to promote their efficiency and ensure the independence of judges. Budget allocations for courts should be decided directly by the National Assembly and People's Councils, rather than by higher courts. In the long term, it would be necessary to re-examine and clarify the functions of the procuracy, which currently has both prosecutorial functions and the function of controlling the judiciary. Ultimately, the procuracy should be transformed into an institution in charge of public prosecution.

Publishing the decisions of the courts is essential to develop the capacity of the judiciary system to interpret the Law and ensure its enforcement. It would also improve the quality of the decision making process by the courts, and thus raise the credibility of courts in society. Allowing greater access by the media to court proceeding could be another way to promote transparency.

Ensuring access to justice, especially for the poor, could be partly accomplished through strengthening the legal and administrative means of defense attorneys. The funding and capacity of the legal aid system should be enhanced. Access to legal support should be simplified for marginalized and vulnerable groups, allowing NGOs to participate in this area.

In brief, Vietnam cannot do everything in order to enhance its national competitiveness at the same time. The top priorities need to be done are following as:

The first priority is to address the shortage of production resources supply (skilled labor, transport infrastructure and electricity supply). The Vietnamese government needs to reform higher education and develop vocational training, improve transport infrastructure and electricity supply, and develop financial market and reform the banking system.

The second priority is to develop an independent and vibrant domestic private sector. The Vietnamese government needs to strengthen state owned enterprise reform and promote development of the private sector, especially small medium sized enterprises (SMEs).

The last one is to strengthen public institution and government effectiveness. The Vietnamese government needs to launch a strong and effective anti-corruption campaign, strengthen public administration reform, and improve framework and enforcement of the legal system.

Chapter 7: Conclusion

National competitiveness is a nation's ability to create and sustain economic growth, and raises the standard of living of its citizens by improving national productivity in condition of a market economy. The competitiveness, productivity and economic growth have been a special interest of policy makers and business leaders as well as scholars and individuals in both developed and developing countries. Vietnam is not an exceptional case. The Vietnamese government has made efforts to maintain its competitiveness, growth and citizen's living standard. The intent of this study is to examine the competitiveness of Vietnam and its determinants. The study has addressed four questions as mentioned previously. The findings of this research are expected to contribute to the improvement of the national competitiveness in Vietnam in particular and the development process of the country in general. They are summarized in the following:

First of all, the determinants of Vietnam's competitiveness and growth were investigated. Relying on recent theories of competitiveness (basically Porter's diamond model), six determinants of national competitiveness were determined, including: production resources, technology development, market conditions, international business and economic activities, government role, and company's strategy and operation. These determinants were tested by using the model of multiple linear regression with hard and survey data. The results showed that the determinants influence Vietnam's competitiveness, productivity, and growth. They have played a significant role in improving Vietnam's national competitiveness and productivity. Particularly, production resources[124], have played the most important role in this process. This is very compatible with Porter's theoretical frameworks. Vietnam has stood in the initial stage of the development processes. Thus, its production resources have become a competitive advantage. It suggests that Vietnam should pay more attention to develop and deploy production resources efficiently.

Secondly, the analysis and assessment of Vietnam's national competitiveness were examined. Based on the six identified determinants of national competitiveness, Vietnam's competitiveness was analyzed and evaluated by using the combination of hard and survey data, including our conducted survey in Vietnam and the collected data from international organisations (such as World Economic Forum (WEF), World Bank (WB), Asia Development Bank (ADB), International Monetary Fund (IMF), and United Nations on Conference Trade and Development (UNCTAD) and domestic organizations (such as General Statistics Office of Vietnam (GSO), Vietnam Chamber of Commerce and Industry (VCCI) and so

---

124 Production resources consist of human resources, infrastructure resources, capital and natural resources.

on). This data was used to analyze Vietnam's competitiveness and compare Vietnam with some selected Asian countries[125]. The analysis and evaluation showed Vietnam's competitiveness progress as well as its productivity in the last decades, and the remaining weaknesses compared to the selected regional countries. Its weaknesses are: shortage of production resources supply, backward and slow technology development, poor competitive markets with a dominance of state-owned enterprises, less attractive investment environment and cumbersome customs procedures, inefficient operation of state-owned enterprises and small range of private firms, and weak public institution and inefficient government governance. These weaknesses have led Vietnam's competitiveness, productivity and economic growth to remain low, especially compared to that of China. In general, the national competitiveness in Vietnam remained low compared with that in the selected regional countries.

Thirdly, based on the above mentioned analyses and assessments, the emerging key issues of Vietnam's productivity and competitiveness were drawn out. They were namely: production resource shortage and low quality[126], outdated technology, bureaucratic and corrupt administration, and the slow reform of state owned enterprises (SOEs). These issues have challenged the productivity, competitiveness, and growth in Vietnam. Vietnam cannot sustain its competitiveness and growth in the long term unless it solves these crucial problems.

Finally, at the same time Vietnam cannot do everything to enhance it's competitiveness. In addition, national competitiveness is a large scope concept relating to many areas of an economy. Therefore, in this study framework, three groups of recomendations were proposed to solve the key issues, which are considered to be the most urgent[127], in order to enhance Vietnam's national competitiveness:

The first recommendation group is to address production resources shortage. In this group, a number of measures were proposed: firstly, Vietnam needs to reform higher education and develop vocational training such as the encouragement of the private sector's participation, the autonomy and accountability of publicly-funded institutions, the establishment partnership between the government, industry, community and learners, and so on; Secondly, the transport infrastructure and electricity supply need to be strengthened. To do so, the Vietnamese government should call for investment of the private sector, reform the Ministry of Transport's

---

125 Some selected Asian countries are China, Thailand, Malaysia, The Philippines, Indonesia and Singapore.

126 Production resources shortage includes: lack of skilled labor force, poor infrastructures (especially transport and electricity), and undeveloped financial market.

127 The most urgent issues are based on our analysis and conducted survey.

State Owned Enterprises and encourage the establishment of new IPPs; Finally, the Vietnamese government should facilitate to develop the financial markets and reform the banking system such as opening the financial sector further and increasing foreign competition, equitizing the SOCBs, and transforming SBV into a modern central bank.

The second recommendation group is to develop an independent and vibrant domestic private sector. In this respect, the Vietnamese government should strengthen the reform of state-owned enterprises and promote the development of the private sector, especially small and medium sized enterprises (SMEs). In regard to SOEs reform, the government needs to speed up the equitization process and reorganization of the unequitized SOEs, separate its administrative and business administration functions, and transfer state ownership right into the SCIC. The state should only hold the controlling shares in the most important fields of the economy.

In order to promote development of the private sector, the Vietnamese government needs to recognize the private sector as the driving force of the economy and create favorable conditions for the development and investment of the private sector without limiting their scale, field, and region. Vietnam should strictly eliminate all forms of discrimination, praise good producers and entrepreneurs, and encourage the development of large private enterprises, private economic groups, and enterprises owned by women. The local governments should establish credit guarantee companies to support SMEs' access to finance which is one of the top concerns.

The last recommendation group is to strengthen public institution and government effectiveness. In this regard, the Vietnamese government should launch a strong and effective anti-corruption campaign, strengthen public administration reform, and improve framework and enforcement of the legal system.

In order to fight corruption effectively, the government encourages all stakeholders (social-political organizations, mass media, enterprises, industrial associations, and individuals) to participate in this campaign. The purpose is to raise awareness about the necessity of fighting corruption, to publicize laws and regulations, and to help mobilize public support. Journalists should be encouraged further to detect corruption cases on their own and have indeed done so in a number of highly visible cases. Conducting the asset declaration of managers, civil servants as well as monitoring their assets in administration agencies and organizations needs to be implemented urgently. Initially, priority should be given to the monitoring of assets of civil servants in such bodies[128] as Tax, Customs, Land, Construction, and Police. E-government needs to be implemented as soon as possible to increase efficiency and to boost transparency. Simultaneously, the competence of local and government officials must be improved and trained. To effectively tackle corruption, the government needs to make rigorous efforts in recruiting highly motivated and talented people, especially for crucial positions to the quality of the business environment.

The government should continue to strongly implement the public administration reform program to strengthen its governance effectiveness and to simplify administrative procedures. Some measures need to be implemented such as: the widening of the one-door model to different levels of government; decentralizing authority to the lowest level possible together with closing inspection and checking by superiors; preventing the trend of being too bureaucratic in public organizations; continuing to eliminate currently unnecessary business licenses and business conditions to facilitate for all investors.

Improving the legal system's framework and enforcement is a measure of strengthening the public institution and fighting corruption. This leads to the building of a transparent society under the rule of law. In doing so, four priorities need to be emphasized. The first one is to reform the law-making process, by facilitating greater participation by citizens, enhancing the representative role of legislative bodies, and improving the skills of legal draftsmen. Second is to ensure the constitutional and legal norms, by monitoring administrative regulations and reducing the number of forms of legal documents. The third priority is to strengthen judicial reviews, building independent administrative tribunals to help ensure the citizens' rights to complain. And fourth is to empower district courts with increasing jurisprudence over civil and criminal cases gradually building a system of high courts for appellation and other specialized courts, on intellectual property issues, for instance.

In summation, the success of the improvement of the national competitiveness and sustained growth in Vietnam depends on how Vietnam will implement the above proposals. Vietnam cannot maintain it's competitiveness and sustain economic growth in the long run unless it solves the key issues. This research provides a comprehensive analysis and proposals to help the Government to make policies to forward enhancing the competitiveness, productivity, and citizens' living standard in Vietnam in the long term.

---

128   These agencies are considered to be the most corrupted following the diagnostic study of the CCIA

Appendices

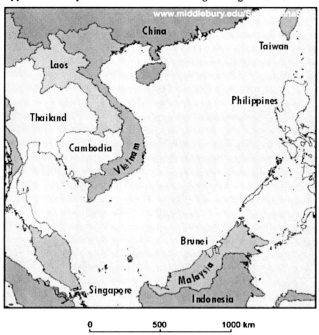

Vietnam is located ideally along the eastern edge of the Indochinese Sea in Southeast Asia and between China and Asia Southeast Association of Nations (ASEAN) countries. The country shares its border with the People's Republic of China in the North, the Lao People's Democratic Public in the Northwest and Cambodia in the Southwest. Vietnam has a long coastline of 3,444 kilometers (excludes islands) and possesses 3,000 islands and a privileged economic area of over 1,000,000 squared kilometers. The country area is 329,560 squared kilometers and the population is 84 million inhabitants in 2006[129]. Vietnam's unification in the year 1975 ended long lasting wars with China, France, Japan and the United State of America. The centrally planed economy was existed in Vietnam during the period 1975-1986.

---

129   CIA- The World Factbook-Vietnam, 2006

Appendix 2: Benchmarking: Competitiveness indices

Table A 2.1

Indices			Production Resources - PR				
Sub-indices			Human Resources (1/4)			Infrastructure Resources (1/4)	
Indicators	GDP per capita, US dollar (PPP) (1/16)	Total population (million unit) (1/16)	Enrollment rate (%), primary (1/16)	Enrollment rate (%), secondary (1/16)	Enrollment rate (%), tertiary, total (1/16)	Telephone subscriber per 100 people (1/8)	Electricity, kWh per head (1/8)
1990	956,922	66,02	106,9	32,22	1,98	0,06	133
1991	1028,82	67,24	104,39	31,32	1,53	0,1	138
1992	1123,87	68,45	108,56	31,79	1,94	0,28	143
1993	1221,39	69,64	110,79	35,49	2,21	0,35	156
1994	1334,92	70,82	112,81	40,54	2,83	0,67	179
1995	1467,92	72,00	114,06	47,04	4,09	1,03	204
1996	1609,5	73,16	114,98	51,96	6,86	1,59	232
1997	1742,27	74,31	113,51	53,75	7,89	2,14	259
1998	1795,47	75,46	112,3	57,35	8,75	2,69	287
1999	1869,7	76,60	108,33	61,5	10,66	3,13	308
2000	1988,54	77,64	106,58	64,59	9,47	4,23	344
2001	2109,52	78,69	104,46	66,57	9,52	5,47	390
2002	2238,05	79,73	102,24	69,11	9,79	6,98	450

Year							
2003	2380,81	80,90	99,94	71,8	10,16	9,07	501
2004	2570	82,03	97,97	74,35	10,16	12,55	563
2005	2782,2	83,12	98,65	76,25	11,02	19	642

Note: Weights of individual indicator and sub-indices are in parentheses.

Original indicators and data sources:

GDP per capita, US dollar, purchasing power parity (PPP), IMF, World Economic Outlook Database, Sep. 2005

Total population (million unit), ADB, Key Indicators 2006

Gross enrollment rate as % of total, primary school, World Bank, Edstats data query, Oct. 2006 and Ministry of Education and training (MOET), Vietnam

Gross enrollment rate as % of total, secondary school, World Bank, Edstats data query, Oct. 2006 and MOET, Vietnam

Gross enrollment rate as % of total, secondary school, World Bank, Edstats data query, Oct. 2006 and MOET, Vietnam

Telephone subscriber (land and cell) per 100 inhabitants, General Statistics Office (GSO), Vietnam, Statistical Yearbook 2000, 2006 and available at www.gso.org.vn

Electricity production per head, kWh, Asia Development Bank (ADB), Key indicators 2006 and own calculation of author

Table A 2.2

Indices	Production Resources – PR			Technology Development - TD			Market Conditions	International Business	
Sub-indices	Capital Resources (1/4)		Natural Resources (1/4)					International Trade (1/2)	
Indicators	Capital formation (1/8)	National savings as % of GDP (1/8)	Mining, quarring as % of GDP (1/4)	Import mean of production (1/3)	Computers/ 1000 people (1/3)	Internet users/ 1000 (1/3)	Private firms[130] as % of total (1)	Openness of econ- omy (1/2)	Exports (US$ mil- lions) (1/4)
1990	12,6	-3,5	6,8	17	0,07	0	5,15	0,48	2404
1991	15,1	4,8	7,2	16,7	0,1	0	8,03	0,50	2087
1992	17,6	10,4	7,1	18,9	0,14	0	13,35	0,52	2581
1993	24,3	13,0	7,35	21,7	0,28	0,01	23,04	0,52	2985
1994	25,5	14,6	7,57	23,5	0,7	0,02	35,37	0,61	4054
1995	27,1	17,1	8,96	25,7	1,37	0,05	44,04	0,66	5449
1996	28,1	15,6	10,94	27,6	2,69	0,1	51,03	0,75	7256
1997	28,3	18,3	11,06	30,3	3,98	0,4	58,45	0,77	9185
1998	29,1	19,6	11,38	30,6	5,23	1,3	65,7	0,77	9360
1999	27,6	23,2	13,02	29,9	6,45	12,9	70,05	0,81	11541
2000	29,6	25,7	14,36	30,6	7,64	25,5	86,39	0,97	14483

130 Including foreign investment firms

Year								
2001	31,2	27,5	14,2	30,5	8,81	127	89,64	0,96	15029
2002	33,2	27,0	13,63	29,8	9,95	186,5	91,47	1,04	16706
2003	35,4	25,8	14,54	31,6	11,24	430,4	93,27	1,15	20149
2004	35,5	27,0	15,29	28,8	12,71	714,4	94,99	1,33	26485
2005	35,4	27,50	15,58	26,2	14,1	857,3	96,48	1,46	32447

Note: Gross capital formation as a percentage of GDP at current prices, Asia Development Bank (ADB), Key indicators 2006

Gross national saving as a percentage of GDP at current prices, Asia Development Bank (ADB), Key indicators 2006 and Ministry of Finance, Vietnam

Mining, quarring, forestry and fishing as a percentage of GDP, General Statistics Office (GSO), Vietnam, Statistical Yearbook 2006; ADB and own calculation of author

Import mean of production as a percentage of total imports, General Statistics Office (GSO), Vietnam, Statistical Yearbook 2006 and own calculation of author

Number of personal computers per 1000 inhabitants, World Bank, Edstats data query, Oct. 2006 and Ministry of Science and Technology

Internet users per 1.000 inhabitants, World Bank, Edstats data query; Ministry of Science and Technology, Vietnam; VDC Company, Vietnam

Number of private own enterprises as a percentage of total enterprises, General Statistics Office (GSO), Vietnam, Statistical Yearbook 2000 and 2006; VCCI and www.vneconomy.vn

Openness of economy = Total Exports plus total Imports divided total GDP; Exports and Imports: Asia Development Bank (ADB), Key indicators 2006; GDP (current price): IMF, World Economic Outlook data, 2005

Total exports (US dollar million), ADB, Key Indicators 2007

Table A 2.3

Indices	and Economic Activities - IBEAs		Government Role - GR				Company's Strategy and Operation - CSO
Sub-indices	Inward FDI performance (1/2)		Government Policy (1/2)		Public Institution (1/2)		
Indicators	Inward FDI stock (US dollar million) (1/4)	Inward FDI stock as % of GDP (1/4)	Government revenue % GDP (1/4)	Government expenditure % GDP (1/4)	Taxes (Bn Dong) (1/4)	Total tax as % of the budget (1/4)	Contributions of private firms[131] as % of total GDP (1)
1990	1 650	25,49	14,7	21,9	4810	78,17	5,35
1991	2 025	26,49	13,1	15,7	10025	86,12	6,50
1992	2 499	25,32	18,3	21,5	18637	71,9	7,94
1993	3 425	25,98	21,0	26,4	27874	80,35	10,70
1994	5 370	32,98	22,0	25,0	35825	76,92	12,10
1995	7 150	34,48	21,9	23,8	43667	79,37	13,74
1996	10 065	40,82	21,7	23,1	52311	82,97	14,79
1997	13 282	49,48	20,0	22,6	55534	82,69	16,29
1998	15 647	57,51	19,6	20,3	59618	82,56	17,27
1999	18 183	63,39	19,0	21,2	66829	83,5	19,50
2000	20 596	66,07	20,1	23,4	79497	82,49	20,58

131 Which include foreign investment firms, but not households and collectives

2001	23 022	70,43	21,2	24,8	91688	82,64	21,71
2002	26 055	74,31	22,3	25,0	106154	84,69	22,06
2003	27 505	70,44	25,3	29,1	127947	85,36	22,70
2004	29 115	63,54	27,4	31,0	155579	83,13	23,62
2005	31 135	61,17	25,6	28,3	188119	80,27	24,88

Note: Inward foreign direct investment (FDI) stock by host country, UNCTAD, World Investment Report 2005

Inward foreign direct investment stock as % of GDP, UNCTAD, World Investment Report 2005

Government revenue as a percentage of GDP, Asia Development Bank (ADB), Key indicators 2007

Government expenditure as a percentage of GDP, Asia Development Bank (ADB), Key indicators 2007

Taxes (Bn Dong), Key Indicator 2007, Asian Development Bank (ADB), available at http://www.adb.org/Documents/Books/Key_Indicators/2007/pdf/Key-Indicators-2007.pdf.

Total tax as % of the budget revenue, GSO, Vietnam, Statistical Yearbook 2000 and 2006; Ministry of Finance, Vietnam.

Contributions of private own enterprises as a percentage of GDP, GSO, Statistical Yearbook 2000, 2006; www.vneconomy.vn. VCCI and own calculation of author

Appendix 3: Standardised competitiveness indicators

Table A 3.1

| Indices | Production Resources - PR | | | | | | |
| Sub-indices | Human Resources (1/4) | | | | | Infrastructure Resources (1/4) | |
Indicators	GDP per capita, US dollar (PPP)	Total population (million unit) (1/16)	Enrollment rate (%), primary (1/16)	Enrollment rate (%), secondary (1/16)	Enrollment rate (%), tertiary, total (1/16)	Telephone subscriber per 100 people (1/8)	Electricity, kWh per head (1/8)
1990	-1,44666	-1,6146	-0,06761	-1,36579	-1,31271	-0,80511	-1,08944
1991	-1,31774	-1,38766	-0,51493	-1,42196	-1,43517	-0,79758	-1,05583
1992	-1,14732	-1,16405	0,22823	-1,39263	-1,32359	-0,76367	-1,02471
1993	-0,97245	-0,94291	0,62565	-1,16169	-1,25012	-0,75048	-0,94754
1994	-0,76889	-0,72442	0,98564	-0,84648	-1,08139	-0,6902	-0,80178
1995	-0,53042	-0,50761	1,20841	-0,44078	-0,7385	-0,62238	-0,64954
1996	-0,27657	-0,29261	1,37237	-0,13369	0,01531	-0,51688	-0,47427
1997	-0,03851	-0,07965	1,11039	-0,02196	0,29561	-0,41327	-0,30467
1998	0,05689	0,13317	0,89475	0,20274	0,52964	-0,30966	-0,12792
1999	0,18998	0,34432	0,18724	0,46176	1,04942	-0,22677	0,00023
2000	0,40308	0,53664	-0,12464	0,65463	0,72558	-0,01955	0,22168
2001	0,61999	0,73112	-0,50246	0,77822	0,73918	0,21405	0,50885
2002	0,85044	0,92398	-0,89809	0,93675	0,81266	0,49852	0,88427

2003	1,10641	1,14153	-1,30799	1,10465	0,91335	0,89224	1,19845
2004	1,44565	1,35063	-1,65907	1,26382	0,91335	1,54782	1,58682
2005	1,82613	1,55213	-1,53789	1,38241	1,14739	2,76291	2,0754

Note: Weights of individual indicator and sub-indices are in parentheses.

Original indicators and data sources:

GDP per capita, US dollar, purchasing power parity (PPP), IMF, World Economic Outlook Database, Sep. 2005

Total population (million unit), ADB, Key Indicators 2006

Gross enrollment rate as % of total, primary school, World Bank, Edstats data query, Oct. 2006 and Ministry of Education and training (MOET), Vietnam

Gross enrollment rate as % of total, secondary school, World Bank, Edstats data query, Oct. 2006 and MOET, Vietnam

Gross enrollment rate as % of total, secondary school, World Bank, Edstats data query, Oct. 2006 and MOET, Vietnam

Telephone subscriber (land and cell) per 100 inhabitants, General Statistics Office (GSO), Vietnam, Statistical Yearbook 2000, 2006 and available at *www.gso.org.vn*

Electricity production per head, kWh, Asia Development Bank (ADB), Key indicators 2006 and own calculation of author

Table A 3.2

Indices	Production Resources - PR			Technology Development - TD			Market Conditions	International Business	
								International Trade (1/2)	
Sub-indices	Capital Resources (1/4)		Natural Resources (1/4)						
Indicators	Capital formation (1/8)	National savings as % of GDP (1/8)	Mining, quarring as % of GDP (1/4)	Import mean of production (1/3)	Computers/ 1000 people (1/3)	Internet users/ 1000 (1/3)	Private firms[132] as % of total (1)	Openness of economy (1/2)	Exports (US$ millions) (1/4)
1990	-2,09826	-2,40972	-1,3406	-1,79635	-1,0764	-0,53518	-1,59123	-1,17311	-0,99214
1991	-1,73977	-1,50003	-1,21835	-1,85484	-1,07027	-0,53518	-1,50435	-1,10631	-1,02715
1992	-1,37193	-0,88352	-1,24891	-1,42586	-1,0621	-0,53518	-1,34388	-1,03951	-0,97263
1993	-0,42503	-0,59414	-1,1725	-0,87989	-1,03351	-0,53514	-1,0516	-1,03951	-0,92798
1994	-0,25033	-0,41957	-1,10526	-0,52891	-0,94775	-0,53511	-0,67968	-0,73893	-0,80997
1995	-0,01152	-0,13719	-0,68043	-0,09993	-0,81093	-0,535	-0,41816	-0,57194	-0,65586
1996	0,12571	-0,30102	-0,07526	0,27055	-0,54139	-0,53482	-0,20732	-0,27136	-0,45631
1997	0,15386	-0,00904	-0,03859	0,79702	-0,27797	-0,53373	0,0165	-0,20456	-0,24324
1998	0,26128	0,14323	0,05922	0,85552	-0,02272	-0,53046	0,23518	-0,20456	-0,2239
1999	0,05799	0,53973	0,56046	0,71903	0,22641	-0,48829	0,36639	-0,07097	0,01698
2000	0,34142	0,81122	0,97002	0,85552	0,46941	-0,4425	0,85927	0,4634	0,34182

132 Including foreign investment firms

2001	0,56513	1,00854	0,92112	0,83602	0,70832	-0,07358	0,9573	0,43	0,40219
2002	0,85824	0,96121	0,7469	0,69953	0,94111	0,14269	1,0125	0,69718	0,58739
2003	1,17663	0,82678	1,02503	1,05051	1,20453	1,02919	1,06679	1,06456	0,96764
2004	1,17956	0,95251	1,25426	0,50454	1,50471	2,06144	1,11867	1,66573	1,66736
2005	1,17702	1,01102	1,3429	-0,00244	1,78855	2,58084	1,16362	2,0999	2,32581

Note: Gross capital formation as a percentage of GDP at current prices, Asia Development Bank (ADB), Key indicators 2006

Gross national saving as a percentage of GDP at current prices, Asia Development Bank (ADB), Key indicators 2006 and Ministry of Finance, Vietnam

Mining, quarring, forestry and fishing as a percentage of GDP, General Statistics Office (GSO), Vietnam, Statistical Yearbook 2006; ADB and own calculation of author

Import mean of production as a percentage of total imports, General Statistics Office (GSO), Vietnam, Statistical Yearbook 2006 and own calculation of author

Number of personal computers per 1000 inhabitants, World Bank, Edstats data query, Oct. 2006 and Ministry of Science and Technology

Internet users per 1.000 inhabitants, World Bank, Edstats data query; Ministry of Science and Technology, Vietnam; VDC Company, Vietnam

Number of private own enterprises as a percentage of total enterprises, General Statistics Office (GSO), Vietnam, Statistical Yearbook 2000 and 2006; VCCI and *www.vneconomy.vn*

Openness of economy = Total Exports plus total Imports divided total GDP; Exports and Imports: Asia Development Bank (ADB), Key indicators 2006; GDP (current price): IMF, World Economic Outlook data, 2005

Total exports (US dollar million), ADB, Key Indicators 2007

Table A 3.3

Indices	and Economic Activities - IBEAs		Government Role - GR				Company's Strategy and Operation - CSO
Sub-indices	Inward FDI performance (1/2)		Government Policy (1/2)		Public Institution (1/2)		
Indicators	FDI stock (US dollar million) (1/4)	Inward FDI stock as % of GDP (1/4)	Government revenue % GDP (1/4)	Government expenditure % GDP (1/4)	Taxes (Bn Dong) (1/4)	Total tax as % of the budget (1/4)	Contributions of private firms[133] as % of total GDP (1)
1990	-1,24876	-1,27916	-1,68397	-0,55413	-1,24786	-0,9165	-1,71549
1991	-1,21311	-1,22505	-2,10013	-2,21495	-1,14843	1,30786	-1,53422
1992	-1,16809	-1,28805	-0,70247	-0,6739	-0,98422	-2,67081	-1,30724
1993	-1,0801	-1,25248	0,05277	0,65991	-0,8081	-0,30655	-0,87218
1994	-0,89538	-0,8758	0,33358	0,2883	-0,65651	-1,26625	-0,6515
1995	-0,72625	-0,79501	0,29265	-0,02596	-0,50699	-0,58075	-0,39299
1996	-0,44931	-0,45362	0,22999	-0,22361	-0,34217	0,42651	-0,22748
1997	-0,14378	0,01254	-0,22073	-0,37476	-0,28072	0,34817	0,00897
1998	0,08091	0,44479	-0,32903	-0,97522	-0,20285	0,3118	0,16344
1999	0,32184	0,76178	-0,48846	-0,73995	-0,06536	0,5748	0,51495
2000	0,55101	0,90596	-0,20007	-0,15925	0,17617	0,29221	0,68519

133 Which include foreign investment firms, but not households and collectives.

2001	0,78146	1,14099	0,09506	0,23486	0,40862	0,33418	0,86331
2002	1,06964	1,34955	0,40456	0,28184	0,68443	0,90776	0,91848
2003	1,20738	1,14147	1,22082	1,39437	1,09995	1,09522	1,01937
2004	1,36033	0,76998	1,7907	1,90835	1,6268	0,47128	1,16438
2005	1,55222	0,64212	1,30474	1,17409	2,24723	-0,32893	1,363

Note: Inward foreign direct investment (FDI) stock by host country, UNCTAD, World Investment Report 2005
Inward foreign direct investment stock as % of GDP, UNCTAD, World Investment Report 2005
Government revenue as a percentage of GDP, Asia Development Bank (ADB), Key indicators 2007
Government expenditure as a percentage of GDP, Asia Development Bank (ADB), Key indicators 2007
Taxes (Bn Dong), Key Indicator 2007, Asian Development Bank (ADB), available at *http://www.adb.org/Documents/Books/Key_Indicators/2007/pdf/Key-Indicators-2007.pdf*.
Total tax as % of the budget revenue, GSO, Vietnam, Statistical Yearbook 2000 and 2006; Ministry of Finance, Vietnam.
Contributions of private own enterprises as a percentage of GDP, GSO, Statistical Yearbook 2000, 2006; *www.vneconomy.vn*. VCCI and own calculation of author

Appendix 4: The Tables of the Regression Results

Table A 4. 1 Model Summary

Model	R	R Square	Adjusted R Square	Std. Error of the Estimate	Change Statistics				
					R Square Change	F Change	df 1	df 2	Sig. F Change
1	,999 (a)	,999	,998	,0498	,999	1007, 770	6	9	,000
2	,999 (b)	,999	,998	,0474	,000	,065	1	9	,804
3	,999 (c)	,998	,998	,0472	,000	,897	1	10	,366

a Predictors: (Constant), CSO, GR, IBEA, TD, MC, PR
b Predictors: (Constant), GR, IBEA, TD, MC, PR
c Predictors: (Constant), IBEA, TD, MC, PR

Table A 4. 2 Coefficients(a)

Model		Unstandardized Coefficients		Standardized Coefficients	t	Sig.
		B	Std. Error	Beta		
1	(Constant)	,000	,012		,000	1,000
	PR	,827	,257	,706	3,221	,010
	TD	,255	,179	,218	1,427	,187
	MC	-,267	,139	-,267	-1,914	,088
	IBEA	,376	,115	,362	3,273	,010
	GR	,050	,054	,040	,935	,374
	CSO	-,059	,230	-,059	-,256	,804
2	(Constant)	,000	,012		,000	1,000
	PR	,776	,155	,663	5,003	,001
	TD	,265	,166	,226	1,595	,142
	MC	-,294	,086	-,294	-3,419	,007
	IBEA	,381	,107	,368	3,553	,005
	GR	,047	,050	,037	,947	,366
3	(Constant)	,000	,012		,000	1,000
	PR	,762	,154	,651	4,960	,000
	TD	,366	,127	,312	2,881	,015
	MC	-,286	,085	-,286	-3,360	,006
	IBEA	,332	,093	,320	3,555	,005

a Dependent Variable: GDPPC

218

Table A 4. 3 Model Summary

Model	R	R Squa-re	Adjus-ted R Square	Std. Error of the Es-tim-ate	Change Statistics				
					R Square Change	F Chan-ge	df 1	df 2	Sig. F Chan ge
4	,757 (a)	,573	,556	,530	,573	32,894	6	147	,000
5	,755 (b)	,570	,555	,531	-,004	1,211	1	147	,273
6	,750 (c)	,562	,551	,533	-,007	2,450	1	148	,120

a Predictors: (Constant), GP, IBEA, MC, TD, CSO, PR
b Predictors: (Constant), GP, IBEA, MC, CSO, PR
c Predictors: (Constant), GP, MC, CSO, PR

Table A 4. 4 Coefficients(a)

Model		Unstandardized Co-efficients		Standardized Coefficients	t	Sig.
		B	Std. Error	Beta		
4	(Constant)	-,689	,320		-2,153	,033
	PR	,471	,109	,336	4,323	,000
	TD	,073	,067	,082	1,100	,273
	MC	,171	,070	,154	2,424	,017
	IBEA	,112	,075	,089	1,493	,137
	CSO	,228	,089	,196	2,566	,011
	GP	,144	,070	,152	2,058	,041
5	(Constant)	-,729	,318		-2,293	,023
	PR	,526	,097	,375	5,452	,000
	MC	,174	,070	,157	2,470	,015
	IBEA	,117	,075	,093	1,565	,120
	CSO	,237	,089	,203	2,669	,008
	GP	,159	,069	,168	2,317	,022
6	(Constant)	-,460	,269		-1,711	,089
	PR	,543	,096	,387	5,634	,000
	MC	,174	,071	,157	2,453	,015
	CSO	,282	,084	,242	3,349	,001
	GP	,149	,069	,158	2,167	,032

a Dependent Variable: VNC

Table A 4. 5 Model Summary, hard data, time series 1990-2005

Model	R	R Square	Adjusted R Square	Std. Error of the Estimate	Change Statistics				
					R Square Change	F Change	df 1	df 2	Sig. F Change
7	,999 (a)	,998	,997	,0501	,998	1492,723	4	11	,000

a Predictors: (Constant), NR, IR, CR, HR

Table A 4. 6 Coefficients (a)

Model		Unstandardized Coefficients		Standardized Coefficients	t	Sig.
		B	Std. Error	Beta		
7	(Constant)	,000	,013		,000	1,000
	HR	,219	,074	,140	2,970	,013
	IR	,524	,032	,519	16,428	,000
	CR	,208	,042	,205	4,980	,000
	NR	,197	,050	,197	3,929	,002

a Dependent Variable: GDPPC

Table A 4. 7 Model Summary

Model	R	R Square	Adjusted R Square	Std. Error of the Estimate	Change Statistics				
					R Square Change	F Change	df 1	df 2	Sig. F Change
8	,660 (a)	,435	,420	,606	,435	28,690	4	149	,000

a Predictors: (Constant), NR, HR, CR, QI

Table A 4. 8 Coefficients(a)

Model		Unstandardized Coefficients		Standardized Coefficients	t	Sig.
		B	Std. Error	Beta		
8	(Constant)	,077	,302		,253	,801
	HR	,192	,076	,181	2,509	,013
	QI	,263	,082	,257	3,197	,002
	CR	,204	,074	,213	2,761	,006
	NR	,263	,061	,291	4,349	,000

a Dependent Variable: VNC

Appendix 5
Survey Questionnaire
Vietnam national competitiveness

Introduction to survey:

Dear Madam or Sir,

My name is Hien Phuc Nguyen, a teaching assistant at Hanoi National Economics University and a PhD candidate in Economic Policy at Leipzig University. A supporting part of my research toward my PhD dissertation is analyzing the determinants of national competitiveness of Vietnam. Apart from WEF data and data from other organizations, I designed and conducted this survey to further analyze the drivers leading Vietnam's national competitiveness.

The survey is structured around the major dimensions of national competitiveness, which are depicted in the following areas: Production Resources, Technology, Market Condition, International Business and Economic Activities, Company's Strategy and Operation, Government Role, Priorities for the Government in the next five years, and Top Priorities for the Company.

The survey will be conducted for a sample of about 300 respondents from business leaders, scholars, and local and government officials across the country. Their responses will be aggregated to produce further analysis featuring the emerging issues and perspective of Vietnam's national competitiveness in the context of international economic integration.

The questionnaire consists of 44 questions and it takes approximately 30 minutes to answer. The sincerity and accuracy of your answers are critical to the success of my survey and research. I greatly appreciate your time and cooperation. Please let me know if you would like to have a copy of my analysis report on the result of the survey, which I plan to finish in January 2007. Be assured that all answers will be treated as confidential.

For any question about this study, please do not hesitate to contact me at my email: hien@wifa.uni-leipzig.de

Yours sincerely,

Nguyen Phuc Hien

Instructions for the following sections of this questionnaire

Please indicate your agreement or disargeement with each of the following statements. Circle the appropriate number, which best expresses your opinion (based on your own experience) about status of your company (located in Vietnam) and Vietnam economy.

1 means " disagree strongly"   5 means " agree somewhat"
2 means " disagree generally"   6 means "agree generally"
3 means " disagree somewhat"   7 means "agree strongly"
4 means " neither disagree nor agree"

You should circle "NI" in answering a question only when the question is irrelevant in the context of your business.

Part 1: Determinants of Vietnam National Competitiveness.

Production Resources

Human Resources

1	The education system meets the needs of a competitive economy	1 2 3 4 5 6 7 NI
2	The overall quality of the education system(grade 1-12) is as high as that of the regional leaders*	1 2 3 4 5 6 7 NI
3	The most talented people remain in Vietnam	1 2 3 4 5 6 7 NI
4	The labor force's health is among the best in the region**	1 2 3 4 5 6 7 NI

Quality of the Infrastructure.

5	The overall quality of general infrastructure is among the best in the region	1 2 3 4 5 6 7 NI
6	The quality of land and ship transportation, in general, is among the best in the region	1 2 3 4 5 6 7 NI
7	The quality of the telephone system (landline and cell), in general, is among the most reliable	1 2 3 4 5 6 7 NI

---

* The leader of the region is Singapore.
** Association of South East Asia Nations (ASEAN) includes 11 member nations (Singapore, Malaysia, Thailand, Brunei Darussalam, The Philipines, Indonesia, Vietnam, Myanmar, Cambodia, Laos and East Timore).

	in the region	
8	The quality of electricity supply, in general, is as highly reliable as that of the regional leaders	1 2 3 4 5 6 7 NI

Capital Resources

9	The level of sophistication of financial markets is generally as high as that of the regional leaders	1 2 3 4 5 6 7 NI
10	The banking system is generally healthy with sound balance sheets like that of the regional leaders	1 2 3 4 5 6 7 NI
11	Banks are responsive to firm's demand	1 2 3 4 5 6 7 NI
12	Obtaining a bank loan in Vietnam with a good plan is the easiest in the region	1 2 3 4 5 6 7 NI

Natural Resources

13	Vietnam's resources are the richest in the region	1 2 3 4 5 6 7 NI
14	Vietnam's location is the greatest resource advantage in the region	1 2 3 4 5 6 7 NI
15	Vietnam's land is the greatest resource advantage in the region	1 2 3 4 5 6 7 NI
16	Vietnam's marine is the greatest resource advantage in the region	1 2 3 4 5 6 7 NI

Technology

17	Vietnam's position in technology, in general, ranks among the regional leaders	1 2 3 4 5 6 7 NI
18	Scientific research institutions are truly region-class	1 2 3 4 5 6 7 NI
19	Firms in Vietnam are willing to absorb new technologies like that of the regional leaders	1 2 3 4 5 6 7 NI
20	Information and communication technology(ICT) development ranks among the regional leaders	1 2 3 4 5 6 7 NI

Market Condition .

21	The competition in Vietnam, in general, is as	1 2 3 4 5 6 7 NI

	fair and healthy as that of the regional leaders	
22	The demand in Vietnam is actively seeking the latest products, technologies and processes like that of the regional leaders	1 2 3 4 5 6 7 NI
23	Anti-trust policy in Vietnam is the most effective and promotes competition in the region	1 2 3 4 5 6 7 NI

International Business and Economic Activities (International Trade and Foreign Direct Investment-FDI)

24	In Vietnam, hidden barriers[130] are not an important problem at all	1 2 3 4 5 6 7 NI
25	The customs regime in Vietnam is among the region's most liberal toward import and export activities.	1 2 3 4 5 6 7 NI
26	Vietnam is the most FDI attracting environment among the regional leaders	1 2 3 4 5 6 7 NI
27	FDI in Vietnam is an important source of new technology	1 2 3 4 5 6 7 NI

Government role

28	The Government treats all economic sectors (private, state-own, and FDI-invested) equally	1 2 3 4 5 6 7 NI
29	The competence of local and government officials, in general, is the best in the region	1 2 3 4 5 6 7 NI
30	Government policies are independent of pressure from special interest groups	1 2 3 4 5 6 7 NI
31	Burdensome administrative regulations are not pervasive	1 2 3 4 5 6 7 NI

Public Institution

32	The legal framework is extremely efficient and follows a clear, neutral process like that of the leaders	1 2 3 4 5 6 7 NI
33	Property rights are clearly defined and protected by law	1 2 3 4 5 6 7 NI
34	The effectiveness of the law-making bodies, in general, is the highest in the region	1 2 3 4 5 6 7 NI

---

130 That is, barriers other than published tariffs and quotas

35	Corruption is as rare as that of the leaders	1 2 3 4 5 6 7 NI

Company's Strategy and Operation.

36	State-owned firms' operation in Vietnam, in general, is highly efficient	1 2 3 4 5 6 7 NI
37	Competitiveness of Vietnam's firms in international markets is primarily due to unique products and processes	1 2 3 4 5 6 7 NI
38	Firms have a close partnership with research institutes and universities in addressing the challenges	1 2 3 4 5 6 7 NI
39	It is easy for a firm to recruit and retain qualified engineers	1 2 3 4 5 6 7 NI
40	Firms, in general, are able to develop new products and /or improve the quality of their existing products	1 2 3 4 5 6 7 NI
41	Firms, in general, have well-developed international brand and sale distribution channels	1 2 3 4 5 6 7 NI

Vietnam national competitiveness, in general, 1 2 3 4 5 6 7 NI
ranks highest in the region

Part 2: Attitudes forward enhancing competitiveness

The most concerning problems (for sole firm)
42. Among the most concerning problems facing your company is.....

8a	Being overstaffed	1 2 3 4 5 6 7 NI
8b	Shortage of skilled labours	1 2 3 4 5 6 7 NI
8c	Scarcity of capital	1 2 3 4 5 6 7 NI
8d	High production costs	1 2 3 4 5 6 7 NI
8e	Low product quality	1 2 3 4 5 6 7 NI
8f	Low efficiency and productivity	1 2 3 4 5 6 7 NI
8g	Weak company brand name and image	1 2 3 4 5 6 7 NI
8h	Weak distribution networks	1 2 3 4 5 6 7 NI
8i	Limited capability for developing new products	1 2 3 4 5 6 7 NI
8j	Lack of information about customers and markets	1 2 3 4 5 6 7 NI
8k	Lack of new market opportunities	1 2 3 4 5 6 7 NI
8l	Difficulty in acquiring land for expansion	1 2 3 4 5 6 7 NI
8m	Unhealthy business environment	1 2 3 4 5 6 7 NI

8n	The pressures of international economic integration	1 2 3 4 5 6 7 NI
8o	Don't know any thing about the regulatory system of the WTO	1 2 3 4 5 6 7 NI
8p	Unwilling to participate in regional and world competition	1 2 3 4 5 6 7 NI
8q	Other, please specify......	1 2 3 4 5 6 7 NI

Top priority of Company (for sole firm)

In this section only:

1 means „ not important at all"

2 means „ slightly important"

3 means „ important"

4 means „ very important"

5 means „ extremely important"

43. Among the most urgent actions that your company plans to take in the next few years is to...

11a	Substantially reduce the production cost	1 2 3 4 5 NI
11b	Purchase new production equipment	1 2 3 4 5 NI
11c	Upgrade the management capability	1 2 3 4 5 NI
11d	Launch an effective marketing program	1 2 3 4 5 NI
11e	Strengthen the distribution network	1 2 3 4 5 NI
11f	Recruit talented employees	1 2 3 4 5 NI
11g	Invest in improving knowledge about market and customers	1 2 3 4 5 NI
11h	Enter new markets	1 2 3 4 5 NI
11i	Look for a foreign partner	1 2 3 4 5 NI
11j	Request a special support or aid from the Government	1 2 3 4 5 NI
11k	Apply ICT(Internet) to doing business	1 2 3 4 5 NI

Priorities for the Government in the next five years

44. Below is a list of actions that government considers to take in order to promote the growth and national competitiveness. Please indicate how important each one is, as priority for government over the next five years.

As noted in the previous section, 1 means "not important at all"....5 means "extremely important".

10a	Making substantial investment in upgrading conditions and quality of primary and secondary education	1 2 3 4 5 NI
10b	Investing in vocational education and training	1 2 3 4 5 NI

	programs to prepare and upgrade workers skills	
10c	Upgrading the quality of transportation in infra-structure	1 2 3 4 5 NI
10d	Upgrading the quality of the information tele-communication infrastructure	1 2 3 4 5 NI
10e	Reducing the cost of telecom and internet ser-vices	1 2 3 4 5 NI
10f	Upgrading the reliability of power suppliers	1 2 3 4 5 NI
10g	Upgrading the quality of the banking system	1 2 3 4 5 NI
10h	Introducing new policies with much stronger in-centives for business investment and expansion	1 2 3 4 5 NI
10i	Promoting the partnership between government and private sector and the networking among firms	1 2 3 4 5 NI
10j	Promoting the image of local business environ-ment in particular, and of Vietnam in general in the global market	1 2 3 4 5 NI
10k	Increasing financial support encouraging the col-laboration between universities/research institutes and the business sector in their research and de-velopment projects	1 2 3 4 5 NI
10l	Speeding up the privatization process	1 2 3 4 5 NI
10n	Enhancing the competence and working ethics of government agencies	1 2 3 4 5 NI
10o	Launching a strong and effective anti-corruption campaign	1 2 3 4 5 NI
10p	Making significant investment in developing an information center for supporting domestic busi-ness in market research and for coordination for-eign market penetration	1 2 3 4 5 NI
10q	Constructing Cluster network	1 2 3 4 5 NI
10r	Other....	1 2 3 4 5 NI

Respondent's full Name:...

Occupation/Position:..

Office/Company's Name:..

Email:...

Appendix 6
Summary of Survey Result

I. Determinant of Vietnam National Competitiveness
As mentioned in the survey questionnaire sample, each respondent circles a number in scale of 1 to 7, for which:

1 means „ disagree strongly"   5 means „ agree somewhat"
2 means „ disagree generally"   6 means „ agree generally"
3 means „ disagree somewhat"   7 means „ agree strongly"
4 means „ neither disagree nor agree"

Respondents circle „ NI" in answering a question only when the question is irrelevant in the context of their business.

In this survey framework, score of 1 is considered as the worst value in the region[131] and score of 7 is the best one in the region or the leader[132] of the region.

We interpret the answers follows:

1.   Production Resources
Human resource.

	Official	Execu-tive	Scholar	Overall
1. The education system meets the needs of a competitive economy (O=41; E=58; S=53)[133]	2.63 (1.35)[134]	2.36 (1.37)	2.79 (.85)	2.6 (1.21)
2. The overall quality of the education system(grade 1-12) is as high as that of the regional leaders (O=42; E=57; S=52)	2.81 (1.25)	2.81 (1.36)	3.17 (1.08)	2.93 (1.24)
3. The most talented people remain in Vietnam(O=42; E=57; S=52)	3.14 (.89)	2.88 (1.07)	3.29 (.69)	3.09 (.92)
4. The labor force's health is among the best in the region(O=43; E=58; S=53)	3.26 (.90)	3.31 (1.12)	3.83 (.91)	3.47 (1.02)

---

131   Association of South East Asia Nations (ASEAN) includes 11 member nations (Singapore,Malaysia, Thailand, Brunei Darussalam, The Philipines, Indonesia, Vietnam, Myanmar, Cambodia, Laos and East Timore
132   The leader of the region are Singapore.
133   Number of respondents, who are officials, executives and scholars, are given in the parentheses; O, E, S stand for official, executive and scholar respectively.
134   Standard deviation is given in the parentheses

Quality of the infrastructure.

5. The overall quality of general infrastructure is among the best in the region (O=42; E=58; S=51)	2.71 (.77)	2.19 (1.05)	2.51 (.80)	2.44 (.92)
6. The quality of land and ship transportation, in general, is among the best in the region (O=41; E=58; S=50)	2.05 (.94)	2.10 (1.18)	2.62 (1.26)	2.26 (1.17)
7. The quality of the telephone system (landline and cell), in general, is among the most reliable in the region (O=41; E=58; S=52)	3.29 (1.25)	2.84 (1.16)	3.06 (.95)	3.04 (1.13)
8. The quality of electricity supply, in general, is as highly reliable as that of the regional leaders (O=43; E=57; S=53)	2.88 (1.11)	2.86 (1.14)	2.66 (.70)	2.80 (1.02)

Capital resource

	Official	Executive	Scholar	Overall
9. The level of sophistication of financial markets is generally as high as that of the regional leaders (O=40; E=58; S=50)	2.83 (1.15)	2.59 (1.21)	2.52 (1.16)	2.63 (1.18)
10. The banking system is generally healthy with sound balance sheets like that of the regional leaders (O=42; E=57; S=52)	3.07 (1.13)	2.67 (1.13)	2.77 (.98)	2.82 (1.09)
11. Banks are responsive to firm's demand (O=39; E=58; S=50)	3.69 (1.17)	3.29 (1.25)	3.76 (1.08)	3.56 (1.18)
12. Obtain a bank loan in Vietnam with a good plan is the easiest in the region (O=42; E=57; S=52)	3.05 (1.14)	2.56 (1.15)	2.85 (1.17)	2.83 (1.20)

Natural resource.

13. Vietnam's resources are the richest in the region (O=40; E=57; S=53)	4.95 (1.01)	4.56 (1.29)	4.42 (.86)	4.61 (1.09)
14. Vietnam's location is the great-	4.60	4.16	4.16	4.28

est resource advantage in the region (O=42; E=57; S=49)	(1.28)	(1.19)	(1.04)	(1.18)
15. Vietnam's land is the greatest resource advantage in the region (O=41; E=58; S=53)	3.51 (1.20)	3.24 (1.27)	2.81 (1.02)	3.16 (1.19)
16. Vietnam's marine is the greatest resource advantage in the region (O=43; E=58; S=52)	4.49 (1.38)	3.98 (1.51)	3.94 1.36)	4.11 (1.44)

2. Technology development

17. Vietnam's position in technology, in general, ranks among the regional leader (O=43; E=58; S=52)	3.04 (1.20)	2.89 (1.39)	2.49 (0.80)	2.80 (1.20)
18. Scientific research institutions are truly region-class (O=41; E=56; S=53)	2.76 (1.18)	2.27 (1.30)	2.58 (1.24)	2.51 (1.25)
19. Firms in Vietnam are willing to absorb new technologies like that of the regional leaders (O=39; E=57; S=50)	3.62 (1.26)	3.49 (1.16)	3.70 (.83)	3.60 (1.09)
20. Information and communication technology(ICT) development ranks among the regional leaders (O=40; E=58; S=52)	3.53 (1.13)	3.29 (1.22)	3.02 (.94)	2.70 (.97)

3. Market condition

21. The competition in Vietnam, in general, is as fair and healthy as that of the regional leaders (O=40; E=58; S=53)	2.95 (1.01)	2.71 (.92)	2.49 (.95)	2.70 (.97)
22. The demand in Vietnam is actively seeking the latest products, technologies and processes like that of the regional leaders (O=41; E=58; S=51)	3.61 (1.07)	3.38 (1.33)	3.53 (1.08)	3.49 (1.18)
23. Anti-trust policy in Vietnam is the most effective and promotes competition in the region (O=41; E=58; S=50)	3.37 (1.24)	2.71 (.88)	3.00 (.83)	2.99 (1.00)

4. International business and economic activities.

	Official	Executive	Scholar	Overall
24. In Vietnam, hidden barriers[135] are not an important problem at all (O=42; E=58; S=53)	3.29 (.97)	3.10 (.79)	3.32 (.93)	3.23 (.89)
25. The customs regime in Vietnam is among the region's most liberal toward import and export activities (O=41; E=58; S=52)	3.15 (1.03)	2.81 (.94)	2.67 (.83)	2.85 (.95)
26. Vietnam is the most FDI attracting environment among the regional leaders (O=40; E=56; S=51)	4.10 (1.17)	3.58 (1.01)	4.08 (.93)	4.72 (1.04)
27. FDI in Vietnam is an important source of new technology (O=41; E=57; S=53)	4.68 (1.25)	4.74 (.99)	4.72 (.93)	4.72 (1.04)

5. Government role

28. The Government treats all economic sectors(private, state-own, and FDI-invested) equally (O=42; E=57; S=53)	3.98 (1.20)	2.96 (1.03)	2.94 (.75)	3.24 (1.09)
29. The competence of local and government officials, in general, is the best in the region (O=42; E=57; S=53)	3.55 (1.17)	2.47 (.92)	2.66 (.85)	2.84 (1.07)
30. Government policies are independent of pressure from special interest groups (O=43; E=57; S=53)	3.84 (1.19)	2.95 (.92)	3.17 (.94)	3.27 (1.07)
31. Burdensome administrative regulations are not pervasive (O=43; E=57; S=53)	3.28 (1.24)	2.29 (.84)	2.58 (.95)	2.67 (1.07)

Public institution

---

135   That is, barriers other than published tariffs and quotas

32. The legal framework is extremely efficient and follows a clear, neutral process like that of the leaders (O=43; E=57; S=53)	3.26 (1.13)	2.52 (1.01)	2.64 (1.07)	2.77 (1.17)
33. Property rights are clearly defined and protected by law (O=42; E=58; S=51)	3.19 (1.27)	2.41 (1.06)	2.84 (1.19)	2.77 (1.20)
34. The effectiveness of the law-making bodies, in general, is the highest in the region (O=41; E=57; S=52)	3.20 (1.14)	2.74 (.95)	2.57 (.80)	2.80 (.98)
35. Corruption is as rare as that of the leaders (O=43; E=56; S=53)	2.65 (1.34)	1.55 (.82)	1.98 (1.20)	2.01 (1.19)

6. Company's strategy and operation

	Official	Execu tive	Scholar	Overall
36. State-owned firms' operation in Vietnam, in general, is highly efficient (O=41; E=58; S=50)	3.17 (1.02)	2.55 (1.04)	2.60 (.82)	2.74 (.99)
37. Competitiveness of Vietnam's firms in international markets is primarily due to unique products and processes (O=41; E=58; S=49)	3.08 (.87)	2.89 (.92)	2.92 (.99)	2.95 (.89)
38. Firms have a close partnership with research institutes and universities in addressing the challenges (O=39; E=58; S=53)	2.81 (1.11)	2.52 (1.04)	2.58 (.90)	2.62 (1.05)
39. It is easy for a firm to recruit and retain qualified engineers(O=40; E=58; S=51)	3.55 (1.37)	2.97 (1.07)	3.28 (.90)	3.23 (1.07)
40. Firms, in general, are able to develop new products and /or improve the quality of their existing products (O=41; E=58; S=49)	3.32 (.97)	3.43 (1.17)	3.28 (.85)	3.35 (1.01)
41. Firms, in general, have well-developed international brand and sale distribution channels (O=41; E=58; S=48)	3.44 (.98)	2.88 (1.06)	3.21 (.92)	3.14 (1.03)

Vietnam national competitiveness (VNC), in general, ranks the highest in the region (O=41; E=58; S=48)	3.39 (1.07)	2.83 (1.10)	2.95 (.96)	3.03 (1.15)

II. Attitudes forward enhancing competitiveness

7. The most concerning problems (for sole firm).

We calculate and rank descending mean score as the following table.
42. Among the most concerning problems facing your company is.....

	Number	Mean	Std.deviation
Shortage of skilled labors	58	5.69	1.301
Scarcity of capital	58	5.50	1.478
Weak company brand name and image	58	5.47	1.366
Limited capability for developing new products	58	5.31	1.417
The pressures of international economic integration	58	5.24	1.261
Low efficiency and productivity	58	5.22	1.312
Weak distribution networks	58	5.21	1.281
High production costs	57	5.04	1.451
Low product quality	58	4.98	1.573
Lack of information about customers and markets	58	4.91	1.614
Difficulty in acquiring land for expansion	58	4.91	1.525
Unhealthy business environment	58	4.90	1.209
Lack of new market opportunities	58	4.76	1.699
Other, please specify......	30	4.57	1.591
Being overstaffed	58	4.31	2.037
Don't know any thing about the regulatory system of the WTO	57	3.95	1.597
Unwilling to participate in regional and world competition	56	3.95	1.519

Note: In the following sections, a list of priorities for company and government are given. Respondents are asked to assess the importance of these priorities involving in enhancing competitiveness.

Respondents circle a number in the scale of 1-5 follows:

1 means „ not important at all"

2 means „ slightly important"

3 means „ important"

4 means „ very important"

5 means „ extremely important"

We calculate and rank descending mean score as tables follow:

8. **Top priority of Company (for sole firm)**

43. Among the most urgent actions that your company plans to take in the next few years is to...

	Number	Mean	Std.deviation
Recruit talented employees	58	4.19	.783
Upgrade the management capability	58	4.07	1.041
Launch an effective marketing program	58	4.07	.953
Apply ICT(Internet) to doing business	58	3.97	.898
Invest in improving knowledge about market and customers	58	3.86	.907
Strengthen the distribution network	58	3.83	.841
Purchase new production equipment	58	3.74	.909
Enter new markets	58	3.69	.940
Look for a foreign partner	58	3.67	.758
Substantially reduce the production cost	58	3.52	1.158
Request a special support or aid from the Government	58	3.07	1.137

9. **Priorities for the Government in the next five years**

44. Among the most crucial actions that the government plans to take in the next few years is to...

	Number	Mean	Std.deviation
Launching a strong and effective anti-corruption campaign	154	4.12	.956
Speeding up the privatization process	154	4.09	1.072
Enhancing the competence and working ethics of government agencies	154	4.07	.886
Introducing new policies with much	154	4.04	.885

stronger incentives for business investment and expansion			
Upgrading the reliability of power suppliers	154	4.01	.886
Investing in vocational education and training programs to prepare and upgrade workers skills	154	3.97	1.009
Upgrading the quality of transportation in infrastructure	154	3.93	1.017
Promoting the image of local business environment in particular, and of Vietnam in general in the global market	154	3.90	.872
Making significant investment in developing an information center for supporting domestic business in market research and for coordination foreign market penetration	154	3.83	.962
Constructing Cluster network	154	3.76	.929
Upgrading the quality of the information telecommunication infrastructure	154	3.73	1.043
Promoting the partnership between government and private sector and the networking among firms	154	3.73	.864
Upgrading the quality of the banking system	154	3.72	1.019
Making substantial investment in upgrading conditions and quality of primary and secondary education	154	3.64	1.137
Reducing the cost of telecom and internet services	154	3.63	.900
Other, please specify......	59	3.63	1.202
Increasing financial support encouraging the collaboration between universities/research institutes and the business sector in their research and development projects	154	3.58	.877

Figure 6. 4: The most concerning problem for doing business

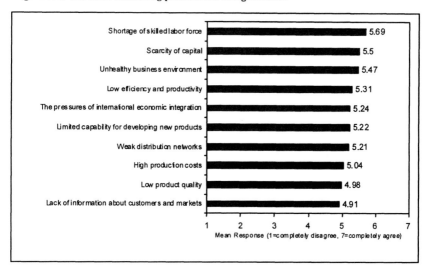

Figure 6. 5: Priorities for the Government in the next five years

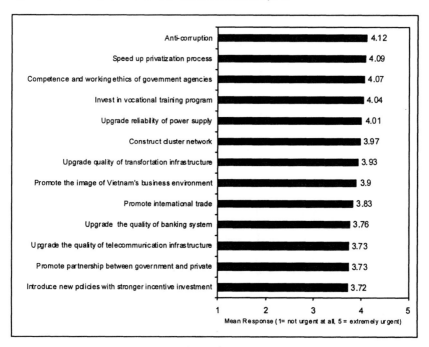

Bibliography

Abdullah, W.A.W. (1995) "The Old and New Competition and Malaysian Manufacturing Firms: A Case Study", *International Journal of Human Resource Management* 6(4): 872-90.

Adams, G., Gangnes, B, and Shachmurove, Y (2004), "Why is China So Competitive? *Measuring and Explaining China's Competitiveness*", Working Paper No 04-6, available at http://www.economics.hawaii.edu/research/workingpapers/WP_04-6.pdf

Asia Development Bank-ADB (2003), Competitiveness in developing Asia in *Asia Development Outlook 2003, Oxford University Press*, available at: http://www.adb.org/Documents/Books/ADO/2003/ado2003.pdf

Asia Development Bank-ADB (2007), Asia Development Outlook 2007, available at: http://www.adb.org/Documents/Books/ADO/2007/default.asp

Asia Development Bank-ADB, Key Indicators 2007, available at http://www.adb.org/Documents/Books/Key_Indicators/2007/pdf/Key-Indicators-2007.pdf

Altenburg, T. (1998), "Building Systemic Competitiveness – Concept and Case Studies from Mexico, Brazil, Paraguay, Korean and Thailand", Working Paper, 3/1998, German Development Institute, Berlin.

Belser, P. (2000), "Viet Nam: On the Road to Labor Intensive Growth", Policy Research Working Paper, No 2389, World Bank, Hanoi.

Bennett, D. and Vaidia, K. (2001), Meeting Technology Needs of Enterprises for National Competitiveness, UNIDO, Vienna. Available at: http://www.unido.org/userfiles/timminsk/featarabmotBennett.pdf.

Bergman and Feser, (1999) Industrial and Regional Clusters: Concepts and Comparative Application, Regional Research Institution, West Virginia University.
Berndt, R (2004), *Competitiveness and Ethic*, Springer, Berlin.

Berry, Albert, (1997) SME competitiveness: the Power of Networking and Subcontracting, Washington D.C, IMF.)

Best, M. H. (1993) "The New Competition, Institutions of Industrial Restructuring, Polity Press.

Blejer, M (2004), The Future of Competitiveness-Enhancing Reforms in Latin America in M. Porter, K. Schwab, X. Sala-I-Martin and A. Lopez-Claros (eds) *The Global Competitiveness Report 2004-05*, Palgrave Macmillan, New York.

Boltho, A. (1996) "The Assessment: International Competitiveness, *Oxford Review of Economic Policy*, 12 (3) pp.16.

Bosworth, D., R. Wilson, T. Hogarth (1995), Impact of EC-Funded R§D Programmes on Human Resources Development and Long Term Competitiveness, Office for Official Pul. of the Europ. Communities, Luxembourg.

Buckley, P.J. (1998), "Measures of International Competitiveness: A critical survey" *Journal of Marketing Management*, quoted from IMD World Competitiveness Yearbook 2005.

Bui, Anh Tuan (2000), Creating Jobs through Foreign Direct Investment (FDI) in Vietnam, Hanoi, (in Vietnamese).

Ceglie, Giovanna, and Dini, Marco. (1999), SMEs Cluster and Networks Development in Developing Countries: the Experience of UNIDO.

Chiang Kao, Wann-Yih Wu, Wen-Jen Hsieh, Tai-Yue Wang, Chinho Lin, and Liang Hsuan Chen (2007), "Measuring the National Competitiveness of Southeast Asian Countries", available at http://www.sciencedirect.com/science/article/B6VCT-4NJ0TH8-9/2/8839addf45e32fad30b6ba0f7b390950.

Cho, D. and Moon, H. (2005), "National Competitiveness: Implications for Different Groups and Strategies", International Journal of Global Business and Competitiveness, 1 (1), pp. 1-11.

Cho, D.S and Moon, H.C, (2000) "From Adam Smith to Michael Porter: Evolution of Competitiveness Theory, *Asia-Pacific Business Series*, Vol.2, World Scientific, Singapore.

Cho, D.S. (1994), "A Dynamic Approach to International Competitiveness: The Case of Korea, *Journal of Far Eastern Business*, 1 (1), pp 17-36.

CIA – The World Factbook-Vietnam, 2006, available at: https://www.cia.gov/library/publications/the-world-factbook/geos/vm.html

Center Institute of Economic Management-CIEM (2003), Enhance the National Competitiveness of Vietnam, Transport Publisher, Hanoi, in Vietnamese.

Cohen and D. Levinthal, (1989), "Innovation and Learning: the Two Faces of R&D", *Economic Journal*, September 1989.

Cohen, D and D.Levinhthal (1989), "Innovation and Learning: The Two Faces of R&D, *Economic Journal*, September.

Commons, J.R. (1970), "The Economics of Collective Action", University of Wisconsin Press, Madison.

Competitiveness Advisory Group – Ciampi Group (1995), "Enhancing European Competitiveness", *first report to the President of the Commission, the PM and the Heads of State*, June.

Competitiveness Advisory Group – Ciampi Group (1995), "Enhancing European Competitiveness", *second report to the President of the Commission, the PM and the Heads of State*, December.

Competitiveness Advisory Group (1996), "Enhancing European competitiveness: Fourth Report to the President of the European Commission, the Prime Ministers and Heads of State, Office for Official Publ. of the EU Communities. Luxembourg.

Cooper, R. (1983), "A Process Model of New Industrial Product Development", IEE *Transaction on Engineering Management*, 30 (1), pp. 2-11.

Cornelius, P., J. Blanke and F. Paua (2003), The Growth Competitiveness Index: Recent Economic Developments and the Prospects for a Sustained Recovery in P. Cornelius, M. Porter and K. Schwab (eds) *The Global Competitiveness Report 2002-03*, Oxford University Press, New York.

Creswell, John W. (2003), "Research Design: *Qualitative, Quantitative, and Mixed Methods Approaches*", Sage, California.

Dapice, D. (2003), "Vietnam's Economy: *Success Story or Weird Dualism? AS-WOT Analysis*", Vietnam Program, Kennedy School of Government, Harvard University.

Dapice, D. (2006), "Fear of Flying: Why is Sustaining Reform so Hard in Vietnam", Vietnam Program, Kennedy School of Government, Harvard University.

240

Dettmann, I. (2005), Export competitiveness- Improving Export Ability of Developing Countries: German Preparation Conference for UNCTAD XI, Bonn: In-Went.

Dictionary of Business and Management (2006), Oxford University Press. Oxford and New York.

Dosi, G. (1984), Technical Change and Industrial Transformation, Macmillan, London.

Dosi, G. (1988), "Sources, Procedures and Micro-economic Effects of Innovation", *Journal of Economic Literature*, 36, pp. 1126-71.

Dunning, J.H (1988), Explaining International Production, Unwin Hyman, London.

Dunning, J.H (1992), "Competitive Advantage of Countries and the Activities of Transnational Corporations", *Transnational Corporations,* 1 (1), pp. 135-168.

Dunning, J.H (1993), Multinational Enterprise and The Global Economy, Addison Wesley, New York.

Easterly, W (2004), Can Foreign Aid Make Poor Countries Competitive? In Porter, M., Schwab, K., Sala-I-Martin, X and Lopez-Claros, A (eds) *The Global Competitiveness Report 2004-05*, Palgrave Macmillan, New York.

Economic and Social Commission for Western Asia (2001), New Technology for Enhancing Competitiveness and Productivity in Selected Sectors, New York: United Nations.

Erber, G (1995), Public Infrastructure, Productivity and Competitiveness: An Analysis of Relative Differences and Impacts with Regard to US and German Industries, Discussion Paper No 115, DIW, Berlin.

Esser, K., Hillebrand, W., Messner, D., Meyer-Stamer, J., (1996) "Systemic Competitiveness: New Governance Pattern for Industrial Development", GDI Book, No 7.

Fagenberg, J., (1996), "Technology and Competitiveness, *Oxford Review of Economic Policy*, 12 (3), pp. 39-51.

Felipe, J. and Sipin, G. (2004), "Competitiveness, Income Distribution and Growth in the Philippines: What Does the Long-run Evidence Show?, ADB, ERD Working Paper No 53.

Felke, R (1998), European Environmental Regulations and International Competitiveness, Nomos Verlagsgesellschaft, Baden.

Fielding, N. and Scheier, M. (2001) Introduction: On the Compatibility between Qualitative and Quantitative Research Methods, Forum: Qualitative Social Research, available at (16/09/2002): http://qualitative-research.net/fqs/fqs-eng.htm

Fisher, E. and Reuber, R. (2001), Industrial Clusters and Business Development Services for Small and Medium Sized Enterprises in Wignaraja, G (eds), *Competitiveness Strategy in Developing Countries*, Routledge, London and New York.

Foster and Rosenzweig 1996, Foster.A.D and M.R. Rosenzweig "Technical Change and Human Capital Returns and Investments: Evidence from Green Revolution" *America Economic Review*.

Franziska, B (2006), „What is Competitiveness", in the Competitiveness Institute (TCI), Spain. Available at http://www.competitiveness.org/article/articleview/774/1/32/

Freeman, C and C.Perez (1988), "Structural Crises and Adjustment, Business Cycles and Investment Behaviour", in Dosi, C. Freeman, R. Nelson, G.Silverberg and L.Soete (eds), Technical Change and Economic Theory, Printer Publishers, London.

Freeman, C. (1982), The Economics of Industrial Innovation, Printer, London

Fröhlich, H.P. (1989), "International Competitiveness: Alternative Macroeconomic Strategies and Changing Perceptions in Recent Years", *The Competitiveness of European Industry*, Routledge, pp. 21-40.

General Statistic Office (2000), Vietnam Statistical Yearbook 2000, Hanoi.

General Statistic Office (2001), Vietnam Statistical Yearbook 2001, Hanoi.

General Statistic Office (2006), Vietnam Statistical Yearbook 2006, Hanoi.

General Statistics Office of Vietnam (2006), The Vietnamese International Merchandise Trade for Twenty Years Innovation (1986-2005), Statistical Pulishing House, Hanoi.

General Statistics Office of Vietnam (2006), Vietnamese Industry in Twenty Years of Innovation and Development, Statistical Publishing House.

Gereffi, G (2002), The International Competitiveness fo Asian Economies in the Apparel Commodity Chain, ERD Working Paper No 5, ADB, available at http://www.adb.org/Documents/ERD/Working_Papers/wp005.pdf

Goldstein, A (2004), Regional Integration, FDI and Competitiveness in Southern Africa, OECD, Paris.

Hämäläinen, T. (2003), "National Competitiveness and Economic Growth: *The Changing Determinants of Economic Performance in the World Economy*", Edward Elgar, Massachusetts.

Hämäläinen, T. and J. Laitamaki (1993), "A Value-added Theory of the Firm: An Explanation for the Destruction of Large Hierarchies in the Computer Industries", paper presented at conference on Strategic Management Society, Chicago, September.

Haque, I. (1995), "Technology and Competitiveness in Haque *et al* (eds.), *Trade, Technology and Competitiveness*, Institute for the World Bank, Washington, pp 11-45.

Harvie, C. (2003). "Competition Policy and SMEs in Asian Transition Economies: The Experience of China" in Tran, V.H. (eds), Competition Policy and Global Competitiveness in Major Asian Economies, Edward Elgar, Cheltenham, UK.

Hasse, R (1988), Econometrics in the Service of Economic Interests: On the Validity of the UNCTAD Calculation of the Trade Effects of the Tokyo Round on Developing, Gustave Fisher.

Hasse, R., Schneider, H. And Weigelt, K. (2005), Lexikon Soziale Marktwirtschaft: Wirtschaftspolitik von A bis Z, Schöningh, Paderborn.

Hiemenz, U. (1999), Growth and Competition in the New Global Economy, OECD, Paris.

Hookway, J and Nguyen Anh Thu (2007), Vietnam Aims to Bolster Private Sector, The Wall Street Journal Europe, Sep. 26th 2007, pp 9.

Howells, J and Michie, J (1997), *Technology, Innovation and Competitiveness*, Edward Elgar Publishing.

Hymer, S.H, (1960), The International Operations of National Firms: a study of Direct Investment, PhD Thesis, Massachusetts Institute of Technology.

IMD (2003), World Competitiveness Yearbook 2003, Bellerive, Lausanne.

IMD (2005), World Competitiveness Yearbook 2005, Bellerive, Lausanne.

IMF, World Economic Outlook Database, September 2005, available at http://www.imf.org/external/pubs/ft/weo/2005/01/data/index.htm

Jenskins, R. (2006), "Globalization, FDI and Employment in Vietnam", *Transnational Corporations*, 15 (1), pp. 115-142.

Jomo, K (2002), Manufacturing Competitiveness in Asia, Routledge Curzon, Kuala Lumpur.

Jomo.K.S, (2003), Manufacturing competitiveness in Asia, p42-75, Kuala Limpur, Malaysia.

Kelle, U. (2001) Sociological Explanations between Micro and Macro and the Integration of Qualitative and Quantitative Methods, Forum: Qualitative Social Research, available at (16/09/2002): http://qualitative-research.net/fqs/fqs-eng.htm

Ketels, C., (2002a), "Location, Location, Location", HBS Working Knowledge.

Keynes, J. M (reprinted in 1997), *The General Theory of Employment, Interest, and Money*, Prometheus Books, New York.

Kitnmantel, E., (1995) "A Multi-Faceted Concept: 35 Years of Free Trade in Europe, Messages for the Future", *Proceeding of EFTA's 35th Anniversary Workshop*, Emil EMS Geneva, p 106-112.

Kokko, A., Kotoglou, K and Karson, A (2003), "The Implementation of FDI in Vietnam: An Analysis of Characteristics of Failed Projects", Transnational Corporations, 12 (3), pp. 40-77.

Krugman, P.R. (1994), "Competitiveness: A Dangerous Obsession", Foreign of Affairs, 73 (2), March – April, pp. 28-44.

Krugman, P.R. (1996) "Making Sense of the Competitiveness Debate, International Competitiveness", *Oxford Review of Economic Policy*, 12 (3), p17-25

Lall, S (2000.a), "Technological Structure and Performance of Developing Country Manufactured Exports, 1985 – 98". *Oxford Development Studies*, 28 (3), pp 337-369.

Lall, S. (2000.b), "Technological Change and Industrialization in Asia newly Industrialized Countries: Achievement and Challenges", in L. Kim and R.R. Nelson "Technology, Learning and Innovation: Experience of newly Industrialized Economies", Cambridge University Press, pp13-68.

Lall, S (2001a), "Comparing National Competitive Performance: An Economic Analysis of World Economic Forum's Competitiveness Index", *Working Paper*, 61 (2).

Lall, S (2001b), *Competitiveness, Technology and Skills*, Edward Elgar, Cheltenham, UK.

Landabaso, M. (2001), "Cluster in Less Prosperous Places: Policy Options in Planning and Implementation" Draft, European Commission: Brussels

Landau, R. (1992), "Technology, Capital Formation, and U.S. Competitiveness" in B. G. Hickman (eds.), *International Productivity and Competitiveness,* Oxford University Press, New York and Oxford, pp. 299-325.

Le, Dang Doanh. (2001) "National Competitiveness and The Competitiveness of Vietnam's Products and Services", VCCI Conference, in Vietnamese.

Leal Filho, W. (2006), Achieving Competitiveness through Innovation: A Challenge for Poland and other New EU Member States, Lang, Frankfurt.

Levin, R.C., A.K. Klevorick, R.R. Nelson and S.G. Winter (1987), "Appropriating the Returns from Industrial Research and Development", *Brookings Paper on Economic Activity*, 3, pp. 783-820.

Levy, B., Berry, A. and Nugent, J. (1999), "Supporting the Export Activities of Small and Medium Enterprise in Levy, B., Berry, A., and Nugent, J. (eds), *Fulfill-*

ing the Export Potential of Small and Medium Firms, Boston, MA: Kluwer Academic Publishers.

Lim, H (1998), Korea's Growth and Industrial Transformation, Macmillan Press.

Lipsey. R (2003), Foreign Direct Investment, Growth and Competitiveness in Developing Countries in P. Cornelius, M. Porter and K. Schwab (eds) *The Global Competitiveness Report 2002-03*, Oxford University Press, New York.

Lodge, G. and Vogel, E. (1987), Ideology and National Competitiveness: An Analysis of Nine Countries, Harvard Business School Press, Boston.

Lopez-Claros, A and Blanke, J (2004), "The Growth Competitiveness Index: Assessing Countries' Potential for Sustained Economic Growth" in Porter, M., Schwab, K., Sala-I-Martin, X and Lopez-Claros, A (eds) *The Global Competitiveness Report 2004-05*, Palgrave Macmillan, New York.

Magee, S.P. (1977), "Information and the Multinational Corporation: An Appropriability Theory of Direct Foreign Investment", in J. Bhagwati (eds), *The New International Economic Order*, The MIT Press, Cambridge.

Maidique, M.A. (1983), "The Stanford Innovation Project", in R.A Burgelman and M.A. Maidique (eds), *Strategic Management of Technology Innovation*, Worchester Polytechnic Institute.

Malesky, E (2005), The Vietnam Provincial Competitiveness Index 2005: Measuring Economic Governance for Private Sector Development, VNCI, Hanoi.

Mansfied, E. (1986), "Microeconomics of Technological Innovation", in R.Landau, R. and N. Rosenberg (eds), *The Positive Sum Strategy: Harnessing Technology for Economic Growth*, National Academy Press, Washington, DC.

Martin, R. and P. Sunley (2003), "Deconstructing Cluster: Chaotic Concept or Policy Panacea?," *Journal of Economic Geography*, 3 (1), pp. 5-35

McArthur, J. and Sachs, J (2002), The Growth Competitiveness Index: Measuring Technologocal Advancement and the Stages of Development in Porter, M., Sachs, J., Cornelius, P., McArthur, J. and Schwab, K (eds) *The Global Competitiveness Report 2001-02*, Oxford University Press, New York.

McKinsey § Company (2003), ASEAN Competitiveness Study, The Final Report to ASEAN Leaders.

246

Ministry of Science and Technology (2003), Vietnam Science and Technology Development Strategy by 2010, available at: http://www.most.gov.vn/mlfolder.2006-07-13.8523759789/mlfolder.2006-07-13.1746877991/

Mori, J. (2005), "Development of Support Industries for Vietnam's Industrialization: Increasing Positive Vertical Externalities through Collaborative Training, Fletcher School, Tuft University.

Mosley, H., Schmid, G., (1993), "Public Services and Competitiveness" in Hughes, K. S. (eds.), *European Competitiveness*, Cambridge University Press, pp. 200-231.

Mowery, D.C. and N. Rosenberg (1979), "The Influence of Market Demand Upon Innovation: A Critical Review of Some Recent Empirical Studies", *Research Policies,* 8(2), pp. 102-150.

Mytelka, L. (1999), Competition, Innovation and Competitiveness in Developing Countries, OECD, Paris.

Nadvi, Khanlid, (1995) Industrial Cluster and Networks: Case Studies of SME Growth and Innovation, UNIDO Small and Medium Industries Brand.

Nelson, R.R. and S.G. Winter (1977), "In Search of a Useful Theory of Innovation", *Research Policy*, 6(1), pp. 36-76.

Nguyen, Phuc Hien, (2002) "Recommendations for Enhancing the Competitiveness of Vietnamese Enterprises in the Context of International Economic Integration, *Development and Economic Magazine*, Vol 65, in Vietnamese.

Nguyen, Thi Phuong Hoa. (2004), FDI and Its Contribution to Economic Growth and Poverty Reduction in Vietnam (1986-2001), Peter Lang, Frankfurt.

Nguyen, Tien Trung (2002), "Vietnam's International Trade Regime and Comparative Advantage, CAS Discussion Paper No 37, CAS, Hanoi.

North, D.C (1990), "Institutions, Institutional Change and Economic Performance", *Cambridge University Press*, Cambridge.

OECD (1991, 1996, 1997), Education at a Glance, OECD, Paris.

OECD (1992), Technology and the Economy: *The Key Relationships*, OECD, Paris.

OECD (1994), The OECD Jobs Study: Evidence and Explanations, Part I, OECD, Paris

OECD (1996a), Technology, Productivity and Job Creation, OECD, Paris.

OECD (1996b), "Regulatory Reform and Innovation", Science Technology Industry, OECD, Paris.

OECD (1996c), Globalization and Competitiveness, OECD, Paris.

OECD (1997), Regional Competitiveness and Skills, OECD, Paris.

OECD (1998), The Competitiveness of Transition Economies, OECD, Paris.

OECD (1999), Foreign Direct Investment and Recovery in Southeast Asia, OECD, Paris.

OECD (2000), Privatization, Competition and Regulation, OECD, Paris.

OECD, (2001), Enhancing SMEs competitiveness, Bologna Ministerial Conference, pp. 105-145.

Ohno, K (2003), Vietnam at Crossroads: Policy Advice from the Japanese Perspective, available at
http://www.vdf.org.vn/Doc/2003-2004/PN01E-KOhnoDec03.pdf

Ohno, K and Nguyen, V.T (2005), Improving Industrial Policy Formation, The Publishing House of Polictical Theory, Hanoi.

Ohno, K and Nguyen, V.T (2006), Business Environment and Policies of Hanoi, The Publishing House of Social Labor, Hanoi.

Olso, M. (1982), The Rise and Decline of Nations, Yale University Press, New Haven

O'Mahony, M and Bart van Ark (2003), "EU Productivity and Competitiveness: An Industry Perspective; Can Europe Resume the Catching-up Process?", Office for Official Publ. of the EU Communities. Luxembourg, pp. 259-273.

Oxfam, summaries of the annual meeting 2000, " Growing pains for the world's economies" session 55 and "A billion illiterates lack access to gains of globalization" session 25.

Painter, M. (2005), "The Politics of State Sector Reforms in Vietnam: Contested Agendas and Uncertain Trajectories", The Journal of Development Studies, Vol 41, pp. 261-283.

Pavitt, K. (1987), 'International Patterns of Technological Accumulation', in N. Hood and J.E. Vahlne (eds), *Strategies in Global Competition*, Croom Helm, London.

Piore, M.J and C.F. Sabel (1984), The Second Industrial Devide, Basic Books, New York.

Porter, M. (1985), *Competitive Advantage*, The Free Press, New York.

Porter, M. (1990), *The Competitive Advantage of Nations*, The Macmillan Press, London and Basingstoke.

Porter, M. (2000b), "Locations, Clusters, and Company Strategy," in G.L. Clark, M.P. Feldman, and M.S.Gertler (eds), *The Oxford Handbook of Economic Geography*. New York: Oxford University Press, 253-274.

Porter, M (2000a), The Current Competitiveness Index: Measuring the Microeconomic Foundations of Prosperity in M. Porter, J. Sachs, A. Warner, C. Moore, J. Tudor, D. Vasquez, K. Schwab, P. Cornelius, M. Levinson (eds) *The Global Competitiveness Report 2000*, Oxford University Express, New York, pp 40-58.

Porter, M. (2003a), "The Economic Performance of Region", Regional Studies, 37 (6§7), pp. 549-678.

Porter, M. (2003b), Building the Microeconomic Foundations of Prosperity: Findings from the Microeconomic Competitiveness Index in P. Cornelius, M. Porter and K. Schwab (eds) *The Global Competitiveness Report 2002-03*, Oxford University Press, New York, pp. 23-45.

Porter, M. (2004a), Building the Microeconomic Foundations of Prosperity: Findings from the Microeconomic Competitiveness Index in Porter, M., Schwab, K., Sala-I-Martin, X and Lopez-Claros, A (eds) *The Global Competitiveness Report 2004-05*, Palgrave Macmillan, New York, p 23-45

Porter, M (2004b), Chinese Competitiveness: Where Does The Nation Stand?, available at http://www.isc.hbs.edu/pdf/CAON_China_2004.06.18.pdf

Porter, M. (2005), "National Competitiveness: Issues for Vietnam", The Presentation at Meeting with Vietnamese Prime Minister Phan Van Khai and his Delegation, available at: http://www.isc.hbs.edu/pdf/Vietnam_2005.06.24.pdf.

Pyke, Frank, (1992) Industrial Development through Small-Firm Cooperation-Theory and Practice, ILO, Geneva.

Rao, S.L (2001), Productivity, Competitiveness and Economic Policies, National Management of All India Management Association (AIMA), Amexcel.
Rapkin, D and Avery, W (1995), "National Competitiveness in a Global Economy", Intenational Political Economy Yearbook, Vol 8, Lynne Rienner, London.

Reiljan, Janno, Hinrikus, Maria and Ivanov, Anneli (2000) Key Issues in Defining and Analyzing The Competitiveness of A Country, *Working Paper No1*, Tartu University Press.

Reich, R. (1990), Who is us? Harvard Business Review, Jan-Feb, pp.2-12
Ricardo, D. (1817 reprinted in 1996), *Principles of Political Economy and Taxation*, Prometheus Books, New York.

Rosenberg, N (1976), Perspectives on Technology, *Cambridge University Press*, Cambridge

Rosenfeld, S., (2002a), "A Governor's Guide to Cluster-Based Economic Development", National Governors Association: Washington, D.C.

Rosenfeld, S., (2002b), "Creating Smart Systems: A Guide to Cluster Strategies in Less Favored Regions" European Commission: Brussels.

Sabel, C. (1990), "Individual's Skills as Information Processing", in A.L Stinchcombe (ed), *Information and Organizations*, University of California Press, Berkeley.

Sachs, J and A. Warner (2000), Globalization and International Competitiveness: Some Broad Lessons of the Past Decade in M. Porter, J. Sachs, A. Warner, C. Moore, J. Tudor, D. Vasquez, K. Schwab, P. Cornelius, M. Levinson (eds) *The Global Competitiveness Report 2000*, Oxford University Express, New York, pp 18-27.

Sala-I-Martin, X and Artadi, E (2004), "The Global Competitiveness Index" in M. Porter, K. Schwab, X. Sala-I-Martin and A, Lopez-Claros (eds) *The Global Competitiveness Report 2004-05*, Palgrave Macmillan, New York.

Salter, W.E.G. (1960), "Productivity and Technical Change", Cambridge University Press, London, pp 133-134.

Schmookler, J. (1966), Invention and Economic Growth, Harvard University Press, Cambridge.

Schumpeter, J. (1934), *The Theory of Economic Development*, Harvard, Cambridge.

Scott, B.R. and Lodge, G.C. (1985), "US competitiveness in the World Economy", Harvard Business School Press, Boston.

Sjöholm, F. (2006), "State Owned Enterprises and Equitization in Vietnam", Working Paper 228, Stockholm School of Economics, Sweden.

Smith, A. (1776, a selected edition 1998), *An Inquiry into the Nature and Causes of the Wealth of Nations*, Oxford University Press, New York.

Stoke, J (2003), *A Guide to Doing Business in Vietnam*, Johnson Stoke § Master, Hanoi.

Strauss, J. (1986) "Does Better Nutrition Raise Farm Productivity" Journal of Political Economy 94, pp297-320, Deolalika 1988 "Nutrition and Labor Productivity in Agriculture: Wage Equation and Farm Production Function Estimates for Rural India" The Review of Economics and Statistics (70), pp. 406-14)

Tedesco, J (1997), The New Educational Pact: Education, Competitiveness and Citizenship in Modern Society, International Bureau of Education (IBE), Paris.

Teece, D. (1987), 'Profiting from Technological Innovation: Implication for Integration, Collaboration, Licencing, and Pulic Policy' in D.Teece (ed), The Competitive Challenge: Strategies for Industrial Innovation and Renewal, Harper & Row, New York.

Tellisuuden Kestkusliitto, Teollisuuden Kilpailukyky (1989), "International Competitiveness and Business Strategies: Sportswear Industry", Helsinki School of Economics, Artto-Project 1988-1989, Nr 27.

251

Thurow, L. (1992), Head to Head: The Coming Economic Battle among Japan, Europe, and America , William Morrow and Co, New York.

Tran, Van Hoa (2003), Competition Policy and Global Competitiveness in Major Asian Economies, Edward Elgar, Cheltenham, UK:

Tung, R.L. (1994) "Human Resource Issues and Technology Transfer", *International Journal of Human Resource Management*, 5(4): 807-24

UNCTAD (1994), World Investment Report 1994, Transnational Corporations, Employment and Workplace, United Nation, available at: http://www.unctad.org/Templates/WebFlyer.asp?intItemID=2431&lang=1

UNCTAD (1995), *World Investment Report 1995*, Transnational Corporations and Competitiveness. New York: United Nation, available at: http://www.unctad.org/Templates/WebFlyer.asp?intItemID=2430&lang=1

UNCTAD (1998), "Promoting and Sustaining SMEs Cluster and Networks for Development-Issues", paper by UNCTAD Secretariat, Trade and Development Board, Commission on Enterprise, Business Facilition and Development, Expert Group Meeting on Cluster and Networking for SEM Development, Geneva.

UNCTAD (1999), *World Investment Report 1999:* Foreign Direct Investment and the Challenge of Development. New York: United Nation, available at: http://www.unctad.org/Templates/WebFlyer.asp?intItemID=1991&lang=1

UNCTAD (2000) The Competitiveness Challenges: Transnational Corporations and Industrial Restructuring in Developing Countries. New York: United Nations.

UNCTAD (2002), *World Investment Report 2002*, Transnational Corporations and Competitiveness, New York and Geneva: United Nations.

UNCTAD (2003), The World Investment Report 2003: FDI Policies for Development: National and International Perspectives, UN, available at: http://www.unctad.org/Templates/WebFlyer.asp?intItemID=2979&lang=1

UNCTAD (2004), Policy Options for Strengthening SME Competitiveness, Eleventh session Sao Paulo, 13-18 June 2004, United Nations.

UNCTAD (2005), The World Investment Report 2005: *Transnational Corporations and the Internationalization of R§D*, United Nation, available at: http://www.unctad.org/Templates/WebFlyer.asp?intItemID=3489&lang=1

UNCTAD 2006, available at:
http://www.unctad.org/Templates/Page.asp?intItemID=3277&lang=1

UNDP (2005), MDGs and Vietnam's Social-Economic Development Plan 2006-2010, United Nation Development Program, Hanoi.

United Nations Industrial Development Organisation (UNIDO) (1993) Indonesia: Industrial Development Review. London: The Economist Intelligence Unit

US Competitiveness Policy Council (1992), "The First Report to the President and Congress", quoted in IMD World Competitiveness Yearbook 2005.

Vietnam Economy- Thoi Bao Kinh Te Vietnam (2007), Economic Forum: Delegates on Vietnam's Development, available at (26/04/2007) at: http://www.vneconomy.vn/ Delegates on Vietnam development.htm

Vietnam Economy-Thoi Bao Kinh Te Vietnam (2006), "What need to be done to the integration of the higher education", VN Economy (12/05/2006) in Vietnamese.

Vietnam Economy-Thoi Bao Kinh Te Vietnam (2007), "Public Administration Reform: Three Priorities", available (26/04/2007) at: http://www.vneconomy.vn/Cai cach hanh chinh.htm in Vietnamese.

Vietnam-US Trade (2007), Vietnam Business Environment, available at http://www.vietnam-ustrade.org/Eng/business_environment.htm

Vo, Tri Thanh (2005): Vietnam's Trade Liberalization and International Economic Integration: Evolution, Problems and Challenges, in: *ASEAN Economic Bulletin* 22, p75-79.

Vu, Minh Khuong (2000), "An Analysis of Efficiency and Competitiveness of Vietnam's Economy", Vietnam Economic Studies, June 2000.

Vu, Minh Khuong (2002), "A Comparative Analysis of Growth Performance of Vietnam vs China", Vietnam Economic Studies, July 2002.

Vu, Minh Khuong and Johnathan Haughton (2003), The Competitiveness of Vietnam's Three Largest Cities: A Survey of firms in Hanoi, Haiphong, and Ho Chi Minh city, available at: http://mail.beaconhill.org/~j_haughton/VnCompetitDec2003a.pdf.

Vu, Minh Khuong (2006), "A Global Perspective on the ICT penetration and Economic Growth in Asia: Issues and Policy Implications" in The Challenges of Economic Policy Reforms in Asia, Center for International Development, Stanford University. Available at http://scid.stanford.edu/events/PanAsia/Papers/papersonly.html.

Vu, Thanh Tu Anh (2005), "Vietnam – The Long March to Equitization", Policy Brief, No 33, The William Davidson Institute, Michigan.

VUFO-NGOs Resource Centre, (2006), VDR/PRSC Consultation Exercise 2007 The Contribution of Non- Government Organizations (NGOs) to the Development of Policy Actions to Help Implement the SEDP 2006-10, Hanoi.

Wallis, J. and D. North (1986), "Measuring the Transaction Sector in the American Economy, 1870-1970", in S.L. Engerman and R.E. Galman (eds), Long-Term Factors in American Economic Growth, *University of Chicago Press*, Chicago.

Warner, A (2004), International Productivity Comparisons: The Importance of Hours of Work in Porter, M., Schwab, K., Sala-I-Martin, X and Lopez-Claros, A (eds) *The Global Competitiveness Report 2004-05*, Palgrave Macmillan, New York.

World Economic Forum-WEF (2000), "The Global Competitiveness Report 2000", Oxford University Press, New York.

WEF (2002) "The Global Competitiveness Report 2001-02", Oxford University Press, New York.

WEF (2003) "The Global Competitiveness Report 2002-03", Oxford University Press, New York.

WEF (2004) "The Global Competitiveness Report 2004-05", Palgrave Macmillan, New York.

Wei, Zhang and Tao Zhang (2005), "Competitiveness of China's Manufacturing Industry and Its Impact on Neighboring Countries", Journal of Chinese Econocmic and Business Studies, No3, pp. 205-229.

Wen-Jen Hsieh and other Vietnamese scholars (2004), "An Analysis of National Competitiveness: A Perspective in Vietnam", available at http://140.116.50.130/apmr/apmrsp/v.pdf.

Wienmann, J., (2006), Vietnam – the 150th WTO – Member: Implications for Industry Policy and Export Promotion, DIE, Bonn.

Wignaraja, G and Joiner, D. (2004), "Measuring Competitiveness in the World's Smallest Economies: Introducing the SSMECI", EDR Working Paper series No 60, Asia Development Bank (ADB).

Wignaraja, G. (2001), *Competitiveness Strategy in Developing Countries*, Routledge, London and New York.

Williams, T. (1996), "New Technology, Human Resources and Competitiveness in Developing Countries: the Role of Technology Transfer", The International Journal of Human Resource Management 7 (4), pp. 832-844.

Williamson, O.E (1985), "The Economic Institutions of Capitalism", The Free Press, New York.

Wolf, S (2003), Private Sector Development and Competitiveness in Ghana, Discussion Paper on Development Policy No 70, ZEF, Bonn.

World Bank 1993, "The east Asia Miracle: Growth and Public Policy", Oxford University Press, pp.318.

World Bank, World Development Report 2000-2005, New York: United Nations.

World Bank (2006a), *Vietnam's Infrastructure Strategy*, World Bank, Hanoi.

World Bank (2006b), *Overview of the Capital Markets in Vietnam and Directions for Development*, Finance and Private Sector Development Department East Asia and Pacific Region, World Bank, Hanoi.

World Bank, (2006c), *Vietnam Development Report 2006: Business*, Joint Donor Report to the Vietnam Consultative Meeting, December 6-7, World Bank, Hanoi.

World Bank (2007a), *Vietnam Development Report 2007: Aiming High*, Joint Donor Report to the Vietnam Consultative Meeting, December 14-15, 2006, World Bank, Hanoi.

World Bank (2007b), Vietnam: Laying the Foundation for Steady Growth, IDA, available at http://www.worldbank.org/ida.

Xiangshuo, Y (1996), China's Trade Policy Reforms and their Impact on Indsutry in Wall, D., Boke, J and Yin Xiangshuo (eds), China's Opening Door, Royal Institute of International Affairs.

Zhu, Y. (2005), The Asian Crisis and the Implications for Human Resources Management in Vietnam, International Journal of Human Resource Management, 16(7), pp. 1261-1276.

SCHRIFTEN ZUR WIRTSCHAFTSTHEORIE UND WIRTSCHAFTSPOLITIK

Herausgegeben von Klaus Beckmann, Michael Berlemann, Rolf Hasse, Jörn Kruse,
Franco Reither, Wolf Schäfer, Thomas Straubhaar, Klaus W. Zimmermann

www.peterlang.de

Walter Leal Filho / Marzenna Weresa (eds.)

Achieving Competitiveness Through Innovations – A Challenge for Poland and Other New EU Member States

Frankfurt am Main, Berlin, Bern, Bruxelles, New York, Oxford, Wien, 2007.
246 pp., num. tab. and graphs
ISBN 978-3-631-56136-2 · hardback € 36.80*

This book attempts to analyse, document and disseminate some basic information on the role of innovation in fostering competitiveness. It tries to consider the various variables that influence the implementation of innovative approaches in market economies, paying at the same time some attention to the barriers that prevent, inhibit or slow down further progress. Among other issues, the book discusses the "new" Lisbon strategy and provides an analysis of the means to implement innovation policy and enhance competitiveness in the European Union and in the new EU States. Moreover, it compares how technological development and international competitiveness influence the 'old' and 'new' EU Member States, also critically analysing Poland's competitive position in the enlarged EU and considering its attractiveness for foreign investors from an income tax perspective. Due to its international scope, this publication is of special interest to educators, scientists and researchers working in the innovation sector. It also provides useful insights to politicians and other academics interested in innovation issues in the new EU member countries.

Contents: The "new" Lisbon strategy · Means to Implement Innovation Policy in the European Union and in the New EU States- Innovation Policy of the European Union · Building Regional Competitive Advantage. Lessons from U.S. Experiences in Poland and Other New EU Member States · Technological Development and International Competitiveness: 'Old' And 'New' EU Member States Compared · Poland's Competitive Position in the Enlarged EU · Expenditures on innovation and their influence on competitive position in the market: empirical evidence from Poland · and many more

Frankfurt am Main · Berlin · Bern · Bruxelles · New York · Oxford · Wien
Distribution: Verlag Peter Lang AG
Moosstr. 1, CH-2542 Pieterlen
Telefax 00 41 (0) 32 / 376 17 27

*The €-price includes German tax rate
Prices are subject to change without notice
Homepage http://www.peterlang.de

Peter Lang · Internationaler Verlag der Wissenschaften